VISIONS OF
RYUKYU

VISIONS OF
RYUKYU

❖

Identity and Ideology
in Early-Modern Thought
and Politics

GREGORY SMITS

University of Hawai'i Press
Honolulu

Library of Congress Cataloging-in-Publication Data
Smits, Gregory, 1960–
Visions of Ryukyu : identity and ideology in
early-modern thought and politics / Gregory Smits.
p.   cm.
Includes bibliographical references and index.
ISBN 978-0-8248-2037-4 (cloth : alk. paper)
1. Ryukyu Islands—History.   I. Title.
DS895.R95S65   1999
952'.29—dc21   98–38468
CIP

Printed by Edwards Brothers, Inc.

For Akiko

Contents

Acknowledgments ix

Introduction 1

CHAPTER 1 The Status of Ryukyu and Its Relations with Japan and China 15

CHAPTER 2 Looking North and Looking West: Shō Shōken and Tei Junsoku 50

CHAPTER 3 Empowering Ryukyuans:
The Theoretical Foundations of Sai On's Ryuku 71

CHAPTER 4 Re-Creating Ryukyu: Sai On and His Critics 100

CHAPTER 5 Contested Visions of Sai On's Ryukyu 133

Epilogue and Conclusions 143

Appendix 1: Ryukyuan Kings 163

Appendix 2: Glossary of Selected Ryukyuan Terms 165

List of Abbreviations 168

Notes 169

Works Cited 201

Index 209

Acknowledgments

It is with pleasure that I thank those who have assisted in the production of this book. Peter Nosco and Gordon Berger offered invaluable advice during the early stages of my research and writing on Ryukyu. As the notes in the chapters that follow indicate, I have relied heavily on the research of various Japanese scholars of Ryukyu, many of whom have assisted me personally at one time or another. Asato Susumu, Dana Masayuki, Higa Minoru, Itokazu Kaneharu, Nakama Yūei, Takara Kurayoshi, Kyan Shin'ichi, Tasato Osamu, Tomishima Sōei, Tomiyama Kazuyuki, and Tsuzuki Akiko have all provided important material and other assistance. Takara Kurayoshi and Tomiyama Kazuyuki especially have provided extensive support and encouragement over the years, for which I am most grateful. Many others have assisted over the years by helping me obtain needed materials, by engaging parts of my work in academic discussion, or by providing general encouragement. They include Elizabeth Byrd, Irene Cermak, Alan Christy, Wm. Theodore de Bary, Gerald Figal, Takashi Fujitani, John Henderson, Masato Matsui, Sharon Minichiello, Mike Molasky, Rick Mulcahey, Rob Oechsle, Laura Phillips, Steve Rabson, Mitsugu Sakihara, Conrad Schirokauer, Koji Taira, Takeishi Kazumi, and Ronald Toby. A Faculty Research Grant from Eastern Washington University assisted with travel to Okinawa. I am grateful to Patricia Crosby of the University of Hawai'i Press for her editorial assistance and general support for this project. Thanks also to Ann Ludeman and Sally Serafim for assisting in the production of this book. Two anonymous readers for the press offered a wealth of valuable suggestions. Needless to say, any shortcomings that remain are entirely my own responsibility.

Introduction

A few years ago, when a box arrived in the mail from a used book store in Okinawa, I noticed that the store's label, affixed to the inside cover of some of the books, had been redesigned. In the old version, the store was located in Okinawa-ken, Ginowan. In the new version, although the store was in the same physical location, its label now proclaimed Ryūkyū-koku, Ginowan. No change in Japan's political boundaries had taken place, but the store's psychological address, if I may use such a phrase, had changed from "Ginowan City, Okinawa Prefecture" to "Ginowan City, Country of Ryukyu." While visiting Okinawa in 1988, I talked to people who had attended college in "Japan" during the late 1970s and early 1980s, who told me of having received compliments on their ability to speak Japanese and use chopsticks when strangers (elderly people, in all examples I heard) found out they were from Okinawa. When I visited the offices of the *Ryūkyū shinpō*, one of the two major Okinawan daily newspapers, a reporter asked me to describe my impressions of Okinawa compared with the rest of Japan, and part of my reply appeared in print the next day. Thinking back on my infrequent and brief visits to Okinawa, I can recall numerous conversations in which Okinawans of various ages and walks of life spoke of *"iwakan"* (a sense of unease) vis-à-vis some aspect of Japanese culture. In 1988, when in an Okinawan restaurant in Tokyo, I overheard a man seated at the next table ask another how long he had been living in Japan *(Nihon)*. It turned out that the sojourner had left Naha four years earlier and had been living in "Japan" ever since.

In mentioning these anecdotes, I do not intend to suggest that all, most, or even many contemporary Okinawans necessarily derive a strong sense of identity as Ryukyuans or Okinawans. Furthermore, inhabitants of Okinawa Prefecture typically imagine Ryukyu or Okinawa in ways that differ widely from one person to the next. Most, of course, are too busy with daily affairs to think much about the matter. The general discourse of contemporary Okinawan life (conversations, letters to the editor in newspapers, advertising, et cetera) resembles that of anywhere else in Japan. One need not listen long or hard, however, to be reminded that the categories "Okinawa" and "Japan," whatever they may be, do not always coexist without tension.

The fit between "Japan" and "Okinawa" is closer today than it was early in this century and much closer than in premodern times. Whether it be the seventeenth century or the twentieth, talk of Okinawan/Ryukyuan identity

Okinawa with principal premodern divisions and cities.

necessarily invoked, directly or indirectly, a non-Okinawan/Ryukyuan Other. Today, it would usually be Japan. In the days of the kingdom, Ryukyuans also constructed visions of Ryukyu in relationship to "Japan," though this term signified several different entities: Satsuma, the bakufu, the Japanese archipelago in general. Owing to complex economic and political relationships described in Chapter 1, and to the fact that premodern constructions of Ryukyuan identity typically involved at least some Confucian elements, "China" (again with multiple possible meanings) also figured as a prominent Other in premodern talk of Ryukyu. This dialogic relationship accommodated considerable ambiguity. Indeed, not even the physical boundaries of the kingdom were clear to all parties, as Toguchi Masakiyo points out: "[After Satsuma's invasion], when it spoke of Ryukyu, the term did not include the region of Amami-Ōshima. When the bakufu spoke of Ryukyu, however, the term included the territory of the original Ryukyu Kingdom, which included Amami-Ōshima."[1]

This book examines different, often competing, visions of Ryukyu from the early seventeenth century through the early nineteenth century and their political consequences. It seeks to center Ryukyu as a historical agent, examining Ryukyuan history mainly from the vantage point of Shuri (capital of the Ryukyu Kingdom), not Edo or Beijing.[2] On the other hand, this study makes no attempt to discover or rescue a timeless "Ryukyuan-ness" from within Ryukyu's past. Visions of Ryukyu were, and continue to be, discursive constructions contingent on changing historical circumstances and subject to contestation from within Ryukyu and without. This book describes the major historical circumstances that informed early-modern discourses of Ryukyuan identity and examines the strategies leading intellectual and political figures deployed in fashioning, promoting, and implementing their visions of Ryukyu.

Preliminaries

In our present era, it is difficult to conceive of human political communities as something other than nations and nation-states. One result is a tendency to project modern nations backward, to regard, for example, seventeenth-century Japan or China as stable, clearly defined political and cultural entities. "Japan" and "China," however, are examples of imagined communities, to use Benedict Anderson's well-known term. Their apparent stability and cultural homogeneity derive in substantial part from customary, contemporary modes of imagining and are subject to contestation and redefinition. The vast critical literature on nationalism has gone far in historicizing and "de-naturalizing" the concept of nation, and many historians of East Asia are taking the implications of this scholarship seriously.[3]

Benedict Anderson, Ernest Gellner, and other theorists of the modern nation have stressed the disjunction between modern nations and the social and political arrangements that preceded them. Their emphasis on nations as radically new discursive constructions has contributed to the desirable end of de-naturalizing the nation. Prasenjit Duara, however, finds this emphasis on

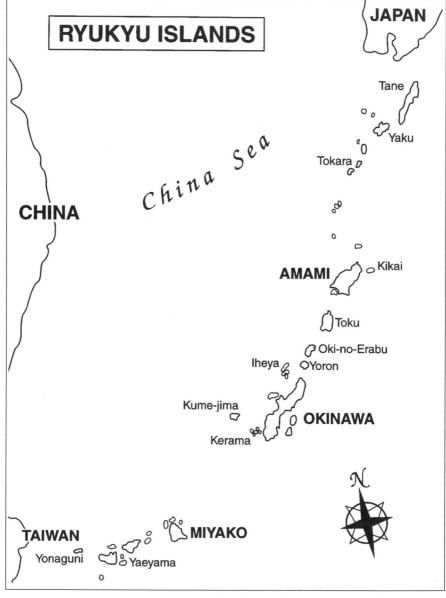

The Ryukyu islands.

the modernity of national consciousness to be problematic, pointing out several ways in which China and India do not fit Anderson's or Gellner's model:

> In privileging modern society as the only social form capable of generating political self-awareness, Gellner and Anderson regard national identity as a distinctly modern mode of consciousness: the nation as a whole imagining itself to be the cohesive subject of history. The empirical record does not furnish the basis for such a strong statement about the polarity between the modern and the premodern. Individuals and groups in both modern and agrarian societies identify simultaneously with several communities that are all imagined; these identifications are historically changeable, and often have conflicted internally with each other.[4]

Although nations typically claim a unified consciousness for their members, the empirical record does not support such a claim in either modern or premodern societies. Furthermore, in both modern and premodern times we can find political communities that have claimed for themselves the status of unified, totalizing subjectivities, even if they never succeeded in actualizing these claims. Nations do not exist as unified subjectivities in any more than a restricted and temporary sense because the various entities that inhabit and identify with a nation often derive sharply different meanings from their relationship with it.[5]

Because nations are not culturally homogeneous, despite their pretensions to be so at some level, they are subject to the instability resulting from contestation over the "true" meaning or essence of the national group. The multiple possibilities for the formation of identities is readily apparent in today's Okinawa. Let us take someone born and raised on the Ryukyu island of Miyako. Vis-à-vis someone from the United States, she might regard herself as Japanese. In dealing with mainland Japanese, she might identify with Okinawa. Many residents of Okinawa Prefecture, however, continue to derive identity, at least in part, from such finely delineated divisions as Shuri versus (other parts of) Naha, not to mention the "main" island of Okinawa versus the "outer islands" (sakishima). A woman who moved to Naha from Miyako as a teenager, and soon thereafter had to visit a hospital, told me of the sense of relief she experienced upon overhearing two elderly women in the waiting room conversing in the language of Miyako—fellow "nationals," at least in that specific context. Similar issues of variable group identities, intra-Ryukyuan cultural diversity, and the differing political agendas and economic interests of specific groups have prevented easy or peaceful closure in implementing early-modern constructions of Ryukyu as a unified subjectivity.

Returning to Duara's argument, earlier, premodern forms of political communities have persisted in historical memory, which has transmitted them across what I will call the modern divide. "There were totalizing representations and narratives of community with which people identified historically and with which they may continue to identify into the modern nation." On the other hand, "premodern political identifications do not necessarily or teleologically develop into the national identifications of modern times."[6] Duara extends his argument to posit a model for understanding historical change in connection with both the continuities and discontinuities associated with modern nation-states and the political communities that preceded them. Drawing in part on the work of Tejaswini Niranjana, Duara proposes a useful metaphor for the transmission of past historical traces to the present: it is akin to translating a foreign language. The past exists in historical memory as dispersed traces, but transmitting these traces into meaningful and convincing narratives entails a reconfiguring process similar to translating one language into another. Linear history is a dialectical relationship between two processes, dispersal and transmission:

> It is in the often conflictual relationship between transmission and dispersal that we can glimpse history outside the categories of the nation-state: at the instant when the transmissive moment seeks to appropriate the dispersive one. Moreover, we are privileged to view this appropriating instant precisely because there is more than one force which seeks to appropriate it—given that there is more than one way to conceive the nation. It is in the contest over the fluid meanings of historical events that we are alerted to how the dispersed meanings of the past are redeployed to construct a linear narrative.[7]

Insofar as Ryukyuans used historical narratives to construct their images of Ryukyu, this study examines the contest over fluid meanings of historical events.

Duara's sophisticated approach preserves many of the important insights of theorists of the nation like Gellner and Anderson, who emphasize discontinuity across the modern divide. At the same time, Duara gives due weight to the continuities with the past via the process of transmitting its dispersed traces. His insights are useful in situating the present study, which focuses primarily on early-modern constructions of Ryukyuan identity. The subsequent chapters examine four such constructions: those of Shō Shōken (1617–1675), Tei Junsoku (1663–1734), Heshikiya Chōbin (1700–1734), and Sai On (1682–1761). All four, albeit with greatly differing degrees of success, sought to conflate culture and polity and to incorporate all Ryukyuans into the resulting political community. In this respect, the projects of these Ryukyuans bears some resemblance to those of their modern counterparts who grappled with issues of Ryukyuan identity after 1879, the year Japan's Meiji state annexed the kingdom and declared Ryukyuans to be imperial subjects.

On the other hand, the intellectual, political, and ideological climate differed greatly in its particulars on either side of Ryukyu/Okinawa's modern divide. The issues of nation, ethnic or cultural characteristics *(minzokusei),* and "race" *(jinshu)* that occupied much of the energies of early twentieth-century Okinawan intellectuals such as Iha Fuyū (1876–1947) and Higashionna (Higaonna) Kanjun (1882–1963) would likely have been inconceivable to any of the four Ryukyuans examined in this study. Their intellectual arena was informed by Buddhism, Confucianism, sinitic modes of ceremonial and symbolic expression, the science of geomancy (C. *fengshui;* O. *funshii*), and other practices and bodies of knowledge that quickly lost ground after 1879.

Yet on both sides of the modern divide, Ryukyu's intellectual and political leaders had to deal with the fact of Japanese political and military power. Thus, the legacies ("traces" in Duara's terminology) of Tei Junsoku, Shō Shōken, Heshikiya Chōbin, Sai On, and other major figures of early-modern Ryukyu, while dispersed by changed political and intellectual conditions, were also transmitted to modern Ryukyuans through the historical scholarship of Iha, Higashionna, Majikina Ankō (1875–1933), and other writers of their generation. This process of transmission was also a process of translation, with the inevitable losses and transformations that such a process entails. Lost, for example, was much of the conflict between the four men and their differing visions, except in the case of Sai On and Heshikiya, where the level of violence was too high to be overlooked. Instead, in modern narratives these Ryukyuans typically took their places, along with some leading early-modern agriculturalists, as the "Great Men" *(ijin)* of Ryukyu, proof to early twentieth-century Okinawans struggling to become Japanese that Ryukyuans had indeed been great in ways that even Japanese would, or at least should, acknowledge.

This book is mainly concerned with early-modern Ryukyuan intellectual and political history. Present-day debates over Okinawa's relationship with Japan, however, always harken back to Ryukyu's status during earlier periods, making it inevitable that this study will become part of these debates as it joins the broader discourse of Ryukyuan/Okinawan history. Therefore, I provide some explicit linkage with modern Okinawa and Japan in the epilogue and concluding chapter. But my main goal is a close examination of prenational modalities of identity construction in early-modern Ryukyu and how these constructed identities shaped Ryukyuan history through their political consequences. A close examination of similar issues in modern Okinawa must await another book.

Because Sai On's vision of Ryukyu eventually prevailed over the others, becoming the ideological basis of the early-modern state by the middle of the eighteenth century, he will figure most prominently in these pages. Sai On appropriated the Confucian tradition in sometimes novel ways to support his political goals. He dealt with Ryukyu's obvious inability to match the military or economic power of China or Japan in part by asserting that the small kingdom could achieve moral parity with its larger neighbors. Existing precariously between China and Japan, Ryukyu's long-term survival and prosperity, Sai On argued, depended in large part on its adoption and adaptation of the Confucian way. In his view, Confucianism provided the only effective means for Ryukyuans to construct their own subjectivity and take charge of Ryukyu's destiny. Sai On, in other words, employed elements of the Confucian tradition in hitherto novel ways, and a study of his thought and political program sheds new light on Confucian praxis. Conversely, it also discloses one variety of an East Asian prenational imagined political/cultural community.

The island kingdom's precarious geopolitical situation, described in Chapter 1, informed the visions of Ryukyu examined here. Ryukyuan identity, however, was not only constructed vis-à-vis extra-Ryukyuan Others. Visions of an ideal Ryukyu typically called for changes in domestic politics, changes that some Ryukyuans resisted. Both Shō Shōken and Sai On, for example, were hostile to aspects of Ryukyu's indigenous shamanic religious practices, though for different reasons. Shō Shōken regarded such practices as embarrassingly backward in the context of Satsuma's critical gaze. For Sai On, shamanic practices ran counter to Confucian-based reason (C. *li*, J. *ri*), wasted precious resources, reinforced superstitions, and were thus a major hindrance to the material and moral improvement of society. Both men, therefore, favored policies to suppress such practices. In short, Ryukyuan identity must be examined from two perspectives. The first is Ryukyu as a distinct, singular entity, interacting with external Others such as Japan (especially Satsuma and the bakufu) and China (especially Fuzhou and Beijing). The second is its internal social and political divisions, which resulted in what we might reasonably call intra-Ryukyuan Others (shamans, for example).

To what extent was Ryukyu a singular, distinct entity? This question admits of no simple answer and is discussed in greater detail in subsequent chapters. On the one hand, Ryukyu was a country with distinct physical boundaries, ruled by a king through a set of government institutions. From this perspective, those living within the king's jurisdiction could all be called

Ryukyuans. Even this rather mechanical framework, however, was subject to ideological and other forms of contestation. Sai On and his allies, for example, successfully sought to refashion Ryukyu's monarch, whose authority to rule had long been based on native religious concepts and Buddhism, into a Confucian sage. This move engendered intense opposition from other elite Ryukyuans, some of whom paid for their opposition with their lives. Even after taking control of the machinery of state, Sai On and his supporters were unable to make much headway in "Confucianizing" the masses of ordinary Ryukyuans in the countryside. Indeed, whether these people would even have derived a strong sense of identity as "Ryukyuans" is doubtful.

The imagined community of Ryukyu, in other words, was, and is, a site of contestation. It is certainly possible to regard the events described in these pages in evolutionary terms—the rise of Confucianism in Ryukyu, for example—and the very narrative form in which this book is cast encourages such a view. One major drawback of viewing the past as a linear, evolutionary development, however, is the elision of conflict, dissonant voices, and difference. On the other hand, contestation and evolution are not necessarily mutually exclusive. The evolutionary development of early modern Ryukyuan institutions, for example, was in large part the result of contestation. Linear narratives often contain an implied teleology as a result of their privileging evolution over contestation. While I would like to avoid this tendency, doing so is difficult. I should say at the outset, therefore, that while I will explain why Sai On's vision prevailed over the others, I do not regard his vision of Ryukyu as predetermined by time, place, and circumstances, the inevitable result of a set of contexts. Other viable imaginings of Ryukyu were possible. Nor, in a similar vein, do I regard my reading of early-modern Ryukyu as having achieved closure. I will be happy if it stimulates other readings of Ryukyuan and Japanese history and if it raises as many questions as it answers.

Terminology

Whatever Ryukyu's connection with Japan may have been during the seventeenth and eighteenth centuries, its institutions, and the practices associated with them, differed significantly from those of the domains and the bakufu. One result of this difference is a set of specialized terms that will be unfamiliar to most English-language readers. Even Ryukyuan terms that superficially resemble Japanese counterparts often designate something quite different. For example, the Japanese term *"sesshō"* indicates a regent for the emperor and most commonly occurs in discussions of Fujiwara power during the Heian period. The Ryukyuan term *sessei* is written with the same characters, and in

Okinawan would actually have been pronounced more like *shisshii*. It also indicates a high officer of state, but the Ryukyuan *sessei* was not a regent for anyone and is probably best rendered "prime minister" in English. Likewise, Ryukyuan *jitō* (district administrators) were an entirely different sort of official from their *shōen*-overseeing terminological counterparts in Kamakura and Muromachi Japan. It is important to bear in mind that terminological resemblances between Ryukyuan institutions and practices and Japanese or Chinese counterparts can be deceptive.

To explain seventeenth- and eighteenth-century Ryukyuan institutions thoroughly would require a separate book. I have therefore provided only enough background information here to explain the matter at hand. A glossary of Ryukyuan terms is also included as an appendix. There are also several key terms that should be dealt with at the start.

First is *early-modern,* which corresponds to the Japanese *kinsei.* Early-modern suggests an early stage on the path of linear evolution to "modernity," whatever that may be. I find this teleological implication problematic in several ways, but looking specifically at Ryukyu, it is doubtful that the kingdom's historical trajectory during the seventeenth through early nineteenth centuries inevitably led to the "modernity" that followed. One could use the Japanese term *kinsei,* but it, too, is implicated in a similar evolutionary teleology. Therefore, I use the term early-modern, but only in the sense of the time period from 1609 to 1879, bounded by invasion of Ryukyu from Satsuma and annexation by Meiji Japan. *Premodern* includes the time period encompassed by early-modern, but it may also indicate time prior to 1609. *Old-Ryukyu* indicates the Ryukyu Kingdom from roughly the late twelfth century to 1609, and is a translation of the Japanese *ko-Ryūkyū.*

Another common term in this book is *royal government.* In a narrow sense it refers to the king and the officials of Ryukyu's central government, located in the capital of Shuri (today part of Naha). More broadly, the term also includes local officials, who, though not holders of aristocratic status, did receive formal appointment from the central government in Shuri.

One of the most problematic terms is *Japan,* which, for early-modern Ryukyuans, often meant the domain *(han)* of Satsuma. In this study, when appropriate, the term appears in quotation marks to indicate its ambivalent status. Educated Ryukyuans and others throughout East Asia certainly had a conception of Japan as a geographical entity. In discussing the spread of Buddhism, for example, Ryukyuans sometimes spoke of its spread from India to China to Japan. As a political entity, however, Ryukyuan elites were more likely to speak of the bakufu and Satsuma separately. Terms like *Yamato* or

Nihon/Nippon in early-modern Ryukyuan texts might indicate Japan as a broad geographical entity, or they might indicate either Satsuma or the baku-fu. The precise meaning would depend on the context.

There are no established conventions for dealing with Ryukyuan terms when writing in English. In Japanese-language dictionaries and other reference works, Ryukyuan words are typically "spelled" in *kana,* and my romanization will consequently be based on romanized Japanese, departing from it in ways that should be readily comprehensible without explanation (e.g., a long *"e"* sound will be *"ee"* as in *ueekata*). I am well aware that modern *kana* is inadequate to represent fully the sounds of the Ryukyuan languages, but my main purpose here is to facilitate documentary inquiry, not necessarily to replicate phonetic accuracy.

Ryukyuan personal names often appear in the literature, both Japanese and English, in two pronunciations: a native Ryukyuan version and a "Japanized" version. An individual bearing a name that in the days of the kingdom that would have been pronounced "Kyan," for example, might use Kyan, Kiyabu, Kiyamu, or Kiyatake today, the latter three pronunciations conforming with likely Japanese readings of the three characters in the name. Likewise, today's Tamashiro was Tamagusuku or Tamagushiku in premodern times. For those who lived in the days of the kingdom, of course, I simply use their actual names as given in the *Okinawa daihyakka jiten*[8] or other authoritative reference works. The names of Okinawan scholars of more recent years, however, pose problems. The historian Higashionna Kanjun (1882–1963), for example, most likely pronounced his name in the Okinawan "Higaonna," at least when among Okinawans, but both the *Okinawa daihyakka jiten* and the *Higashionna Kanjun zenshū* list his name as being "spelled" in the Japanese reading "Higashionna." I therefore use Higashionna, with apologies to Okinawan nationalists who may be offended at my lack of resistance to the hegemony of Japanese. Because some English-language works list his name in the Okinawan pronunciation, however, I provide alternative pronunciations in parentheses in his and similar cases the first time the name appears in the text and in the bibliography.

The problem with naming conventions does not end with personal names. Place names often have dual pronunciations, and in those cases (the majority) in which the Japanese pronunciation is standard today, I employ it. Therefore I write "Yomitan," despite the fact that in premodern Ryukyu, those living there likely called their village "Yuntan." Likewise, I write "Kumemura," not "Kuninda." Like personal names, place names also follow the pronunciation given in the *Okinawa daihyakka jiten.*

Most problematic are specialized Ryukyuan terms, which often appear in a variety of readings within the Japanese scholarly literature, even within the writings of the same person. Most terms do tend to be "spelled" one way or the other—either in their native pronunciation or in Japanese pronunciation—but there is no consistent rule. For example, the Japanese reading *"noro"* (official priestess) is more common than the Okinawan *"nuru,"* even in specialized literature. On the other hand Okinawan *"ueekata"* (a status rank) is more common than the Japanese *"oyakata,"* perhaps in part because the meaning of the Okinawan term is so different from its Japanese counterpart. In this study, therefore, I adhere rigidly to the primary pronunciation given in the *Okinawa daihyakka jiten,* whose editors grappled with the terminological questions and disputes discussed here. Whenever a common alternative form exists, or, in the case of Ryukyuan words, when a knowledge of the Japanese-style pronunciation may aid the memory or comprehension, I provide the term in parentheses using the abbreviations "J" for Japanese and "O" for Okinawan (not "R" for Ryukyuan because there are several mutually unintelligible Ryukyuan languages, and the terms with which we will be concerned are generally known by their Okinawan pronunciations). "C" indicates Mandarin Chinese, and "S-J" indicates a Sino-Japanese compound.

Many of the primary sources used and quoted in this study were written by Ryukyuans, not in a Ryukyuan language, but in either some form of Japanese or classical Chinese. When parenthetically indicating the original word or phrase in translated passages, I use Chinese if the text was originally written in Chinese, and Japanese if the original text was in that language. For example the term *substantive learning* would be *"(jitsugaku)"* if the original was in Japanese, and *"(shixue)"* in the case of a Chinese text. Outside of quoted passages, specialized Confucian terms will appear in their Chinese pronunciation, but the Japanese pronunciation will be given once in parentheses the first time the word appears. For example, "Heaven" would appear as *"tian* (J. *ten)."* A term that is primarily associated with Japanese religious or philosophical traditions, however, will be given in Japanese. For example, the nearly untranslatable *tentō* (also *tendō*) is peculiarly Japanese in the context of such Sengoku or early Tokugawa texts as *Honsaroku* or *Shingaku gorinsho,* and thus writing *"tiandao"* would make little sense.

Overview

The first chapter examines Ryukyu's complex relations with Japan (Satsuma and the bakufu) and China (Fuzhou and Beijing) during the seventeenth century. Satsuma's invasion of the kingdom in 1609 rendered Ryukyu's precise political status ambivalent. Owing in large part to major events outside of Ryukyu, most important the Manchu conquest of China, Ryukyu attained a substantial degree of autonomy through the Satsuma/bakufu policy of governing the kingdom indirectly. A complex web of trade and diplomacy connected Beijing, Fuzhou, Ryukyu, Satsuma, and the bakufu, the major features of which this chapter examines. Although relations between Ryukyu and its neighbors continued to evolve throughout the eighteenth and nineteenth centuries, by the end of the seventeenth century, an enduring pattern of interactions was firmly in place. Subsequent changes took place within this pattern, and this chapter is intended to contextualize those that follow.

Chapter 2 examines the thought and careers of Shō Shōken and Tei Junsoku. Shō Shōken saw Ryukyu as, ideally, a loyal vassal of Japan (via Satsuma). As Ryukyu's first official historian, he read this lord-vassal relationship far back into the past and blamed Satsuma's invasion on Ryukyu's failure to live up to its proper obligations to Satsuma/Japan. For Shō Shōken, Ryukyuan acceptance of its relationship with Satsuma was the key to a prosperous future for the kingdom. As prime minister, he implemented policies that promoted the mastery of Japanese cultural forms among Ryukyuan elites. By contrast, Tei Junsoku looked to China, less as a political entity than as a universal cultural ideal. He saw Ryukyu as a participant in China's glorious literary and cultural tradition and vigorously promoted Chinese studies in Ryukyu. Tei Junsoku served the kingdom as a diplomat. Although his vision of Ryukyu was substantially different from that of Shō Shōken, there was relatively little conflict between the Japan-centered view and the China-centered view during the seventeenth century because each tended to inform different segments of Ryukyuan society and politics. During the eighteenth and nineteenth centuries, however, the level of conflict between Sino- and Japan-centric views tended to increase.

Sai On was a product of the program of Chinese studies that Tei Junsoku helped develop. Beginning his political career in the eighteenth century, Sai On developed a sophisticated, nuanced view of Ryukyu that combined elements of Shō Shōken's frank recognition of Japanese power and Tei Junsoku's glorification of Chinese culture as a universal standard. More important, Sai On went beyond both of the earlier views by developing what might be called a Ryukyu-centered view. By implementing an ideal Confucian society, Sai On argued, Ryukyuans could take control of their destiny and create a prosperous country fully on a moral par with its larger neighbors. Chapter 3 examines Sai On's vision with an emphasis on its theoretical foundations.

The theoretical side of Sai On's vision of Ryukyu contained almost revolutionary implications for politics if put into practice. Sai On was a master politician who eventually became Ryukyu's most powerful minister. In that capacity he worked to implement his vision of Ryukyu with considerable success. His attempt to transform Ryukyu into his version of an ideal Confucian society engendered opposition from at least three major groups: the traditional Shuri aristocracy, a segment of the residents of Kumemura, Ryukyu's center for Chinese studies, and the peasantry. Chapter 4 examines Sai On's political program and the intra-Ryukyuan opposition to parts of it.

Although it faced significant opposition, Sai On's vision of Ryukyu had powerful backers. Activist kings Shō Boku (r. 1752–1795) and Shō On (r. 1796–1802) continued the process of Confucianization that Sai On began, sponsoring, among other institutions, a civil service examination system and a national university and school system. Shō On formally declared that merit in the form of knowledge of Confucian literature would henceforth become the basis for the selection of government officials. Ironically, the spread of Confucianism throughout all segments of Ryukyu's upper classes caused violent protest on the part of Kumemura, whose residents feared losing their monopoly on Chinese learning. Chapter 5 examines these events and chronicles the steady decline of Ryukyu's economic fortunes during the nineteenth century. By the time of the kingdom's end, chronic and increasingly severe financial problems had eroded Sai On's Ryukyu from within.

The Epilogue and Conclusions chapter carries the narrative of Ryukyuan/Okinawan history close to the present, with emphasis on the Meiji and Taishō periods. By outlining some of the major issues in modern Ryukyuan/Okinawan identity, it seeks to provide a bridge across Ryukyu/Okinawa's modern divide, linking the present study with recent and contemporary issues. It also draws conclusions by linking this study with issues in Ryukyuan history, Confucianism, Japanese history, and the construction of imagined communities.

CHAPTER 1

The Status of Ryukyu and
Its Relations with Japan and China

This chapter examines dimensions of the complex web of relationships between Ryukyu, China, and Japan during the seventeenth and eighteenth centuries. It was within this environment that men such as Shō Shōken, Tei Junsoku, Sai On, and Heshikiya Chōbin created their visions of Ryukyu. The precise status of early-modern Ryukyu has been a much discussed and often emotional question ever since the kingdom's demise. Even today, Ryukyuan nationalists often rummage through the seventeenth and eighteenth centuries in their search for "facts" that might justify separating "Ryukyu" (whatever it might be) from "Japan" (whatever that it be). The question of early-modern Ryukyu's status will not be settled definitively here, but I do hope to provide a sense of the complexity and ambiguity of that status. Ryukyu's ambiguous status vis-à-vis Satsuma, the bakufu, and China created an enabling tension that produced a range of possible ways of envisioning Ryukyu. Terms such as "country," "nation," "independent country," or "Japan" that seem obvious and natural to many in today's world become problematic when employed to describe early-modern Ryukyu and its relations with surrounding lands.

By the eighteenth century, the mechanics of early-modern Ryukyu's relationship with other countries had settled into a pattern. Although the details of this pattern changed throughout the eighteenth and nineteenth centuries, its basic outline remained the same. This chapter examines the major contours of that outline using a topical approach as opposed to a chronological narrative.

Satsuma's "Great-hearted Deed"
On the fifth day of the fourth month of 1609, Ryukyuan defenders of Shuri castle surrendered to an invading army from Satsuma. The majority of Satsuma's soldiers soon left Ryukyu, bringing King Shō Nei (r. 1587–1620) and major Ryukyuan officials back with them to Kagoshima. During the king's two-year absence, Satsuma officials left behind to oversee Ryukyu's

affairs undertook a detailed survey of all islands to determine their productive capacities. Meanwhile, the king traveled to Sunpu to meet Tokugawa Ieyasu and then went on to Edo for a formal audience with the shōgun, Hidetada. Upon their return to Kagoshima, Satsuma's officials presented the Ryukyuans with formal documents of surrender.

The surrender documents consisted of two oaths, one signed by the king and the other by his leading officials, and a set of fifteen broadly worded injunctions. The first item was similar in both oaths, and in the official English translation prepared by Japan's Meiji government in the 1870s, it reads:

> The islands of Riu Kiu have from ancient times been a feudal dependency of Satsuma; and we have for ages observed the custom of sending thither, at stated times, junks bearing products of these islands, and we have always sent messengers to carry our congratulations to a new Prince of Satsuma on his accession.[1]

Here Satsuma's daimyō, Shimazu Iehisa, depicts Ryukyu and its king as long having stood in relation to the Shimazu clan as had the heads of states participating in tributary relations with China stood in relation to the Chinese emperor. That no such relationship had existed prior to 1609 undoubtedly made the document a particularly bitter pill for Shō Nei and his officials to swallow. In an important sense, Satsuma's military power had transformed Ryukyu's past.[2]

The oath goes on to explain that the king and his court were "very guilty" of neglecting their duty to Satsuma. Indeed, their neglect eventually required Satsuma to send an army of chastisement. "A prisoner in [Satsuma's] mighty land," the king "had lost all hope of returning to [his] home." Fortunately, however, ". . . our merciful Prince [Shimazu] has shown his loving kindness; and taking pity on master and servants whose country seemed all lost to them, gave them his leave to return to their homes; not only so, but also allowed themselves to govern some of their country's islands."[3] The phrase "some of" indicates Satsuma's decision to seize the northern Ryukyu islands and incorporate them into its own territory. So "thankful" were the Ryukyuans for such benevolence and generosity from Satsuma's virtuous rulers that king and ministers swore: "So will we forever be the humble servants of Satsuma, and obedient to all commands, and never will be traitors to our Lord."[4]

The oath signed by Ryukyu's major officials was similar to the king's. The officials, too, "know not how to show our thankfulness," and swore forever to "remain the loyal subjects of Satsuma." In addition, their oath contained the following substantive item, enjoining them to give their highest loyalty to Satsuma's rulers:

If, peradventure, any man of Riu Kiu, forgetful of this great-hearted deed, ever in times to come, plans a revolt against you, yea, if it were our Chieftain himself who should be drawn to join [in] revolt, yet we nevertheless obedient to the commands of our Great Lord, will never be false to our Oath by abetting a rebel, be he lord or churl.[5]

Like their king, Ryukyu's top officials were presented with Satsuma's re-creation of Ryukyu's past upon which to affix their seals and signatures. One did not.

Tei Dō (Jana Ueekata, ?–1611), commander of the defeated Ryukyuan forces and supporter of the pre-invasion policy of ignoring Japanese demands, continued to resist Satsuma even as a prisoner. In secret he wrote a letter addressed to the Ming court, which he entrusted to Ryukyuans bound for China. The letter got as far as Fuzhou, where resident Ryukyuan officials intercepted and destroyed it. No doubt an appeal for help of some kind, the letter is no longer extant. As a final gesture of protest, Tei Dō refused to sign the surrender documents, for which he was beheaded. Satsuma would tolerate no open defiance of its "great-hearted deed." From this time on, all thoughtful Ryukyuans would have to face the vexing problem of adapting themselves and their visions of Ryukyu to the realities of life under Satsuma's domination.

The Fifteen Injunctions *(Okite jūgo ka jūo)* that accompanied the surrender oaths included several noteworthy items. The first and sixth articles specified that trade with China or elsewhere outside Ryukyu be conducted only with Satsuma's permission. The second article required that stipends or other official compensation be granted based on merit, not heredity. The fifth article specified that the number of shrines and temples "not be excessive." The Council of Three *(Sanshikan)* alone is charged with administering Ryukyu, stated the ninth article. The twelfth specified that Satsuma be notified in the event that excessive taxes were levied on the common people. The thirteenth article forbade any merchant ship to sail from Ryukyu to a foreign country.[6]

The injunctions were of a broad, general nature and indicate certain conditions that Satsuma hoped would prevail in Ryukyu. Tomiyama Kazuyuki has criticized the tendency of earlier generations of historians of Ryukyu to place too much importance on this and other sets of injunctions from Satsuma. That Satsuma issued the injunctions does not necessarily mean that Ryukyuans followed all or any of them. Certain Ryukyuan practices remained contrary to several of the Fifteen Injunctions well into the seventeenth century if not later.[7] Tomiyama's point is valid. It is also important to note, however, that the trajectory of change in Ryukyuan society throughout its early-modern period was in the direction outlined in the Fifteen Injunctions. For example, although two centuries passed before its fullest implementation, the principle of merit in the selection of government officials gained increasing ground against heredity. In another example, Buddhism and native forms of religion came under ever increasing attack by Confucians. Some of these Confucians eventually succeeded in making their views state ideology, and mastery of certain Confucian concepts and texts thus became the basis of determining "merit" in selecting officials. Although Satsuma rarely micro-managed Ryukyu's internal affairs, reform-minded Ryukyuans required Satsuma's direct and indirect support were they to have any hope of accomplishing their aims. Satsuma's support consistently went to those Ryukyuans whose policies supported the letter or spirit of the Fifteen Injunctions.

Early Evolution of Ryukyu-Satsuma Relations

When Shō Nei and his officials arrived in Edo, bakufu officials praised Shimazu for his success and permitted him to receive "tribute" payments from Ryukyu. The bakufu confirmed Shimazu's control over Ryukyu, but only within the bounds of facilitating the bakufu's own policy toward Ming China. Shōgun Hidetada told Shimazu, "Because the king of Chūzan has ruled Ryukyu for many generations, it is not permissible to set up someone from another household as king."[8] The bakufu, while recognizing Satsuma's control over Ryukyu, also imposed limitations on Shimazu's authority to direct Ryukyu's internal affairs. Although Satsuma intended to use Ryukyu for the domain's benefit, it had to be wary of possible bakufu interest in Satsuma's activities connected with Ryukyu.

Shō Nei and his officials returned home to Shuri, Ryukyu's capital, and took up their old posts. Satsuma removed the northern Ryukyu islands of Kikai, Amami-Ōshima, Tokunoshima, Okinoerabu, and Yoron from the king's jurisdiction and incorporated these territories into its own domain. Initially, Satsuma sought to make even the territories remaining under Shuri's ostensible control as much like Japan (or Satsuma) as possible with respect to culture. In 1613, for example, Satsuma ordered that "The various customs and practices of Ryukyu are not to differ from those of Japan."[9] Satsuma also purged any Ryukyuan officials thought to be sympathizers of Tei Dō, who in death became the scapegoat for having caused Satsuma's invasion.[10] As replacements, Satsuma promoted those with extensive knowledge of Japan. The overall aim of the purge was to prevent Ryukyuan opposition to Satsuma.[11]

The failure of the bakufu's trade negotiations with Ming in 1615, however, enhanced Ryukyu's potential importance for bakufu policy. For the time being, at least, the bakufu had no alternative but to trade with Ming indirectly, via Ryukyu and Satsuma. This new situation was a major reason for Satsuma's 1616 reversal of the Japanization policy it had announced only three years previously. In a letter to Shō Nei, Shimazu Iehisa stated that for Ryukyu to follow Satsuma in every way would be detrimental to Ryukyu's continued existence as a country. Ryukyu was to preserve its separate identity for the sake of maintaining its relationship with China. Shimazu's new policy explicitly prohibited Ryukyuans from adopting certain Japanese customs. Furthermore, Satsuma granted the king primary political authority in the administration of Ryukyu's internal affairs within certain general bounds. In 1617, additional regulations forbade Ryukyuans to wear Japanese hair or clothing styles and in general to act "like Japanese" *(Nihonjin no nari)*.[12]

By the mid-1630s, the general framework of Ryukyu's relationship with Satsuma and the bakufu was in place. An important 1624 directive from Satsuma repeated some earlier policies and also authorized additional leeway for Ryukyu in administering its judicial affairs. The relevant five-article declaration stated:

1. Stipends for the Council of Three and other officials are hereafter to be commensurate with their positions.
2. Capital punishment and banishment are to be carried out in accordance with circumstances, without making inquiries to Satsuma.
3. It is strictly forbidden to take Japanese names or wear Japanese clothing.
4. Within our domains [Satsuma, Ōsumi, northern Ryukyu islands], agricultural festivals are not to interfere with time spent harvesting. Areas under your control are to be [regulated regarding this matter] as is appropriate.
5. People from other *kuni* [here meaning other Japanese domains] are forbidden to go to Ryukyu.[13]

The second article granted the king full juridical authority within his own territories. From his examination court documents, Takara Kurayoshi points out that Ryukyuans charged with crimes in Satsuma's territories were not tried in Satsuma but were sent to Ryukyu to be dealt with according to its "national laws."[14]

Also significant in these articles is the prohibition against Japanese names and clothing along with the prohibition against other Japanese going to Ryukyu. By returning a large measure of internal administrative control to the royal government, prohibiting the outward appearance of Japanese influence among Ryukyuans, and preventing other Japanese from visiting or residing in Ryukyu, Satsuma was laying the foundation for a new Ryukyu. It was a Ryukyu ultimately under Satsuma's control but also nominally a separate

country. Nearly all historians of Ryukyu agree that Satsuma's major interest in
Ryukyu was profit from the tribute trade with China. Satsuma quickly learned
that in order for this trade to go on smoothly, it was necessary that Ryukyu
appear entirely free of Japanese domination or influence in Chinese eyes.

The final element in the general framework binding Ryukyu, Satsuma,
and the bakufu together was Ryukyu's de facto incorporation into the *bakuhan*
(bakufu-domains) system. Kamiya gives the date for this event as 1634, for it
was then that Iemitsu formally recognized Ryukyu's *kokudaka* (assessed productivity) as belonging to Shimazu's domain. Simultaneously, however, the
shōgun also recognized Ryukyu's tributary relationship with China.[15] When a
new shōgun took office, he would issue a document known as *ryōchi hanbutsu,*
which reconfirmed the daimyō in their holdings. The document Hidetada
issued to Shimazu Iehisa in 1617 did not include Ryukyu's *kokudaka,* whereas
all those issued from 1634 and thereafter did. Kamiya points out that a major
incentive for the bakufu's incorporation of Ryukyu into the *bakuhan* system
was to ensure control over the kingdom's foreign trade.[16] Bakufu officials
regarded this control as necessary, in part because of Ryukyu's longstanding
ties with China.

Ryukyu in a Changing International Order

The Ming dynasty fell in 1644, after several decades of decline. After consoli-
dating their power in China proper, the Qing emperors began to push the
boundaries of the Chinese empire outward. By the turn of the eighteenth century, Qing China was a vast, wealthy, militarily powerful empire. Bakufu and
other Japanese officials watched these developments on the continent with
great interest and no small degree of concern. The Ming-Qing transition
affected Ryukyu as well, both directly through its tributary relations with
China and indirectly through Ryukyu's changed importance to Satsuma and
the bakufu. From the middle of the seventeenth century, Ryukyu found itself
in the midst of a complex network of economic, military, and political interests that stretched between China and Japan.

Many educated Koreans and Japanese regarded China's new Manchu
rulers as barbarians. Recalling what happened the last time a "barbarian" conquest dynasty came to power in China (the Yuan dynasty, which invaded Japan),
many in Japan voiced concerns over possible Qing military action. This concern
continued into the eighteenth century. The influential scholar Kumazawa
Banzan (1619–1691), for example, was convinced of an imminent attack on
Japan by the Manchus and wrote about this matter in several of his essays. In
Daigaku wakumon he stated: "The urgent duty of the present is to store up mil-

itary provisions. The Tartars [Manchus] have taken China and will soon be coming to Japan."[17] Maehira Fusaaki points out that scholar and bakufu advisor Arai Hakuseki (1657–1725) was apprehensive over the possibility that Japan and China might be drawn into conflict over Ryukyu. As a result, he sought information on Ryukyu, which became the basis for his two essays on Ryukyuan history and conditions.[18] In 1712 bakufu officials wrote to Satsuma seeking specific information on Qing armor, weapons, and related items. Satsuma in turn sent the following notice to Ryukyu's Council of Three: "Regarding things such as officers' uniforms, armor, and weapons of Great Qing, according to bakufu request, though we have books from which we can see the appearance of the officers' uniforms and can get by with them, in China, you are to search for books dealing with armor and weapons and should ask the Chinese with whom you interact to provide them for you."[19] Many Japanese were uneasy about Qing military power, and Ryukyu, with its close ties to China, turned out to be an ideal source of first-hand information about Qing China.

Bakufu concerns about Qing military power affected its policy toward Satsuma and Ryukyu. In 1646, for example, when the powerful Ming loyalist general Zheng Chenggong asked Japan for military assistance in resisting the Manchus, Senior Councillor (rōjū) Abe Shigetsugi asked Satsuma to obtain a report from Ryukyu on conditions in China. In response to Satsuma's request for clarification about whether trade should continue between China and Ryukyu despite the ongoing turmoil, the bakufu responded that the status quo should continue. Bakufu officials had two reasons for this policy. First was a reluctance to lose a valuable source of information about China. Second was fear that forcing one of China's tributary states to break off relations would give the Qing an excuse to attack Japan.[20]

In 1655, the bakufu formally approved tribute relations between Ryukyu and Qing, again, in part to avoid giving Qing any reason for military action against Japan.[21] An apprehension shared by both Satsuma and the bakufu just before the start of Qing-Ryukyu relations was whether the Manchus would insist on Ryukyuan officials conforming to Qing customs such as wearing the queue. Were the new dynasty to lord over Ryukyu, both Satsuma and the bakufu feared losing control. Although these fears proved unfounded, starting in the middle of the seventeenth century, the bakufu began to place the primary responsibility for Ryukyuan affairs in Satsuma's hands, thereby distancing itself from a possible source of trouble. One result, of course, was for Shimazu's control over Ryukyu to expand relative to that of the bakufu.[22] But the need to maintain good relations with Qing China also dictated that Satsuma be discreet in how it exercised that control.

Soon after the rise of the Qing, the bakufu articulated a policy of governing Ryukyu indirectly.[23] The king's officials would take care of Ryukyu's internal administration, and they would conduct the kingdom's external affairs according to Satsuma or bakufu guidelines. This way, Japanese control over Ryukyu would be kept completely out of China's sight. Reflecting this policy, Satsuma issued new and more detailed regulations in 1657, reaffirming royal administration of Ryukyu's affairs. Kamiya points out that it was after this time that the pace of internal restructuring of the kingdom intensified, as did efforts to conceal the nature of the relationship between Japan and Ryukyu from China.[24]

The bakufu-Satsuma policy of promoting Ryukyu-Qing relations was effective in maintaining a flow of goods and information from China, although there were some unanticipated adverse consequences. Anti-Qing naval forces based (at different times) in Guangdong, Fujian, and Taiwan preyed on Ryukyuan shipping throughout the 1660s and 1670s to the point that Ryukyuan ships had to be armed with rifles and cannon. In a letter to Nagasaki officials explaining a 1670 attack on a Ryukyuan vessel, anti-Qing warlord Zheng Jing stated that he regarded Ryukyu as an enemy country because, though once loyal to the Ming, it had gone over to the side of the Qing. The letter gave no indication that Zheng saw Japan as Ryukyu's protector or overlord, suggesting the policy of concealing Ryukyu's true relationship with Japan was at least partially effective.[25]

Japanese officials watched the 1673 Revolt of the Three Feudatories with great interest. While the revolt was under way, Shimazu sought bakufu approval for virtually everything Ryukyu did in the realm of foreign relations, an indication of the high degree of concern this event generated in Japan.[26] As they had done earlier when the outcome of the battles between Qing forces and their enemies was unclear, Ryukyuan envoys sailing for China during the time of the revolt brought with them two sets of official correspondence. One was addressed to "Great Qing" and the other to the restorers of "Great Ming." Upon arrival in Fujian, they would quickly ascertain the present situation from Ryukyuans already there and burn one of the two sets. By such means, the Ryukyuans appeared to the Qing emperor as never having doubted his control. Once, the Kangxi emperor even commended Ryukyu for its "loyalty" during the difficult time of the revolt.[27] Satsuma was delighted when Qing forces finally prevailed, and in a letter to King Shō Tei (r. 1669–1709), Shimazu Mitsuhisa was barely able to contain his happiness.[28] With the Qing dynasty firmly in control, Satsuma hoped to be able to increase its trade with China and thereby relieve ongoing financial woes.

Immediately after its invasion of Ryukyu, Satsuma instructed Ryukyuans traveling to China as follows: "There is to be no mention of Ryukyu's having come under Satsuma's control while you are in China. Also, it is forbidden to speak about actual conditions in Ryukyu to any Chinese."[29] Chinese officials, however, eventually learned that Satsuma had invaded Ryukyu and grew suspicious of Japanese influence in the kingdom's affairs. When Ryukyuans presented their second post-invasion tribute items to China in 1611, for example, a supervising official in Fujian sent the following message to the Ming court: Your servant is attached to the agency that supervises the Ryukyuans. An entire year has already gone by, but [Ryukyu] was invaded by Japan and [the invaders] have now gone back [to Japan]. . . . The tribute they present now includes a sharp increase in the quantity of Japanese goods such as sulphur and horses."[30] Ostensibly as a favor to Ryukyu to allow it to "recover" from Satsuma's invasion, in 1612 the Ming court reduced the frequency of tribute embassies from one every two years to one every ten years.

Satsuma pressured Ryukyu to persuade Ming to restore the tribute missions to their former frequency. Some progress took place in 1622, when the Ming court increased the frequency to once in five years. Higashionna points out that the liberal payment of bribes to Chinese officials with cash provided by Satsuma helped accomplish this change.[31] It was not until 1633 that the Ming court restored tribute missions to their former frequency of once every two years. Owing to problems in obtaining Ryukyuan cooperation, however, and to the weakening and fall of the Ming dynasty, Satsuma was unable immediately to capitalize on this restoration of the tribute trade.

Satsuma's Uses of Ryukyu

Satsuma sought to use its relationship with Ryukyu to enhance its wealth and prestige. This undertaking proved more complex and less successful than originally anticipated because of the need to deal with a web of changing conditions within and between China, Ryukyu, the bakufu, and Satsuma itself. It was with respect to trade that Satsuma encountered the greatest problems. Its plans were to provide capital, mainly in the form of silver, to fund Ryukyuan purchases of Chinese goods. Domain officials then intended to sell those goods at market centers in Japan at a substantial profit. The major problem throughout most of the seventeenth century following the "normalization" of Ryukyu's tribute trade with China in 1633 was what Uehara calls "sabotage" by Ryukyuan officials in China. For example, Ryukyuan officials hid or pocketed much of the silver that Satsuma provided to fund the 1634 voyage. Furthermore, many goods that Ryukyuans did purchase were of poor quality.[32]

Always in financial difficulty, Satsuma experienced a particularly severe period of financial crisis from the late 1630s through the late 1660s. This crisis was in part the result of acute problems such as crop failures and military impositions from the bakufu. It was also the result of longer-term factors such as difficulty adjusting to the new market economy then spreading throughout Japan. An additional cause of the financial crisis was a lack of profit from Ryukyu's tribute trade.[33]

In 1663, Shō Shitsu (r. 1648–1668) became the first Ryukyuan king to receive investiture from the Qing court. The investiture envoys brought an imperial edict stating that tribute embassies were to be sent once every two years, that they should consist of 150 people, and that two official envoys, plus a retinue of fifteen attendants, would be allowed to travel to Beijing. To express his thanks to the Qing court, the king sent Chatan Ueekata Chōhō (Shō Kokuyō) as an Envoy of Gratitude. Eso Ueekata also went along as an Envoy of Congratulation, since the Kangxi emperor had just ascended the throne. Thus began the most serious instance of Ryukyuan sabotage of Satsuma's economic interests, the Chatan-Eso Affair. The incident is worth describing at some length, for it sheds light on the state of Satsuma-Ryukyu relations at the time.

It began with the Ryukyuan ship encountering dangerous wind conditions and an attack by a band of pirates as it entered the harbor of Fuzhou. Eso and most of the crew panicked and fled the ship, but some Ryukyuans remained on board to defend the cargo. There, they realized that the pirates, while dressed like Chinese, were really Ryukyuans. After fending off the pirates, some of the Ryukyuan crew decided to make off with the cargo themselves. Kyan Chikudun, who had led the initial resistance against the pirates, along with several crew members who remained loyal, gave up their resistance. They left the ship and headed for the Ryukyuan courier station to make a report. Ashore, the guilty members of the vessel's crew robbed and killed Kyan and his group to cover up their crimes. Meanwhile, the original pirates made off with items from the ship including the most valuable piece of cargo, a gold wine jar provided by Satsuma to be presented as a gift to the new emperor. The jar changed hands between Ryukyuans several times under unsavory circumstances that included theft, poisoning, and blackmail before being sold to a Chinese and lost.[34]

These matters did not become known to the royal government until 1665, when Chatan returned. The royal government sent two envoys to Satsuma to report the matter, and Satsuma responded by sending officials to Ryukyu who questioned various suspects, some under torture. The next year these officials moved the investigation to Satsuma, where over twenty Ryukyuans were questioned. In the fall of 1666, those questioned returned to

Ryukyu. The next year, Satsuma handed down judgments. Chatan and Eso were to be executed and their children and families banished to remote places. The text of the judgment contained the following points:

1. The theft of the jar was the result of [Chatan and Eso's] failing to carry out their duty, and they were at fault for not holding an inquiry at the scene;

2. Possession of poison is prohibited in both Japan and China, and the two were at fault for the delay in reporting the poisoning of Miyazato [one of the Ryukyuan victims];

3. Improper procedures were followed in allowing the group of Ryukyuan pirates to approach the vessel;

4. As numerous crimes were committed by your [Chatan and Eso's] subordinates, you should have had them punished immediately upon returning, but instead you had them sent off to various places to lay low and delayed reporting the matter;

5. Regarding Eso: No matter the difficulties or circumstances, the person in charge is never to abandon a cargo, and your doing so was cowardly.[35]

As Uehara points out, the fact that Ryukyuans themselves were involved in stealing the tribute cargo was a grave matter because it had the potential to imperil Ryukyu-Qing relations. Because Chatan was not prosecuted initially, Satsuma suspected a coverup by Ryukyu. When accused of such, the royal government claimed that its lack of vigor in pursuing the case was the result of the prime minister (sessei, O. shisshii) and one member of the Council of Three having become ill. Other than the execution of Chatan and Eso, Satsuma left it to Ryukyu to mete out justice to the lesser offenders, but the royal government did not pursue the matter.[36]

There were numerous lesser incidents in which money and goods were lost under suspicious circumstances. In each case Satsuma reacted with angry letters and by setting up new trade procedures. It is significant, however, that even for misconduct as extreme as the Chatan-Eso Affair, Satsuma was relatively restrained in its intervention. It had little choice but to rely largely on a royal government that was less than enthusiastic about cooperating with its recent conquerors. Satsuma could bring great force to bear on Ryukyu, and it certainly had no reservations about doing so if such actions would advance its interests. But for all its power, Satsuma was constrained by its need for Ryukyuan cooperation as well as by the need to conceal Japanese military power from Chinese eyes.

Angry letters to the royal government and the occasional use of force proved insufficient for generating a profit from Ryukyu's tribute trade. Still,

Satsuma continued to look to that trade as potentially the best way to extricate itself from its financial difficulties. In the 1670s and 1680s, the domain developed a more effective set of policies to gain Ryukyu's cooperation in making the trade profitable. In 1672 Satsuma again revised trade practices, implementing verification procedures designed to ensure that the goods brought back to Ryukyu from China matched records indicating the amount of money spent on those goods. What is more important, in 1683, Satsuma restructured taxes. Under the new system, Ryukyu paid Satsuma one *shō,* seven *gō* of rice for every *koku* produced.[37] This rice was freely convertible to other goods according to a set schedule (Table 1), most of which were Chinese products. This new system created an incentive for Ryukyu to provide Satsuma with high-quality Chinese products.[38]

In 1685, Satsuma made further efforts to obtain high-quality Chinese goods at reasonable prices by issuing additional regulations. The first specified that henceforth all Ryukyuan officials sent to China must be knowledgeable of its actual conditions and should have experience purchasing goods there. The

ITEM	RICE
10 *kin* [≈6 kg.] jar of longan fruits	4 *shō*
1 *kin* [≈.6 kg.] jar of *mochi*	2 *shō*
50 *kin* [≈30 kg.] of sapan wood	3 *shō*
100 *kin* [≈60 kg.] of silk	1 *koku* 8 *to*
1 large rug	5 *shō*
1 medium rug	3 *shō*
1 5-bundle, white Chinese paper	5 *shō*
1 20-bundle, yellow Chinese paper	2 *to* 5 *shō*
1 60-bundle, straw Chinese paper	2 *to* 5 *shō*
1 7-bundle, cotton paper	4 *shō*
50 *kin* of ginned cotton	5 *shō*
small, 10-*kin* jar of alum	4 *shō*

Table 1 Partial conversion list.

second regulation ordered Ryukyuan buyers to inspect carefully the quality of all items at the time of purchase and to reject any inferior items. The third mandated greater diligence with regard to goods purchased in Fujian. It also specified that any goods purchased be arranged and ready for shipment in time to get them on the next ship back to Ryukyu. The most important regulation was the fourth. Hitherto, private trade by Ryukyuans in China had been prohibited, but now Satsuma permitted limited private trade as a material incentive for Ryukyuans to be more reliable and cooperative.[39] Satsuma's officials no doubt realized that Ryukyuans would not work diligently for Satsuma's interests without some benefit to themselves. This added incentive, and the requirement that only knowledgeable Ryukyuans conduct the trade, also helped create conditions favorable to the study of Chinese language and culture in Ryukyu.

There was more to Satsuma's use of Ryukyu than trade with China. The domain's leaders adroitly used Ryukyu's relationship with the Qing to leverage the bakufu in various ways. An excellent example is Shimazu Yoshitaka's successful 1710 campaign to have his court rank raised. Shimazu's argument stated in part that Ryukyu ranked second only to Korea in China's tributary system, and its king was also a vassal of Satsuma. The increase in rank, he claimed, was necessary for Shimazu to be of suitably high status to deal effectively with Ryukyu's king. Shimazu further argued that his firm control over Ryukyu was necessary to ensure that it would not join forces with the Qing empire against Japan.[40] Even as late as the Tenpō era (1830–1844), when again Shimazu petitioned for increased court rank, part of the argument stressed the need to maintain control over Ryukyu: "As for maintaining control over Ryukyu, although it is indeed a small country, because it has diplomatic relations with Qing, it places great value on matters such as court rank. . . . [Low court rank would] raise doubts and lead to numerous obstacles *(samatage)* in governing [Ryukyu]."[41] The result of these arguments was an increase in rank from Junior Fourth to Senior Fourth. There were numerous other instances during the nineteenth century when Satsuma used the possibility of a rupture in Ryukyu-Chinese relations to get its way vis-à-vis the bakufu.[42]

There were other ways that Satsuma used its relationship with Ryukyu to bolster the domain's prestige. Ryukyuan embassies traveled to Edo periodically for such purposes as offering congratulations to a new shōgun or thanking the shōgun for approving a new Ryukyuan king, a practice called *Edo nobori.* These embassies were an important part of bakufu foreign relations, as Toby and others have pointed out.[43] The embassies, which consisted of one- to two-hundred officials, retainers, and musicians, would sail from Naha to Satsuma. From there they would travel by land to Edo. The embassies were impressive spectacles that attracted attention all along the route. Crowds invariably gathered to gawk at the oddly attired Ryukyuans. The several extant *Ryūkyūjin odori* attest to the impression the Ryukyuans conveyed to Japanese audiences. Also known as *Tōjin odori,* these were dances by Japanese in imitation of the Ryukyuans. At least three such dances are still performed annually in parts of Kagoshima Prefecture.[44] The essential point here is that Satsuma, whose samurai escorted the Ryukyuans, was able to show off its unique status as the only domain that controlled a foreign king. Satsuma took every opportunity to emphasize the foreignness of the Ryukyuans, who were under instructions to feign ignorance of Japanese language and customs while en route to Edo. Similarly, the Shimazu daimyō took every opportunity to exaggerate the importance of the small kingdom in the eyes of other daimyō and the shōgun.

In 1709, this practice of actively enhancing Ryukyu's importance encountered a temporary setback. When Tokugawa Ienobu became shōgun, Satsuma prepared for Ryukyu to send a congratulatory embassy. Unexpectedly, the bakufu informed both Shimazu and the Ryukyuan Council of Three not to bother.[45] The year 1709 was a particularly bad one for Ryukyu. It suffered from repeated typhoons, crop failures, and famine, natural disasters that reduced a large portion of the population to eating bark.[46] On top of these problems, the royal palace burnt down. As Uehara points out, the order from the bakufu not to send an embassy was therefore good news for the hard-pressed royal government. It was, however, quite vexing for Satsuma.[47] The domain petitioned the bakufu to resume former practices, pointing out that among China's tributary states, Ryukyu ranked second only to Korea. Therefore, went the argument, the Ryukyuan kings' official displays of subordination to the shōgun enhanced bakufu prestige. Satsuma also pointed out that cessation of the *Edo nobori* embassies would make Ryukyuans think that Satsuma's prestige had gone down in bakufu eyes, which would make it more difficult to govern the kingdom.[48]

Satsuma's petition initiated a dialogue between Ienobu's top advisor, Manabe Akifusa, and Shimazu about the precise relationship of Satsuma's control over Ryukyu. Ultimately, the bakufu restored the practice of *Edo nobori,* but provided its own rationale: the show of ritual submission by the Ryukyuans was an important element in asserting the bakufu's military authority as *kōgi,* the source of political authority in the realm.[49] The Ryukyuans would be allowed to come, in other words, because the practice would enhance bakufu authority. By stating its own rationale instead of that provided by Satsuma, the bakufu was saying, in effect, that Ryukyu was like the various domains in terms of its relationship to shogunal authority.

This move prompted Satsuma to make several changes to boost Ryukyuan prestige and enhance the kingdom's image as an important foreign country. First, the head and assistant envoys assumed more impressive titles. In 1712, the king's official diplomatic title was changed from *kokushi* (roughly "administrator") to *kokuō* (king). Finally, before 1726, only the highest Ryukyuan officials traveled to Edo clad in Ming-style Chinese robes, but starting that year, all Ryukyuans in the embassy wore such robes.[50]

Incidents such as these reveal something of the complex network of diplomatic, political, economic, and ceremonial relationships in which Ryukyu was enmeshed. In the first instance, of course, Satsuma used Ryukyu to enhance its own prestige. To whatever extent the Ryukyuan envoys may have bolstered the prestige of the bakufu, they bolstered Shimazu's prestige even more. The argument that the bakufu's receiving embassies from Ryukyu was necessary to enable Satsuma to control the kingdom was a variation of the argument Shimazu used to obtain higher court rank, and it may, of course, have been nothing more than a strategy to win bakufu approval. On the other hand, we have seen the great difficulty Satsuma encountered trying to gain the cooperation of Ryukyuan officials. Furthermore, owing to the necessity of hiding the nature of Satsuma's relationship with Ryukyu from Chinese eyes, the domain had no real choice but to control Ryukyu indirectly through cooperative royal government officials. In this respect, the enhanced authority conferred on Satsuma by active bakufu interest in Ryukyu may indeed have increased Satsuma's leverage over Ryukyu.

An incident in 1690 nicely illustrates Satsuma's difficulty in managing Ryukyu's foreign affairs. In that year, the Qing court settled on three items that it would require Ryukyuans to bring as tribute: copper, sulphur, and tin. The last item was added at the behest of Qing officials who thought that Ryukyu's tribute allotment had previously been too low. Ryukyuan envoys in China agreed to the new conditions, but the addition of tin caused trouble for Satsuma. Not only was tin unavailable in Ryukyu, it was also unavailable in Satsuma. The domain thus had to purchase tin on the open market, which was both costly and required bakufu approval. For the tribute mission of 1692, Satsuma had no choice but to send tin. Along with the tin, it also sent a memo specifying that in the future Ryukyuan envoys must consult with Satsuma before agreeing to any similar trade conditions.[51] As this matter shows, Satsuma had little leverage over the activities of Ryukyuans once they arrived in China.

The bakufu used Ryukyuan embassies as an opportunity ritually to display its authority. Satsuma used Ryukyu to maintain its prestigious role as overlord of a foreign king and guardian of an important link between China and

Japan.[52] It is also important to note that the treatment Ryukyu received from Satsuma and the bakufu enhanced the prestige of its king as well. With a total assessed productivity of 90,000–100,000 *koku,* and actual production roughly twice that amount, the Ryukyu Kingdom was only as large as a medium-sized Japanese domain.[53] The diplomatic treatment it received from the bakufu was vastly out of proportion to its small size. For their own very different reasons, therefore, the bakufu, Satsuma, and Ryukyu's royal government all stood to gain by enhancing Ryukyu's image as a foreign country distinct from Japan.

As mentioned previously, Ryukyu was also valuable to Satsuma as a source of useful information. Throughout the Tokugawa period, the bakufu sought information about East Asian and world affairs. Tokugawa Japan's foreign relations were limited and carefully controlled, but the popular notion that Japan was a "closed country" (i.e., *sakoku,* a word of European origin) is hardly tenable, as Toby's study of Tokugawa foreign relations makes clear. Because the bakufu lacked official diplomatic ties with the Qing court and because of its considerable military power, accurate information about developments in China, particularly in Beijing, was a valuable commodity. Ryukyu was in a position to obtain this information, and Satsuma was in a position to pass it on to the bakufu.

The bakufu had a number of routes for obtaining information about conditions in foreign countries. Two were through Nagasaki, with Chinese and Dutch merchants providing the information. Another source of information was Korea, which conveyed information to Japan about conditions on the continent via Tsushima. The final route for information about China was via Ryukyu and Satsuma.[54] Maehira Fusaaki has examined Ryukyu's role as a conduit of information to Japan in some detail. He concluded that "it is reasonable to surmise that one of the reasons the *bakuhan* state consistently set Ryukyu up as a foreign country and maintained it as a conduit for intercourse with China was not only for obtaining goods through trade, but also because Ryukyu was required to function in the peculiar role of 'information importer.'"[55]

Starting in 1678, whenever a Ryukyuan embassy returned from China, the kingdom dispatched to Satsuma an envoy with the title *Kara no shubi go-shisha* to report the latest information. Satsuma also set up an agency within the domain, the Tōgakuhō, to collect and study information about China, which came mainly from Ryukyu. In 1716, for example, several Ryukyuans from Kumemura, the kingdom's center for Chinese studies, went to Satsuma on orders from the Tōgakuhō. Upon their arrival, Satsuma officials went to Ryukyu's embassy in Kagoshima to interview the Ryukyuans about current conditions in China.[56]

The information route via Ryukyu was less valuable for its quantity than for its quality. Maehira points out that Ryukyuan information was superior in terms of factual accuracy, because the information passed on to Satsuma came from Ryukyuans who had lived in China and had first-hand knowledge of conditions there.[57] The Japanese interpreters in Nagasaki, by contrast, received information from Chinese traders second or third hand because the traders rarely spent much time in inland areas and almost never went to Beijing. In Ryukyu's case, twenty Ryukyuans spent forty days every two years in Beijing. Furthermore, many of those Ryukyuans could speak Mandarin Chinese (*guanhua*), in contrast to the Nagasaki interpreters, who knew only coastal dialects.[58] Also, there were typically one- to two-hundred Ryukyuans temporarily residing in Fujian at any given time.

From the above discussion it is clear that the Ryukyu Kingdom was of value to both Satsuma and the bakufu in various ways. It was potentially valuable to Satsuma as a source of added wealth. It had symbolic importance for both Satsuma and the bakufu in its role as a subordinate foreign country. It was also of great value to both Satsuma and the bakufu as a source of accurate information about conditions in China. In all of these cases, Ryukyu's value to Tokugawa Japan was a function of its close connection with China via regular participation in tributary relations with the Qing court. To maintain those ties it was essential that the fact of Japanese control be kept secret from Chinese officials.

This requirement of secrecy vis-à-vis China produced several concrete effects. First, it prevented Satsuma or the bakufu from maintaining a large presence in Ryukyu. Substantial military forces were out of the question, and Japanese were prohibited from visiting Ryukyu except on official business. Before Satsuma's invasion, groups of Japanese merchants and sailors commonly resided in Ryukyu between voyages, but after the kingdom came under Satsuma's control, its subjects actually had less day-to-day contact with Japanese people than before.

Satsuma was in a difficult position with respect to Ryukyu. On the one hand, it needed to maintain firm control to ensure that the funds it provided for the purchase of goods in China were properly spent. On the other hand, it could not keep a large force of retainers in Ryukyu to enforce its dictates. Naturally, it had even less control over what Ryukyuans did while in China. It was always to Satsuma's advantage to tighten its control over Ryukyu, but circumstances required that the domain maintain a substantial physical and cultural distance from Ryukyu. It was mainly for this reason that Ryukyu continued to function as a quasi-independent country throughout the Tokugawa period.

By the latter half of the seventeenth century, Satsuma's officials began to realize that if they were to control Ryukyu effectively, it would not be through the threat of force alone. The possibility of force was an important element in Satsuma's control and was always present in the background. The stick of coercive force, however, was increasingly accompanied by the carrot of economic incentives. Another control strategy that Satsuma employed was to promote and support those Ryukyuan officials who were sympathetic to the domain's interests. Shō Shōken, for example, came into office as prime minister in the wake of the Chatan-Eso Incident. The main reason he achieved some success as a political reformer was strong Satsuma backing.

Economic Matters I: Ryukyu, Satsuma, Bakufu

In 1681, the Ming loyalist holdout Zheng Jing died. Two years later, Taiwan fell to Qing forces. Firm Qing control of coastal areas prompted China's rulers to eliminate trade restrictions on Chinese vessels in 1684. One result was a sharp increase in the number of Chinese ships sailing to Nagasaki. According to Robert Sakai, these developments made Ryukyu less important as a conduit for Chinese goods into Japan. The price of Chinese goods fell in the Kyoto market, and Satsuma "was hard-hit by this development."[59] Uehara, however, sees the matter differently. He points out that the increased volume of Chinese trade led to bakufu-imposed restrictions on the number of Chinese and Dutch vessels. These circumstances tended to reduce prices for Chinese goods in China, but kept them high in Japan, thus working to Satsuma's benefit.[60] The question of whether the developments of the 1680s were to Satsuma's benefit will not be resolved here. What is important for our purposes is to understand the complexity of the larger economic environment in which the relationship between Ryukyu and Satsuma was situated. As political and market conditions within this larger environment changed, so too did the details of the Ryukyu-Satsuma relationship.

In the late seventeenth century, Satsuma's trade in Chinese goods caught the bakufu's attention. The first instance was in 1661, when Satsuma's agents purchased a large quantity of woolen goods from a Chinese delegation then in Ryukyu to invest King Shō Tei (r. 1669–1709). The domain tried to sell these goods unobtrusively in Osaka, Nagasaki, and Kyoto, but they were too numerous to go unnoticed by the bakufu. Although there were no immediate repercussions, in 1685 the bakufu ordered Satsuma to produce a detailed report of its China trade activities. The next year, the bakufu sent an order restricting the trade between Satsuma and Ryukyu to a value of 2,000 *ryō* a year. This was a 1,000 *ryō* reduction based on the figure of 3,000 *ryō* that Satsuma had reported to the bakufu. The bakufu also prohibited Satsuma from selling goods that competed with bakufu goods obtained through trade at Nagasaki.[61] Satsuma appealed the restriction, but to no avail, and it was therefore forced to cut back on its purchases of Chinese goods.[62]

Despite these restrictions, Satsuma continued to show a strong interest in the China trade. In 1689, for example, after obtaining bakufu permission, the domain opened a shop in Kyoto as an outlet to sell Chinese goods obtained via Ryukyu. Satsuma issued orders to its personnel in Ryukyu to curtail private, unofficial trade in Chinese goods to avoid arousing the bakufu's suspicion.[63] Additional bakufu decrees in the eighteenth century made the original 1686 limitations on Satsuma's trade with China via Ryukyu more inclusive and restrictive. The bakufu also clamped down more tightly on Chinese trade at Nagasaki in the early eighteenth century. The result was an upsurge in smuggling both at Ryukyu and Nagasaki.[64] Concerned that illegal trade might cause the bakufu to shut down the domain's shop in Kyoto, Satsuma enacted several procedural reforms to tighten the accountability and control of Chinese goods coming through Ryukyu.[65] In the seventeenth and eighteenth centuries, Satsuma officials were careful at least to appear to abide by bakufu regulations with respect to trade. The domain government, however, had to contend with the individuals who actually conducted the trade, both from Satsuma and Ryukyu. For these men, the opportunities for personal enrichment through unauthorized channels were many.

Another problem that beset Ryukyuan trade with China and Satsuma was the bakufu's currency debasements. Through a series of three debasements, the silver content in the coins minted by the bakufu went from 64 percent in 1695 to a mere 20 percent in 1711. In 1697 Ryukyu sent an envoy to Satsuma to explain that the newly minted Genroku coins were not suitable for trade. The quality of Chinese goods coming into Satsuma via Ryukyu declined, and Ryukyu petitioned Satsuma several times starting in 1702 to provide coins of pre-1695 silver content. Satsuma, in turn, asked the bakufu to provide such coins. Instead of sending the desired coins, the bakufu responded in 1712 by issuing a set of five injunctions called *Otazune jōjō*. The essence of these injunctions was that Satsuma limit its trade to reduce the outflow of silver to foreign countries.[66] The domain appealed, saying in various ways that maintaining Ryukyu's connection with China was less important for economic reasons than it was for political reasons, an argument we have already seen in other contexts. Satsuma suggested that if Ryukyu could not meet its obligations to Qing owing to inferior coins, the situation might lead to international unrest. This line of argument worked, and the bakufu granted Satsuma permission to mint coins of the former purity for use in Ryukyu's tribute trade. Satsuma was delighted to inform Ryukyu that it was the domain's influence and effort that had managed to secure the proper coinage, and it took the opportunity to exhort Ryukyu not to be negligent in the China trade.[67] Again we see Satsuma skillfully manipulating Ryukyu's connection with China to obtain concessions from the bakufu.

Economic Matters II: Ryukyu's Tribute Trade

It was once common for historians of Ryukyu to assume that its tribute trade with China was profitable for the royal government. Even in a comparatively recent work, Miyata Toshihiko argues that the trade with China was so profitable that it was "a matter of life and death" for Ryukyu.[68] The consensus among most scholars today, however, is that the early-modern tribute trade was a net financial loss for the royal government.[69] To take an example, Araki Moriaki provides detailed trade figures for the year 1720. Total royal government expenses for a tribute voyage amounted to the equivalent of 237.7773 *kan* of silver.[70] Profits from the sale of silk purchased in China, however, amounted to only 156.7014 *kan*. Revenues from the sale of Ryukyuan sugar made up most of the 81.0759 *kan* deficit, though the royal government was still 2.4449 *kan* short in the end.[71] The potential for profits in some aspects of Ryukyu's tribute trade with China was more than offset by a variety of direct and indirect expenses.

Ryukyu's tributary relations with the Qing court also involved Chinese investiture of Ryukyuan kings. Of great symbolic value, Chinese investiture enhanced royal authority and thus worked to the advantage of the royal government, Satsuma, and the bakufu for reasons already discussed. Investiture, however, was terribly expensive, requiring years of prior preparation and post-investiture financial difficulty in most cases. Sakai explains some of the economic considerations:

> The costs incurred for the investiture of the king probably outweighed any benefits derived from the commercial transactions which accompanied the event. The Chinese mission usually numbered between five hundred and eight hundred people, including about two hundred military escorts. All of these people came to the Ryukyus with cloth goods, utensils, and commodities for private sales. On this occasion, it was the turn of the Ryukyuans to play the gracious hosts, sprucing up the capital city, housing and entertaining their guests and plying them with gifts. . . . The costs of investiture usually were subsidized by the Satsuma government.[72]

Other financial costs of Ryukyu's relationship with China included the need to build and maintain large ships and, indirectly, the need to maintain a community of specialists in Chinese affairs, namely Kumemura. As Sakai noted above, Satsuma bore some of the financial burden. Still, Ryukyu's tributary relationship with China was a net financial loss for the royal government, and it maintained these relations because of their political "profit."

Ryukyu's ties with China were the major reason for its existence on Japan's periphery as a quasi-independent kingdom. Relations with China were indeed "a matter of life and death," to use Miyata's phrase, but not because those relations involved profitable trade. Relations with China were a *political* necessity for the kingdom's continued existence.[73] This is not to say that financial profit from the tribute trade was nonexistent. Araki points out that of three entities, the royal government, the Ryukyuan aristocracy, and Satsuma, the latter two generally profited from the trade with China. In this regard, the Ryukyuan aristocracy were like parasites on the royal government.[74] Since these aristocrats were government officials, they obviously had a strong personal incentive to maintain the trade. Financial profit, therefore, indirectly played into the overall political "profitability" of Ryukyu's tribute trade with China.

Ryukyu's Relationship with China

Ryukyu's relations with China included more than just participation in tributary relations, but because Ryukyu's active participation in the tributary system was the formal basis of its relationship with China, it is the starting point of our analysis of Ryukyu-Qing relations. The general nature of the Chinese tributary system in the Ming and Qing dynasties is well known and need be discussed only briefly here. The Qing court conducted a wide variety of foreign relations, not all of which fit the classic pattern of the tributary system described by Fairbank.[75] Ryukyu's relations with China, however, did fit this pattern. The English term "tributary system" suggests a marked degree of political subservience. In the Chinese world order, however, this subservience took the form of ritualized cultural subordination and deference to the Chinese emperor. Participation in the Chinese tributary system, in other words, did *not* imply Chinese political control over any tributary state. Also, tributary states normally could expect no military assistance from Chinese armies should they be invaded. There were, of course, exceptions, such as Ming assistance to Korea after Hideyoshi's armies invaded in 1592. But China provided this assistance because the invasion directly threatened its own interests. In other words, it was better for the Ming court to fight Japanese armies in Korea than to do so in China proper. When foreign envoys bowed before the Chinese emperor, they were in effect acknowledging the *cultural* superiority of the Chinese emperor, not his *political* authority over their states.

In return for presenting items from their own countries as a ritual display of cultural subordination, tributary countries reaped a variety of benefits. First, the emperor would normally show his benevolent generosity by bestowing gifts on the foreigners worth much more than their own "tribute" goods. Furthermore, tribute missions to China were an opportunity to trade legally with Chinese merchants. It was this opportunity for trade that typically provided the largest incentive for states to participate. Participation also provided opportunities for cultural exchange for states like Ryukyu that valued Chinese high culture and learning. The Chinese emperor formally recognized the rulers of participating states by sending envoys to confer official titles, most typically that of king *(wang)*. This recognition was ceremonial and its lack would not normally adversely affect the authority of most non-Chinese rulers within their own territories. For a small country like Ryukyu, however, the cultural prestige of China translated into enhanced authority for the king and his court.

China, in effect, purchased the participation of surrounding states by offering them incentives to enter into tributary relations. This mode of foreign relations enabled Chinese emperors, officials, and scholars more easily to maintain the fiction of China as the center of the civilized world order. China also received important information from tribute envoys about the world outside its borders. Ryukyuan envoys, for example, notified Ming officials of Hideyoshi's impending invasion of the continent approximately two years in advance. Perhaps most important from China's perspective, by offering sufficient incentives for a country to participate in tributary relations, that country was less likely to attempt to obtain Chinese goods through military force.

China maintained a residence for Ryukyuans in Fujian, which served as the base of Ryukyuan trade and diplomacy in China. Although the normal frequency of missions was once every two years in Ryukyu's case, the number of voyages between Ryukyu and China was actually much greater during the Qing period. As soon as the ship or ships that transported a tribute embassy would return to Ryukyu, a second ship loaded with trade items would sail from Ryukyu the following year to pick up the embassy on its return from the Chinese capital. Therefore, there was normally one regular voyage to Fujian every year. Additionally, Ryukyu sent embassies on special occasions, such as to congratulate a new emperor upon his ascension.

During the Ming dynasty, the items Ryukyu typically presented as tribute were sulphur, horses, and cloth. From the late seventeenth century, Ryukyu's tribute consisted of set quantities of sulphur, presented in Fuzhou, and copper and tin, presented in Beijing. Ryukyuans conducted private trade at Fuzhou, which Chinese officials supervised to prevent the purchase of prohibited items.[76]

The best extant description of the details of a Ryukyuan tribute embassy is to be found in an 1853 work, *Tsūkō ichiran*. Hayashi Akira (1800–1859), head of the Hayashi family Confucian academy in Edo, produced this work under orders from the bakufu by compiling and editing documents concerning East Asian trade and diplomacy. The following summary of the activities of Ryukyuan tribute embassies is based on the description in *Tsūkō ichiran*.[77]

Generally, there were two tribute ships, the first with a crew and passengers of about one hundred twenty and the second with a crew and passengers of seventy. Upon arriving in Fuzhou, the ships would dock, off-load their cargo into small boats, and proceed upriver to the Ryukyuan trading center. Chinese officials, some of them military officials armed with swords and some of them scholar-officials, guarded the trading center. People were free to come and go as they pleased during the daytime but not at night. A tribute embassy normally arrived in Fuzhou during the third month, stayed at the Ryukyuan embassy for about seven months, and set out for Beijing by the start of the tenth month. Only about twenty Ryukyuans would go to Beijing, while the rest remained at the embassy in Fuzhou.

The first half of the journey was by land, the second by canal. The return trip took the Ryukyuans overland to Shandong and then to Fujian by water. Each prefecture provided guards, servants, and musicians for the Ryukyuan party while it passed through the area. When traveling overland, the officials rode in palanquins, and their servants traveled on horseback or in carts. The Ryukyuans were lodged in officials' quarters along the way and given excellent treatment. Each prefectural office provided whatever travel expenses the Ryukyuan party incurred. The party would arrive in Beijing in the twelfth month and remain there for roughly forty days.

In Beijing, the Ryukyuans performed the ceremonial acts of subordination to the emperor at the Hall of Supreme Harmony just after sunrise. On the appointed day tribute embassies from other countries were usually present as well. Each went before the emperor in order of their status in Chinese eyes: Korea, Ryukyu, Vietnam, Burma, followed by others. Ryukyuan envoys presented the tribute items: 12,600 *jin* ("catties," one being roughly 1.3 pounds) of sulphur (already handed over in Fujian), 3,000 *jin* of copper, and 1,000 *jin* of tin. The emperor then bestowed return gifts on the king and all Ryukyuan officials who made the passage to China. During their stay in Beijing, Chinese officials treated the Ryukyuans to elaborate banquets.

Besides tribute embassies, Ryukyu maintained formal relations with China in the realm of education. *Kanshō* were Ryukyuans studying in China at the National Academy *(Guozi jian)*. Four Ryukyuans were allowed residence at a time. After entering the academy, the Chinese government supported them, providing robes, caps, shoes, sleeping gear, paper, brushes, and so forth. In 1688, the Kangxi emperor ordered that "when Ryukyu sends the sons of its ministers to the academy to study, they are to be well provided for upon their arrival."[78] Xu Gongsheng points out that during the Qing period Ryukyuan students were often highly motivated and received a rigorous education. They not only excelled in their own studies but even participated in the broader Chinese affairs on occasion. For example, in 1761 some Ryukyuan students presented a book of poems to the court that they had written in honor of the dowager empress' seventieth birthday. Ryukyuan students also regularly participated in Confucian temple rites.[79]

The curriculum at the National Academy in the Qing era included the study of such works as Zhu Xi's commentary on the Four Books *(Sishu jizhu)*, *Sishu zhijie,* a later commentary on the Four Books and the Neo-Confucian anthology *Reflections on Things at Hand (Jinsilu)*. Also included were commentaries on certain of the Five Classics, such as the *Liji jizhu,* a collection of commentaries on the *Book of Rites,* and the *Zo zhuan* commentary on the *Spring and Autumn Chronicles*.[80] The Ryukyuans also studied literature, poetry, and history. Those students who applied themselves left the academy with a knowledge of the Four Books, Zhu Xi's interpretation of them, the basics of Cheng-Zhu Neo-Confucian concepts, and familiarity with the broader Chinese corpus of classical literature.

For those who could not become *kanshō* and wanted to pursue an education in China, either classical or technical, or both, other options were available. By the eighteenth century, it had become standard practice for young men in Kumemura to spend time studying in China, though not all of them stayed long or applied themselves diligently.[81] Residing at the Ryukyuan trading center, they studied at nearby schools and temples. The largest group of Ryukyuans pursuing an education in China at any given time were Kumemura residents studying in Fujian at their own expense. Typically, four such students sailed to China with each tribute voyage, and eight sailed on the ship that came to pick up the tribute embassy the following year. The royal government sent and supported additional students who went to Fujian with specific orders to study a particular subject or learn a particular skill. There were always several such students in Fujian, whose objective was to obtain as much useful knowledge as possible in the shortest time.[82] Sai On was such a student. Early in his career, he studied geomancy with a teacher in Fujian at royal government expense.[83]

Ryukyuans in Fujian studied a variety of subjects, including geomancy, astronomy, geography, calendar making, agriculture, law, protocol, production techniques, and medicine. For example, in 1677 Yō Shunshi of Kumemura received orders to study the calendar in Fujian. He soon became ill, however, so his brother Yō Shun'ei took up the project. The result was a guidebook on the calendar, which the royal government printed and distributed to each district office. This guide may have been inadequate, however, for in 1687, Sai Chōkō received orders to go to Fujian and study the calendar. Upon his return to Okinawa in 1682, he became head calendrical official and distributed guidebooks on the calendar throughout the country.[84]

In 1623 Gima Shinjō (1557–1644), an agricultural official instrumental in encouraging sweet potato cultivation in Ryukyu, went to Fujian to study sugar production techniques. He became the first Ryukyuan to produce brown sugar from cane.[85] Then, in 1663, Taketomi Jūrin (Riku Tokusen) went to Fujian to study techniques for producing white sugar; he disseminated what he had learned upon his return to Okinawa.[86] Other production techniques that Ryukyuans studied in Fujian included sweet potato cultivation, tea production, weaving techniques, metallurgy, casting, tile baking, and umbrella manufacturing.[87] The study of geomancy and physiognomy among Ryukyuans began in the seventeenth century with students in Fujian.[88]

A clear barometer of China's importance to Ryukyu was the area adjacent to Shuri known as Kumemura (O. Kuninda; S-J. Tōei). King Satto (r. 1350–1395) of Chūzan established Kumemura in 1392 as an area for Chinese immigrants to settle. These immigrants and their descendants conducted Ryukyu's relations with China and other foreign countries.[89] Residents of Kumemura served as ambassadors, traders, navigators, and interpreters. For reasons beyond the scope of this study, the quantity and quality of trade with China rapidly declined after 1570, and Kumemura declined to the same extent. The records of Chinese investiture envoys suggest something of this change. For example, early in the reign of Shō Sei (r. 1527–1555), investiture envoy Chen Kan commented on a group of Kumemura *kanshō* as follows: "Of late, Sai Teimi, Tei Fu, Ryō Shi and Sai Kan were all excellent students. They went north to China to study, received the instruction of famous scholars and have now become officials and interpreters. When they advance to meet people, they are correct in their deportment and composed in their speech."[90] In contrast to Chen's praise of the quality of Kumemura scholars, investiture envoy Xia Ziyang saw the Kumemura of the 1590s in a state of decline:

I have heard that during former times in Ryukyu, those sons of officials who were sent to study at the National Academy totaled thirty-six surnames in all. Now, all that remain are the six lineages of Sai, Tei, Rin, Tei [different character], Ryō and Kin, and even these are not prospering. Even the exam to study at the National Academy has become meaningless.[91]

In what he calls the "crisis of Kumemura," Dana explains that around the time of the Satsuma invasion the population of Kumemura had decreased to the point that Kumemura itself was in danger of dying out—a "lantern in the wind."[92]

Within the context of Ryukyu's seventeenth-century international situation, Kumemura took on renewed importance. Beginning in 1633, along with the reversion of the tribute trade with China to its ordinary frequency, the royal government began taking concrete steps to revitalize Kumemura. This revival probably had indirect support from Satsuma as well, for Dana points out that the domain expressed its displeasure over Kumemura's deteriorated condition.[93] One of the first steps the royal government took was the formalization of a system of titles for Kumemura residents to guarantee their social prestige. More important, beginning in the 1650s, a guaranteed rice stipend accompanied each rank.[94] Since nearly all male residents of Kumemura held formal rank, the royal government was in effect paying the residents of Kumemura to pursue Chinese studies. Although the stipends were terribly small by Japanese standards, members of the Ryukyuan upper classes were fortunate to have any stipend at all. Particularly after 1712, when the number of *yukatchu*,[95] formally recognized members of the upper class, increased sharply, competition for government posts intensified. As a result, the many *yukatchu* who could not find government posts went without stipends. The primary duty of all male residents of Kumemura was to pursue Chinese studies, and that the royal government, always under financial pressure, spent so much of its revenue to support the residents of Kumemura is good indication of the increased importance of Ryukyu's relationship with China.

The most important resource for reviving the fortunes of Kumemura was people. In 1633 the royal government offered incentives for the brightest and most talented Ryukyuans to found households in Kumemura and devote themselves to Chinese studies and matters related to diplomacy. By the end of the seventeenth century this policy, along with the financial support mentioned above, resulted in many of Okinawa's most talented individuals residing in Kumemura. This concentration of talent is one reason why, in the eighteenth century, Kumemura moved beyond its role as a center of Chinese studies and diplomacy and came to dominate domestic politics as well.

By the end of the seventeenth century, the royal government's policy of reviving the fortunes of Kumemura was a clear success. From a mere 305 people in 1654, the population increased fivefold by 1729. In a show of royal support for Kumemura, King Shō Tei held a banquet in Shuri castle, to which the residents of Kumemura were invited, celebrating its new prosperity.[96]

A final dimension of Ryukyu's relationship with China is the connection between investiture by the Chinese emperor and royal authority. Ryukyu's monarchs had valued the Chinese emperor's formal recognition of their royal status since the earliest documented reigns. Tomiyama points out that during the Sanzan Period (1314–1429), when several "kings" competed for territory, each expended great effort to obtain ceremonial robes from the Ming court to enhance their authority. The same was also true with the Chinese calendar. By possessing robes, the calendar, and related items, a political leader could control prestigious and sophisticated (i.e., Chinese) rituals and use that control to his advantage.[97]

In the early-modern period, investiture was not only an aspect of maintaining good relations with China. It also enhanced the king's authority vis-à-vis his ministers and the authority of the central government over provincial officials. In his study of ritual connected with the investiture of Ryukyu's kings, Tomiyama points out that the kings of Ryukyu were granted the rank and accoutrement of a Chinese *junwang,* the same rank received by the kings of Korea and Vietnam. So powerful was this symbolic authority, and so deeply entrenched had investiture become in royal tradition, that in Tomiyama's assessment, "if a king did not receive investiture, he could not be king."[98]

Maehira points out that investiture was a group ceremony in which the crown prince and leading ministers played key roles. Furthermore, the investiture envoys' processions had a major impact on the common people, who turned out to watch in large numbers. He also points out that the formal investiture document from the emperor became akin to a sacred cult object, transcending its physical composition of mere ink and paper and even the literal meaning of the words it contained. During his reign, the king wore the crown and robes received from the Chinese emperor on formal occasions because of their authoritative effect.[99]

Ryukyuan officials were appointed via writs of investiture known as *jireisho,* which bore the king's seal. These documents conveyed the king's authority downward. There was also a complementary bottom-up process of recommendation for officials at all levels. In an article on this otherwise little-studied process, Tomiyama describes how peers or those of the next higher administrative level would recommend a candidate for appointment to office. The written form of this recommendation was known as *okazugaki* (O. *ukazi-*

gachi). Officials at each higher level would then review and approve (or disapprove) the *okazugaki* until it eventually reached the king. At this point the king would issue a *jireisho* formally appointing the person to office.[100]

At the highest levels of office, such as the Council of Three or the head of Kumemura, a majority vote by high-status persons determined the occupants.[101] Such elections, says Tomiyama, were *okazugaki* writ large. This process of bottom-up recommendation did not stop at the level of the Council of Three. In a sense, it even included the king himself. The documents sent to China requesting a king's investiture included the Chinese-language equivalent of an *okazugaki,* bearing the names and seals of important ministers as submitters of the document. The practice started with Shō Sei, when the Ming court wanted written proof that he was the legitimate successor to the throne. In this important respect, therefore, the king, too, was recommended for his position. Investiture by the Chinese emperor was the formal approval of the recommendation.[102]

Increased Influence of Chinese Culture

After Ryukyu came under Satsuma's domination, the study of Japanese language and culture became part of the education of elite Ryukyuans. In many respects, however, the events of the seventeenth century described above served to reduce Japanese cultural influence among the Ryukyuan *yukatchu* and increase the cultural influence of China. It was to the mutual advantage of Ryukyu, Satsuma, and the bakufu for Ryukyu and its people to appear as much unlike Japan and Japanese as possible, which, when in Japan, typically meant appearing "Chinese." It was also to the advantage of Ryukyu, Satsuma, and the bakufu that some Ryukyuans master Chinese cultural forms to maintain the vital diplomatic and trade connections with China. The royal government's active participation in reviving Kumemura attests to the need for a community of experts in Chinese culture.

By the end of the seventeenth century, Chinese cultural forms began to affect the royal government in significant ways. Tomiyama has compared royal rituals from Old-Ryukyu[103] with the forms into which they evolved during the early-modern period. In the case of rites venerating "Heaven" (C. *tian,* J. *ten*)[104] performed by the king on new year's day, the older version reflects strong Japanese influence. The Japanese elements were explicitly removed in 1719 and the entire ceremony was modeled after the Chinese emperor's veneration of Shangdi at the Altar of Heaven (discussed at greater length in Chapter 4). Chinese influence was apparent in other areas. For example, in 1683 Wang Ji, the envoy sent to invest Shō Tei, was shown into the Sūgenji temple. This temple was one of several that serves as a site of memorial tablets for Ryukyu's past kings. Wang reported feeling ill at ease because the tablets appeared all out of order. Based on a sketch he made, the tablets were indeed arranged in an order contrary to Chinese norms. In 1719, investiture envoy Xu Baoguang again saw the inside of Sūgenji. This time, however, the tablets were arranged according to Chinese custom. Tomiyama points out that between 1690 and 1730 there was intense discussion within the royal government, and between the government and scholars in Kumemura, about proper procedures regarding the royal memorial tablets. Opinions varied widely, but the final decisions of the government were generally in the direction of conforming with Chinese norms.[105]

Despite Ryukyu's long history of contact with China, Confucianism in any form did not become a major force in upper-class Ryukyuan life until the seventeenth century.[106] In 1673, Ryukyu's first Confucian temple was constructed with support from the royal government. Thereafter, the head of Kumemura presided over the spring and autumn rites held there. He was the highest official at these rites, which were of little importance outside Kumemura. Beginning in 1719, however, the Confucian rites in Kumemura took on greater symbolic and political importance. The king personally dispatched members of the Council of Three, Ryukyu's highest governing body, to perform the spring and autumn rites.[107] This act transformed what had once been the rites of a small community of experts on China into rites of the entire kingdom. It was also in the late seventeenth century that geomancy (C. *fengshui*, O. *funshii*) made its way into Ryukyu.[108] Geomancy quickly spread from Kumemura to affect many aspects of life among the Ryukyuan *yukatchu*.

Knowledge of China—its history and high culture—came to be expected of all Ryukyuan elites by the eighteenth century. In 1753, the royal government published a collection of questions and answers about China, Ryukyu, and Ryukyu's relationship with Japan. Written in Japanese for a wide audience of *yukatchu*,[109] a large part of the document consists of answers to questions about Ryukyu that Chinese might ask of Ryukyuan visitors. The document also includes a lengthy quiz about a wide variety of things Chinese to aid Ryukyuans in preparation for conversing with Chinese. Some of the many questions include:

1. During the reign of which king was Confucius born? . . . Also, what types of decorative trees are planted around his tomb and approximately how much area do they cover?
2. In China, when a husband and wife separate, is it customary for the man to look for another wife or for the wife to look for another husband?
3. Who first attached names to edible things? [answer: Cang Jie]

4. During the reign of which ruler was the practice of people wearing robes and caps first established? [answer: Yellow Emperor]

5. During the reign of which ruler did people first establish houses and agricultural fields? [answer: Shennong]

6. On what basis is the severity and leniency of punishments decided in China?

7. As for Chinese women, how did it become customary for them to make their feet small?

8. [In China's central government,] what are the duties and responsibilities of each of the Six Boards?

9. How many countries are there whose kings receive investiture from envoys sent out by the Chinese emperor?[110]

By the late eighteenth century, Chinese cultural forms had spread from the narrow confines of Kumemura to the larger *yukatchu* population of Shuri. Strange as it may sound at first glance, one result of Japanese *political* domination of early-modern Ryukyu was an increase in the *cultural* influence of China.

To keep matters in perspective, we should bear in mind that most Ryukyuans were illiterate peasants, not *yukatchu*. The cultural traditions of these peasants had little or no connection with the high culture of either Japan or China and did not begin to change in any fundamental way until the coercive forces of the Meiji state were brought to bear on Okinawans to forge them into imperial subjects.[111]

Living a Lie

We have seen that for Ryukyu to maintain its tribute trade with China, the fact of Japanese domination of the kingdom had to be hidden from Chinese eyes. Kamiya, Maehira, and others have pointed out that by the late seventeenth century, the policy of masking the Japanese-Ryukyu relationship significantly intensified.[112] During Shō Tei's investiture ceremonies in 1683, Shimazu instructed Japanese who happened to meet Chinese envoys or traders to say that they were from "Takarashima" under Ryukyuan control. In 1719, Satsuma officials forbade any contact whatsoever between Japanese and Chinese in Ryukyu.[113] The eighteenth-century compilers of *Kyūyō,* one of the kingdom's official histories, maintained the fiction that Ryukyu had only the most indirect contact with Japan:

> . . . [After the Satsuma invasion,] we ceased intercourse with countries such as Korea, Japan, Malacca, and Java. Our country stood alone and was unable to meet its needs. Fortunately, there are merchants on the Japanese-held islands of Tokara.[114] They arrive in our country, engage in trade, and

their coming and going has not stopped. Our country, moreover, by depending on Tokara, can meet its needs and has returned to tranquility. Therefore, our inhabitants call Tokara "Takarashima" [Treasure Island].[115]

Were a Chinese investiture envoy to read this passage (a possibility), it is unlikely he would have suspected Satsuma or other Japanese domination of Ryukyu. Were a Satsuma official to read the passage (also a possibility), it serves to lavish praise on Satsuma (Tokara), Ryukyu's "Treasure Island."

Some of the regulations Satsuma imposed while Chinese envoys were in Ryukyu included:

1. When the investiture ships are in port, should a local ship arrive in Naha, [various Ryukyuan officials] are to investigate, seize, and hide anything that might cause problems, such as items bearing Japanese era-name dates or Japanese names and Japanese books.
2. There is to be no singing of Japanese songs and no use of the Japanese language. Should the Chinese envoys say anything to you in Japanese, act as if you do not understand.
3. Make it appear that no Japanese customs are practiced.[116]

That these items and practices had to be prohibited, of course, attests to the continuing influence of at least some forms of Japanese culture in early-modern Ryukyu.

When the Chinese envoys were in Naha, all Satsuma officials went by ship to Unten harbor and hid themselves in the village of Gusukuma. If by some odd chance the Chinese envoys were to indicate a desire to visit Gusukuma, a contingency plan would go into effect: Ryukyuans would take the Chinese to the neighboring village of Makiminato and tell them the place was Gusukuma.[117] Perhaps the most extreme example of Satsuma's concern with hiding its control over Ryukyu took place in 1838. Satsuma's resident official, Takata Sōgorō, had died in Ryukyu, and domain officials decided that his remains would be interred there, not in Satsuma. Satsuma officials did not want to take even the slight risk that the ship carrying the remains back home would be blown off course and cause suspicion by landing in China.[118]

In the eighteenth and nineteenth centuries, a number of guidebooks circulated to help Ryukyuans going abroad prepare suitable answers to possible questions. One such 1854 book, *Ikokujin ni hentō no kokoroe,* is notable for its blatant lies. First it contains the above-mentioned claim that Ryukyuans had no direct contact with Japanese. The work also instructs Ryukyuan travelers to say that the northern islands of Amami-Ōshima, seized by Satsuma after its invasion, have long been part of Ryukyu, not Japan. The existence of Japanese books in Ryukyu was to be explained by their having been obtained via the fictitious Tokara merchants.[119]

Despite all these precautions, the unexpected sometimes took place. For example, investiture envoy Wang Ji was walking around the Gōkokuji temple and happened to find a bell with the Japanese era-name date Genna 2 on it. Not knowing what it meant, he simply recorded the matter in his records, suggesting that the bell might have dated to the early Tang period. Much later, the envoy sent to invest Shō Boku (r. 1752–95) brought up the matter again (it was standard procedure for envoys to read the records of their predecessors before sailing to Ryukyu). He correctly concluded that the date must have been Japanese because Ryukyu had no contact with Tang China.[120]

Ryukyuans who traveled abroad or dealt with foreigners in Ryukyu had little choice but to cooperate with Satsuma in masking the nature and extent of their country's relationship with Japan. Ryukyuans traveling to Edo enhanced their prestige by appearing foreign and exotic in Japanese eyes. In their own country, they scrambled to keep any sign of Japan out of the eyes of Chinese visitors. To preserve their ties with China, and thus some measure of independence vis-à-vis Satsuma and the bakufu, Ryukyuans had to live a lie in the arena of international relations. With Ryukyuans of the time lying about the status of their country, is it possible now to say what the truth of that status was?

Cultural and Political Status of Ryukyu

The first problem in trying to ascertain Ryukyu's status in the seventeenth and eighteenth centuries is the lack of an adequate vocabulary. In the age of nation-states, it is common to regard the "nation," an imagined community in which cultural and political boundaries are thought to be congruent, as natural and unproblematic. It is neither. Furthermore, as Anderson and others have pointed out, although nationalists themselves would have us believe that nations (or at least *their* nations) have existed since the misty dawn of history, to the critical eye of the historian, nations are a relatively recent construct in human history.[121] In the seventeenth century, Ryukyu, Satsuma, Japan, and China were not nations. States existed in these places, of course, as did various cultural traditions. We also find cultural ethnocentrism and a sense of "us versus them," although this consciousness was just as likely between different social classes *within* a state's borders as between subjects of different states. Large-scale, popular imaginings of shared, horizontal cultural communities congruent with state boundaries were not present in East Asia until the middle or end of the nineteenth century. Of course, states and cultures were still important in East

Asia before the time of nations, with Satsuma and the bakufu's use of Ryukyu's cultural foreignness being an excellent example. Premodern East Asians certainly imagined themselves members of communities, but the usual mode of imagining differed in certain key respects from modern national imagining.

The territory of the kingdom of Ryukyu was a single political entity, but it was far from a single cultural entity. First, culture varied as a function of geography, even within the island of Okinawa. From one major island to the next, the cultural difference was even more striking. For example, any of the dialects of Okinawan would have been incomprehensible to an ordinary resident of Miyako or Yaeyama. Other aspects of culture, such as religious practices and music, also showed marked variation from one Ryukyu island to another. Local officials, who normally had basic familiarity with the Okinawan of Shuri, were the means by which Ryukyu's central government communicated with outlying areas.

Of equal or greater importance was that culture varied as a function of social status and education. To take the example of language, well-educated Ryukyuans such as Tei Junsoku would have studied the Japanese spoken at the shōgun's court. Interestingly, it was in this language of Edo that Ryukyuan officials spoke when talking with officials in Satsuma—a foreign language for both parties, as the *Satsuma fudoki* suggests:

> Regarding the speech of Ryukyuans, when they meet a Chinese *(tōjin)*, they speak in Chinese *(Morokoshi no kotoba)*. When they speak to Japanese *(Nihonjin)*, they speak in [the] Japanese [of the Shōgun's court] *(Nihon no kotoba)*, which they comprehend much better than the language of Satsuma *(Satsuma kotoba)*. It is said that they study Japanese *(Yamato kotoba)* in their country.[122]

Owing to Ryukyu's relative political and economic weakness vis-à-vis both Japan and China, its officials studied spoken and written forms of Japanese and Chinese. They often achieved a high degree of proficiency in either or both languages. Inseparable from the study of these languages was the study of the classical cultural traditions of Japan and China. In this area, too, many elite Ryukyuans attained a high degree of mastery.

Tei Junsoku, for example, spent many years in China and excelled at Chinese poetry. In 1713, after having traveled to China four times, he went to Japan as Chief of Correspondence of the Ryukyuan embassy to congratulate the new shōgun, Tokugawa Ietsugu. While in Edo, he exchanged poems with Arai Hakuseki and discussed Confucian philosophy with Arai and Ogyū Sorai. On the way back to Kagoshima, he visited Sesshō Konoe Iehiro in Kyoto to exchange poems.[123] A Ryukyuan such as Tei Junsoku would have had a much greater cultural affinity with Chinese and Japanese literati than with most other Ryukyuans. Although Tei Junsoku and a fisherman in Miyako would have been subjects of the same king, they would not have been able even to carry on a conversation without an interpreter. Vast cultural gaps between social strata within the same political entity were the norm in Ryukyu, Japan, and China during the seventeenth and eighteenth centuries.[124]

It is impossible, therefore, to identify a single, common Ryukyuan culture in the early-modern period, if Ryukyuan is taken to include all major cultural forms within the territories of the Chūzan king. Only if we were to limit our definition of Ryukyuan to the *yukatchu* in and around Shuri would a few generalizations about culture become possible. In short, the cultural status of early-modern Ryukyu is impossible to define except to say that the kingdom contained a number of distinct cultures and subcultures. Because all of these cultures differed significantly from any of the cultures of Japan or China (while typically containing elements derived from China and Japan), it is reasonable, though not particularly significant, to say that early-modern Ryukyu was culturally distinct from Japan and China. Although Tei Junsoku would have had much more in common culturally with Arai Hakuseki than with a peasant in Yaeyama, Tei would have had even closer cultural ties with other Ryukyuan *yukatchu*.

Regarding the kingdom's political status, most scholars of Ryukyuan history writing in the past fifteen years describe Ryukyu as a "foreign country *(ikoku)* within the *bakuhan* system." Takara elaborates as follows:

> Although it was subject to the strong restrictions and constraints of the *bakuhan* system, the Ryukyu Kingdom was not a region within Japan, nor was it in the same category as the domains. It had to defer to Satsuma's directives, but never became a colony. While being attached to Satsuma and the bakufu, it preserved its previous status as a foreign country *(ikoku)*.[125]

Ryukyu was not a fully independent country vis-à-vis Japan, but it was still a foreign country. To the extent that "foreign" suggests a degree of separation, and thus independence, I refer to early-modern Ryukyu as a "quasi-independent country." The ambiguity in the prefix "quasi" usefully points to the fact that Ryukyu was in some ways a part of Japan and in other ways apart from Japan. The prefix also accommodates Ryukyu's ritualized cultural subordination to the Chinese emperor. Tokugawa-period Japanese writers unanimously referred to Ryukyu as a foreign country. Kumazawa Banzan, for example, in the context of comparing Japan *(Nihon)* with "other countries" *(ta no kuni)* wrote: "[The countries to the east of China] are the most superior in the four seas. Of the nine such countries, Korea, Ryukyu, and Japan are the best, and out of these three, Japan is most excellent."[126] Toby provides ample evidence from the perspective of bakufu foreign relations that the bakufu regarded Ryukyu as a foreign country much as it regarded Korea as such.[127]

The term "foreign country" itself, however, can be deceptive when applied to Tokugawa Japan and its surroundings. From the standpoint of Japan, Tokugawa writers commonly characterized Ryukyu as *ikoku, iiki,* or some variation of *takoku.* The *"i"* in the former two terms suggests difference in the form of strangeness. This difference could mean "foreign" in the sense of territory outside one's jurisdiction, and it often did, but such a meaning was derivative from the basic meaning of cultural difference. The *"ta"* in *takoku* meant something separate or other than one's own, and perhaps most closely approximates the modern legal sense of a foreign country. The word *"kuni"* is perhaps most problematic, since, as Mark Ravina points out, it often meant a domain *(han)* in Tokugawa Japanese usage, as did the term *kokka,* today inevitably rendered "country" or "nation."[128] Clearly Ryukyu was "foreign" to Japan in several key senses of the term. Still, the logic and ideologies that informed this foreignness often did not conform to or correspond with modern conceptions of sovereignty.

All Ryukyuan political leaders and intellectuals had to deal with the fact of Satsuma's political domination of their country. Ryukyu's precise relationship with Satsuma and the bakufu contained a high degree of ambiguity, and the nature of the relationship evolved in response to changing international circumstances. Some latitude existed, therefore, for Ryukyuans to shape and define that relationship as subjects. The following chapter begins an examination of this Ryukyuan subjectivity by analyzing two seventeenth-century Ryukyuan visions of Ryukyu.

CHAPTER 2

Looking North and Looking West
Shō Shōken and Tei Junsoku

Ryukyuan officials had difficulty adjusting to the severe social dislocation of the immediate post-invasion years, a time when Satsuma governed the kingdom with a particularly heavy hand. As Takara points out, there was a substantial gap between the perceptions of Ryukyu's officials and Satsuma's expectations. This gap occasionally resulted in major errors on the part of the royal government, a good example being the case of Christians discovered in Yaeyama in 1623–1624. The royal government dealt with the matter by exiling those involved, but Satsuma regarded the punishment as excessively mild. Its officials ordered the Christians to be rounded up and burnt at the stake.[1]

There appears to have been no organized resistance to Satsuma's rule at any level of Ryukyuan society. Nevertheless, the difficulty that Ryukyuan officials had in adjusting to military defeat and its consequences impaired the royal government's ability to maintain law and order generally. A constant difficulty in the early seventeenth century was maintaining standards of discipline among royal government officials. One result was mishaps such as the Chatan-Eso Incident. Another was an upsurge in officials' patronage of prostitutes. Prostitution spread from the cities to the countryside, and repeated government prohibitions had no effect. It was the neglect of duty and squandering of funds, not issues of sexual morality, that the royal government found most problematic. Takara points out that, in some cases, high officials with stipend lands dissipated their wealth on prostitutes and then appealed to the government for salary increases. Some district administrators (*jitō*) even entrusted administrative affairs to their favorite prostitutes.[2]

In this time of low morale, wedding and funeral ceremonies became increasingly extravagant, even in rural villages. There were cases of families selling one of their members into indentured servitude to pay the expenses. Spending on prostitutes and lavish ceremonies, coupled with weak central government control, led officials to demand excessive labor service from peasants. One way that officials forced compliance with these demands was by forcing high-interest loans on peasants. When, as was often the case, they could not repay the loans, local officials demanded labor service instead. The resulting drain on peasant energies and morale contributed to a decline in agricultural productivity, and the frequency of peasants abandoning their land and moving to Naha or Shuri rose sharply.[3] The first half of the seventeenth century was a time of poverty and indirection in Ryukyu at all levels of society. It was also a time of confusion abroad as the Qing dynasty replaced the Ming in China.

By the second half of the century, several Ryukyuans took the initiative in reconstructing their society. This chapter examines two such Ryukyuans, the political reformer Shō Shōken and Confucian scholar, poet, and diplomat Tei Junsoku. Each man attempted to put into practice his vision of an ideal Ryukyu, and these visions were quite different. One looked west to China, the other north to Japan.

Shō Shōken

In his youth, Shō Shōken[4] studied the Confucian classics under Tomari Jochiku (1569–1655). Tomari, the leading student of Satsuma Zen monk and Confucian scholar Nanpo Bunshi (1556–1620),[5] went to Ryukyu in 1632. There, he stayed for two years teaching the *yukatchu* of Shuri to read classical Confucian texts in Japanese style (as *kanbun*) using Nanpo Bunshi's punctuation system.[6] King Shō Hō (r. 1621–1640) and Shō Shōken were among Tomari's students. Many passages from *Mirror of Chūzan*, Shō Shōken's history of Ryukyu, are direct quotes or close paraphrases of Nanpo Bunshi's writings.[7] Later in life, Shō Shōken traveled to Satsuma on three different occasions, residing there a total of four years. During those years, he befriended Niiro Matazaemon, who later became the domain official in charge of Ryukyuan affairs. In both his political and intellectual life, Shō Shōken looked to Satsuma as a model.[8]

Shō Shōken became prime minister *(sessei[9]* or O. *shisshii)* in 1666, a position second only to the king in the formal line of authority and limited to royal relatives. Strong backing from Satsuma further enhanced Shō Shōken's power within the royal government. Satsuma had pressured Shō Shōken's predecessor, Prince Gushikawa, into resigning as a result of his lack of vigor in prosecuting those involved in the Chatan-Eso Incident.[10] To replace Gushikawa, Satsuma officials sought a prime minister willing actively to cooperate with them. Shō Shōken was a good choice.

Our main source of information about Shō Shōken's activities in office is *Directives of Haneji (Haneji shioki),* a collection of his decrees and their rationale. The first item in *Directives of Haneji* indicates the circumstances under which Shō Shōken accepted the post of prime minister. An official from the inner palace visited Shō Shōken's residence in the capacity of a royal envoy. The envoy conveyed a message of Satsuma's support for Shō Shōken to succeed Prince Gushikawa as prime minister, and the envoy told Shō Shōken to proceed to the palace at once to accept the position. But he did not. Instead, Shō Shōken stated his refusal to accept the post on the spot, telling the envoy that for such an important post as prime minister it was inappropriate for a royal household official to convey the message of appointment. The next day, Inoha Ueekata, member of the Council of Three, conveyed the same message to Shō Shōken, who immediately accepted the post.[11]

By the way in which he accepted the appointment, Shō Shōken gave notice of his intention to change established practices. He made a clear distinction between "private" matters connected with the royal household and inner palace and "public" matters connected with governing. For example, he sought to remove female religious officials from the public realm by eliminating or marginalizing their participation in state ceremonial. Takara points out that Shō Shōken entered office to do battle with entrenched tradition and customs connected with the affairs of the inner palace. Support from Satsuma enabled Shō Shōken to make some progress in his attempts to reform Ryukyuan institutions and social practices.[12]

Shō Shōken decreed changes in certain customary practices immediately upon taking office. Normally, a new prime minister would give gifts of meat, wine, and other items to the king, dowager queen, the queen, and various female palace officials. Shō Shōken modified the practice to include only token gifts to the king and dowager queen. In making the change, he noted Ryukyu's strained financial circumstances and added that "furthermore, if Satsuma were to hear about [this custom], what would it think?" He also required other high officials such as district administrators and members of the Council of Three to follow his example. Shō Shōken prohibited lower officials from presenting gifts to a new prime minister or other high official, declaring that such practices blur the distinction between public (ōyake) and private (watakushi).[13]

Another of Shō Shōken's decrees soon after his taking office was a prohibition of female palace officials conveying royal messages of appointment. According to Directives of Haneji: "Tomorrow, the duties of the Council of Three are to be scheduled. It has been customary for the king's words to be transmitted by female palace officials, but as the Council of Three[14] is an esteemed body, this is not appropriate. Henceforth, the messenger corps is to take care of such matters."[15] Throughout the Ryukyu islands, women were generally regarded as having spiritual power superior to that of men. Since the late fifteenth century, a hierarchy of female religious officials running parallel to that of male officials exerted significant influence on affairs of state in certain circumstances. Throughout his career, Shō Shōken attempted to relegate the activities of female officials to minor roles as clear subordinates to their male counterparts.

In a study comparing administrative reform in Satsuma and Ryukyu, Umeki Tetsuto points out that Shō Shōken continued those Ryukyuan practices he considered viable in the new conditions of the seventeenth century and tried to eliminate the others. In their place, Shō Shōken looked to the administration of Satsuma as a model for changes in Ryukyuan institutions.[16] An entry in the *Kyūyō* for 1667 describes a major realignment of the government that took place during Shō Shōken's tenure as prime minister: "Since former times, those appointed [to the Monobugyō] were of *zashiki* rank. This year, the situation was changed so that [Monobugyō officials] shall have the same court rank as *jimoku* (commonly called *'mōshikuchi'*) officials."[17] The Mōshikuchihō was the division of the royal government concerned mainly with matters of ceremony and royal household affairs. Most of its departments had longer histories and greater prestige than those within the Monobugyō, the other major division of government. By contrast, most departments of the Monobugyō were of relatively recent vintage, many having been created after 1609. The Monobugyō dealt with taxation, finance, the management of resources, and other matters connected with Ryukyu's material wealth. Shō Shōken enhanced the power and prestige of the Monobugyō relative to the Mōshikuchihō as part of his overall effort to weaken entrenched interest in the "inner" or "private" domains of government.

In attempting to improve Ryukyu's material standard of living, Shō Shōken pursued a number of reforms in the countryside. First, he tried to prevent abuses of peasant labor by local officials and district administrators that hampered the peasants' ability to farm productively.[18] Second, he sought to reorganize agricultural villages, moving some to new locations, splitting others up, and changing boundaries. Umeki describes the details of this policy and points out that Shō Shōken's reorganization of agricultural lands was nearly identical with a similar policy carried out previously in Satsuma.[19] Finally, Shō Shōken launched an ambitious program to use tax incentives to bring additional land under cultivation. He inaugurated this program after consultation with Satsuma, and it resulted in a modest increase in agricultural efficiency and new wealth.[20]

Another of Shō Shōken's approaches to improving Ryukyu's material standard of living was to reform customs and attitudes, particularly among the *yukatchu*. By so doing, he sought to reduce household expenditures, reduce corruption, and increase diligence among government officials. He promoted what Takara has called an *"ishiki kakumei,"* or "revolution in consciousness."[21] Shō Shōken criticized the lavish spending on weddings, funerals, and ancestral rites as a waste of resources. In a letter to the Council of Three in 1673, he wrote:

> Weddings, funerals, festivals, and other ceremonies, regardless of high or low status, have recently become too extravagant. Regarding the financially debilitating effect these practices have on everyone, new regulations for both high and low were established. Recently, however, I hear that these ceremonies have [again] become too extravagant. [description of particular practices]. . . . But people unthinkingly carry out ceremonies beyond their means. By thinking only of filial piety, they are ignorant of the fact that they have exceeded their means, which is in fact unfilial, and stupid and benighted in the extreme. From this time on, you are to inform others that the above-mentioned ceremonies are to be conducted in accordance with one's means.[22]

Here we see not only Shō Shōken's views on the conduct of household ceremonies, but also his frustration that previously enacted regulations failed to have the effect he desired.

These early attempts to regulate funerals are detailed in *Directives of Haneji*. Promulgated jointly by the prime minister and Council of Three, they include precise specifications of which items and how many were permitted for use in funerals of different status levels.[23] In justifying such restrictions, Shō Shōken wrote, "If because of [extravagant funerals] one's children and grandchildren become economically hard-pressed, they will take their official duties lightly, which is ridiculous in the extreme."[24] Takara points out that the need for funds to pay for lavish funerals and weddings was a major cause of officials' abuse of the peasants under their control.[25]

Along similar lines, Shō Shōken promulgated an edict entitled "Ryokōshū no shukugi sadame" in 1667, which put specific limitations on the rites officials were permitted to conduct for purposes of ensuring the safe passage of vessels to China. It had been customary to perform an elaborate series of public and private religious rites in connection with vessels sailing to other countries. The stated reason for scaling back those rites was that their costs led officials to neglect their duties. Maehira interprets this prohibition as part of a post-invasion trend in Ryukyu to place less emphasis on rites *(girei)*, and more on practical politics *(genjitsu seiji)*.[26] Two years prior to enacting these restrictions, Shō Shōken ended the practice of the king's personal participation in religious rites connected with overseas voyages. After 1665, a representative participated in the king's stead.[27] This example is but one of many in which Shō Shōken sought to eliminate royal participation in certain religious ceremonies. In this case, the primary reason seems to have been financial. In other words, eliminating direct royal participation downgraded the status of the rites, which paved the way for a reduction in the scope and extent of their practice. In several other cases, the primary motivation seems to have been concern over royal dignity.

In Old-Ryukyu, royal authority was closely interwoven with the power of female religious officials to confer spiritual power (seji) on the king. After Ryukyu failed to prevent or repulse Satsuma's invasion, the influence of the native religion weakened among many elites after 1609.[28] Nevertheless, until the conscious attempt by Sai On and others to cast the king into the mold of a Confucian sage during the eighteenth century, the native religion, mixed with Buddhism, remained closely connected with royal authority. In many of the religious rites in which the king participated, he played a ritually subordinate role to that of the high priestess (kikoe ōgimi). A Kyūyō passage dated 1673 explains that until then, the king would regularly go to the high priestess' palace and perform a variety of rites before the hearth deity (hi-no-kami O. hii-nu kang) under her direction. The passage goes on to explain how this practice changed: "For the first time, changes were made ending the king's travel to the high priestess' palace. Instead, an envoy was dispatched to stand in as a celebrant at the various sacred sites."[29] It was typical of Shō Shōken's approach not to attempt an outright ban on major religious rites with deep roots in the kingdom's past, but to modify them by removing the element of direct royal participation.

Perhaps the best example of this approach was Shō Shōken's successful attempt to prevent the king from traveling twice yearly to Kudakajima with the high priestess to worship the deities there.[30] Worship at Kudakajima was and is the most sacred rite in native Okinawan religion. Shō Shōken's detailed argument against the practice is found in *Directives of Haneji*.[31] It begins with a description of the danger to the king such a journey would entail because Kudakajima is located more than one *ri* (roughly, "mile") out to sea with no safe harbor nearby and because the worship took place at times when strong winds were likely. The next point in his argument is that because the custom of the king's worshiping at Kudakajima was not based on any wise or sagely teachings, should people from "large countries" see this behavior, they would "laugh with derision." In other words, Shō Shōken sought to invoke fear of the ridicule of Ryukyuan customs by visitors from Satsuma. He then explained that the royal procession to Kudakajima and the subsequent worship there placed a severe financial burden on the residents of eight nearby districts.

The final part of the argument is Shō Shōken's so-called *Nichiryū dōso ron,* or "theory of a common ancestry of Ryukyuans and Japanese." Although it was once common for general histories of Ryukyu to mention this theory as Shō Shōken's major intellectual contribution to his age, the entire relevant discussion consists of but part of one passage in a series of five. The theory reads:

> My own opinion is that we Ryukyuans were originally people who came from Japan. The reason is that today, many of our place names, as well as the names of rivers and mountains, the five phases, the five relationships, animals, and plants, are the same as those in Japan. The reason our two languages are so different is simply that a great distance separates us from Japan, and the two places had no contact for a long time. I likewise think that the five grains came from Japan at the same time our people did. . . .[32]

The worship at Kudakajima was to celebrate and commemorate the spontaneous generation of grain on the island, thought to have been a gift from the native deities. Here, Shō Shōken has indeed hypothesized a common origin of Japanese and Ryukyuans, but he did so in order to argue for a non-divine origin for the five grains. This point is all the more clear from the concluding sentence of the above passage, which has typically been left out in discussions of the *Nichiryū dōso ron:* "Therefore, I do not think it matters who conducts the above-mentioned ceremony."[33]

In several essays, Takara has rightly criticized historians who have taken Shō Shōken's brief statement as a well-conceived theory about Ryukyuan-Japanese ancestry. The passage must be read, he says, in its context as part of the argument against royal participation in worship at Kudakajima.[34] "What was the real intention," asks Takara, "behind this *Nichiryū dōso ron* suddenly inserted at the end of the critique of the king's worshiping at Kudakajima? With only a few exceptions, most researchers have not concerned themselves with this question."[35] What Shō Shōken was doing, says Takara, was attacking the very mythical foundations of Kudakajima worship, stating that the grains came not from the gods but from Japan.[36] Clearly it was not Shō Shōken's primary intention to present a theory of common ancestry for its own sake. Takara has restored the *Nichiryū dōso ron* to its original context and makes a convincing case for Shō Shōken's authorial intent. But there is more to the meaning of any text than the author's primary intention.

The *Nichiryū dōso ron* passage, together with the stated fear that "people from large countries" would laugh at the king's going to Kudakajima to worship, indicate Shō Shōken's tendency to regard Satsuma as a benchmark and his concern that Ryukyuans not appear foolish in its eyes. In a passage in

Directives of Haneji, despairing over a lack of support from other Ryukyuan officials for taking steps against the activities of *yuta* (female shamans), Shō Shōken lamented, "I am saddened that there is nobody of like mind throughout the country. It is the one to the north that knows me."[37] Shō Shōken sought to make Ryukyu respectable in Satsuma's eyes.

Exploring this dimension of Shō Shōken further, we find that, on several occasions, he expressed a sense of embarrassment over how officials in Satsuma might regard conditions in Ryukyu. For example, in the context of criticizing Ryukyuan officials' patronage of prostitutes to the point of interference with their public duties, Shō Shōken stated that "furthermore, . . . as word of our officials' lax attitudes toward public service has even reached Satsuma, it is an unavoidable shame for the whole country."[38] Shō Shōken's frequent contact with officials from Satsuma undoubtedly exposed him to derogatory views of Ryukyu and its inhabitants. A late seventeenth-century biography of Tomari Jochiku by a scholar from Satsuma contains the following description of his sojourn in Ryukyu:

> [Tomari] also took to the seas and went to Ryukyu, where he served as a teacher. The diminutive barbarians of Ryukyu *(Liuqiu xiaoyi)* were ignorant of propriety and righteousness. [Tomari] Jochiku arrived and taught them human ethical relationships. After that, customs in Ryukyu increasingly inclined toward what is correct, and for the first time, Ryukyuans began to distinguish themselves from birds and beasts. Jochiku stayed in Ryukyu a long time, but was uncomfortable in a distant foreign country and returned to Satsuma.[39]

At least some of Satsuma's elites viewed Ryukyuans as cultural inferiors, which helps explain Shō Shōken's desire to change Ryukyu in ways that would make it more acceptable in the eyes of "the one to the north."

During the same year Satsuma handed down its verdicts in the Chatan-Eso Affair, Shō Shōken and the Council of Three issued a directive specifying qualifications for government office. It stated that *yukatchu* seeking employment as government officials must be conversant in each of the following areas: the literary arts, arithmetic, writing skills, native music, medicine, culinary arts, protocol, equestrian skills, Chinese music, calligraphy, the tea ceremony, and flower arrangement. If one lacked knowledge of even one item, the directive stated, he would have difficulty finding employment.[40] Ikemiya Masaharu views Shō Shōken's educational directive as an effort to promote education in Japanese cultural forms among the Shuri elite.[41] Mastery of these various skills and areas of knowledge would provide Ryukyuans with the type and degree of cultural refinement comparable to that of educated Japanese. Again we see Shō Shōken attempting to put Ryukyuan elites on a cultural par with Japanese counterparts.

Taking a somewhat different approach, Ōshiro Tatsuhiro ends up making the same point. He points out that although the Chatan-Eso Incident took place before Shō Shōken assumed office, he was prime minister at the time Satsuma handed down its verdicts. At this time, Satsuma directed the royal government to state its views on the matter, but it remained completely silent, doing nothing more than carrying out the sentences Satsuma ordered. Shō Shōken, too, appeared to remain silent, the statement on qualifications for office being the only directive he issued that year. In a novel interpretation of Shō Shōken's directive, Ōshiro regards it as the effective equivalent of a statement on the Chatan-Eso Incident.[42] Shō Shōken, in other words, directed future generations of Ryukyuans to become familiar with Japanese high culture to appear more acceptable in Japanese eyes and to work better with Japanese officials.

Shō Shōken's attempts to remake Ryukyu went beyond the realm of government administration and policy. He also attempted to reconstruct Ryukyu by constructing its past. The overall message of Shō Shōken's narrative of Ryukyu's past was that its relationship with Satsuma extended far back in time and was best characterized as that between lord and vassal. In 1650, he began work on Ryukyu's first official history, *Mirror of Chūzan (Chūzan seikan)*. Because writing a history is less a process of discovering a past already there than an act of creating a past in the context of the present, by examining certain aspects of this work we can gain further insight into Shō Shōken's view of seventeenth-century Ryukyu and its relationship with Satsuma.

Mirror of Chūzan arranges time as a succession of royal reigns. Although it does not deal with the reign of Shō Nei in depth, an overall summary of Ryukyuan history at the beginning of the work contains a brief analysis of the events surrounding Satsuma's invasion. The first statement under Shō Nei's reign is that Ryukyu first became a subordinate state *(fuyō no kuni)* of Shimazu, lord of Satsuma, over a hundred years previously, during the Eikyō period (1429–1441). Next we are told that Shō Nei became worried about policy matters and called his officials together, among whom was one named "Jana" (this Jana was Tei Dō, whose title was Jana Ueekata, but here the first character for his name, *"ja,"* appears not as the original one standing for the morpheme "gratitude," but one standing for the morpheme "evil").[43] As a result of this evil minister, Ryukyu lost its sincerity *(makoto),* which brought on the invasion and capture of the king. Two years later, Shimazu Iehisa, "emanating benevolent humanity *(jin)* and steeped in ritual decorum *(rei)*" set the king free to return to Ryukyu. At this point began the annual payment of a tribute tax to Satsuma.[44] The invasion, in other words, was the result of rudeness on the part of Ryukyu toward Shimazu, its lord of nearly two centuries. Although we are not told what this rudeness was, it was all the doing of the evil minister Jana. Shō Shōken's *Mirror of Chūzan* filtered economic, political, and military struggle out of the whole affair. Fortunately, Shimazu's benevolence permitted the king to return to his throne, a benevolence that included Ryukyuan tax payments to Satsuma.

Shō Shōken's narrative strongly implies that had Ryukyu adhered to the behavior befitting a vassal of Lord Shimazu, military conflict would never have taken place. The narrative also implies that neither Ryukyu generally, nor the king personally, ever favored offending Shimazu, their lord of many generations. The fault was all that of one man, Jana, for leading the king and the rest of his officials astray in opposing Satsuma. Therefore, the narrative implies, for Ryukyuans to oppose Satsuma would be contrary to proper ethical relations. Let us reject the role of Jana, Shō Shōken urged other Ryukyuans, and faithfully serve our overlord Shimazu.

Mirror of Chūzan contains several noteworthy stylistic features. First, it is written mainly in Japanese, although the overall summary of Ryukyuan history is in classical Chinese, as are relevant quoted passages such as Chinese imperial edicts. By contrast, all of the several subsequent official histories were written in classical Chinese. In *Mirror of Chūzan,* the honorific title affixed to the names of the kings of the second Shō dynasty is *kō* (roughly, "duke"), not the more impressive *ō* ("king"). In Dana's view, this usage reflects a fear of offending Satsuma. Also, at that time, Satsuma referred to Ryukyu's kings as *kokushi* (administrator of the country), not *kokuō* (king).[45] Significantly, Shō Nei, king at the time of the invasion, appears without any honorific suffix.[46] In these stylistic details, we see further indication of Shō Shōken's acceptance of Ryukyu's subordination to Satsuma.

According to Dana, the two underlying themes in *Mirror of Chūzan* are Confucian ethics and the fact of Satsuma's control. Regarding the former theme, he points to Shō Shōken's frequent portrayal of a lack of virtue resulting in loss of rulership.[47] On this point, Dana is essentially correct. Instead, of saying "Confucian ethics," however, it would be more accurate to say "*tentō* thought" *(tentō shisō)*. *Tentō* is a term that defies neat translation. Also pronounced *tendō,* it literally means "way of heaven," but in Japanese texts of the Kamakura and Muromachi periods, the term often indicates a willful entity with transcendent qualities. Often, *tentō* was vaguely defined, sometimes to the point of standing for the cosmos itself. This entity rules heaven and earth, and grants earthly rulers their power.[48] The other basic meaning of *tentō* is the sun. Even in spoken Japanese today, the term *o-tentō-san (-sama)* is a way to refer to the sun, and some scholars of Old-Ryukyuan thought have argued that the Okinawan term for the sun, *teda* (O. *tiida* or *teta*), derived from the Japanese *tentō*.[49] *Tentō* was also a standard translation for Deus in Christian texts.

Tentō thought was a major intellectual and religious tradition in Japan's middle ages that combined elements of Confucianism, Buddhism, Chinese correlative cosmology, and native beliefs, and it remained influential in Japanese intellectual circles into the seventeenth century.[50] The Zen-Confucian syncretic teachings of Satsuma scholars like Nanpo Bunshi were rooted in older Muromachi-period intellectual traditions. Considering Shō Shōken's close links with Satsuma and the teachings of Nanpo Bunshi and Ryukyu's long tradition of associating political power with the sun, it is hardly surprising that *tentō* thought serves as the main causal mechanism in *Mirror of Chūzan*.

As in most Japanese texts based on *tentō* thought, Shō Shōken saw *tentō* as punishing earthly rulers grown arrogant and fond of luxury. One such Ryukyuan king, according to *Mirror of Chūzan*, was Satto. Although generally regarded as a good king, Satto allegedly became addicted to luxury and lost the proper degree of humility in his latter years. As a result: "At night when the ruler was [asleep] in the upper chambers, in order to chastise him for his extravagance, *tentō* made his left hand touch a poisonous snake."[51]

Regarding Shō Toku (r. 1461–1469), last king of the first Shō dynasty, who conducted costly military campaigns against the advice of his ministers, *Mirror of Chūzan* relates: "Since assuming office, Shō Toku had not cultivated the virtue befitting a ruler. His mind became unruly from hunting and fishing day and night. Engaging in nothing but violence, cruelty, and lack of the Way, he harmed the people even more than did Jie and Zhou."[52] A detailed account of Shō Toku's evil deeds and *tentō*'s displeasure with them follows this passage. Japanese *tentō* texts often portrayed *tentō*'s retribution as affecting not the evil ruler himself but a descendant one or two generations removed. Likewise, *Mirror of Chūzan* explains the rise of the second Shō dynasty and its first king, Shō En, as follows: "Because *tentō* has the characteristic of despising evil and loving goodness, it quickly killed [Shō Toku's] heir and established Shō En, who had sagely virtue."[53] In other words, it was the goodness-loving *tentō*, not Shō En or his supporters, that killed the son of the warlike Shō Toku.

Floods, famine, epidemic disease, and similar natural disasters were classic signs of *tentō*'s displeasure with a ruler's virtue. Of particular importance for understanding Shō Shōken's thought is his portrayal of King Gihon (r. 1249–1260), the last ruler of his line:

> King Gihon . . . ascended the throne at age forty-four. The next year, there was a great famine in the realm. The year after that it continued, and there was an outbreak of epidemic disease. Half the people died. . . . The outbreak of disease derived from the ruler's lack of virtue. . . . It was proper for him to relinquish the throne. . . . King Gihon abdicated after being on the throne eleven years [age 54], handing it over to Eiso. . . . King Gihon's virtue [in abdicating] was like that of Yao. King Eiso's virtue [in taking the throne] was like that of Shun.[54]

Although *tentō* was not pleased with Gihon for some unspecified moral shortcoming, Shō Shōken ends up comparing him favorably with Yao, among the greatest of ancient China's legendary sage rulers. How could it be that Gihon was a Ryukyuan Yao, while other last kings in their lineages, Bunei and Shō Toku for example, were simply evil rulers whom *tentō* punished?

One reason is that for Shō Shōken, *tentō* was a transcendent ruler of the cosmos, unlike certain Confucian conceptions of *tian* (J. *ten*, "heaven") in which *tian* inheres in humans as part of their fundamental natures. The transcendent nature of *tentō* meant that its decrees are beyond the power of humans to change. Therefore, recognition of and resignation to such decrees were signs of sagely virtue. While Bunei and Shō Toku continued in their evil ways until the end, Gihon received clear signs of *tentō*'s displeasure and resigned himself and his throne to its will. Gihon did the only right thing: bowing to the will of a superior power.

In Shō Shōken's explanation of Satsuma's invasion of Ryukyu, it was Ryukyu that had been lacking in virtue when Shō Nei came under the sway of the evil minister Tei Dō (Jana). Righteous Satsuma had no choice but to send an army of chastisement. It is possible to read the above story of Gihon allegorically, with hapless, defeated Ryukyu like Gihon, with many of its people killed in 1609 by the irresistible force of Satsuma-as-*tentō*. Just as Gihon ascended to a par with Yao by accepting the will of *tentō*, greatness for Ryukyu would consist of accepting the fact of Satsuma's domination and cooperating with it.

It is, of course, impossible to be certain of the extent to which Shō Shōken consciously constructed his version of Ryukyu's past to make such a point. His career and writings taken as a whole, however, leave little room for doubt that his reaction to Satsuma's control was to urge his countrymen fully to accept it. He urged Ryukyuans to master Japanese culture, embrace Satsuma's control, and cooperate with their new (or old, according to *Mirror of Chūzan*) overlords to the north. This position was perfectly reasonable given Shō Shōken's education and experience and the desperate need at the time to revitalize Ryukyu's society, economy, and government. Shō Shōken saw Ryukyu's relationship with Satsuma as that of vassal and lord. His ideal Ryukyu would accept this relationship, fulfill its duties within it, and prosper thereby. The destiny of Shō Shōken's Ryukyu lay to the north.

Tei Junsoku

Shō Shōken's ideal Ryukyu looked much like Japan. Tei Junsoku's ideal Ryukyu looked much like China. Tei Junsoku was a scholar, poet, and diplomat who devoted much of his career and personal wealth to promoting Chinese studies in Ryukyu. In recognition of a lifetime of service, the royal government bestowed on him the honor of high rank, but he had virtually no influence on the political policy of his day. After his death, Tei Junsoku became a symbol of selfless virtue and a moral exemplar in Ryukyuan hagiography.

Tei Junsoku eventually became district administrator of Nago, an honorary rank equivalent to a member of the Council of Three, but he did not distinguish himself as a politician. Indeed, what brief record there is of his official performance when faced with difficult circumstances suggests little aptitude for such matters.[55] A writer of Chinese poetry whose reputation extended from Beijing to Edo and a vigorous promoter of Chinese studies, Tei Junsoku served the royal government in diplomatic assignments. Because diplomacy in East Asia was, at least on the surface, a variety of *li* (J. *rei,* ceremonial, ritualized conduct) between states, his literary refinement made him ideal for such work. Owing to a widespread reputation for moral excellence, Tei Junsoku became known as Nago *seijin,* "Sage of Nago."

Tei Junsoku spoke Chinese fluently and spent many years there during the course of five visits. At age twelve, he began his formal education in Kumemura under the instruction of a local scholar. At twenty-one he went to China to study at his own expense, returning to Ryukyu four years later in 1687. The next year, he received formal status rank in Kumemura and began working as a teacher at a salary of 2.5 *koku.*[56] A year later, he was back in China to serve as an official at Ryukyu's trading center in Fuzhou. When he returned to Okinawa in 1691 after a two-year stay, he brought back several sets of seventeen Chinese historical works in 159 volumes, printed at his own expense, which he donated to the Confucian temple library. In 1693, at age thirty-one, he won a poetry competition sponsored by the crown prince, Shō Jun. Two years later, Tei Junsoku was back in China as an interpreter for a tribute mission and traveled all the way to Beijing. He wrote poetry throughout the trip to and from Beijing and later compiled these poems to create his most famous work, *Setsudō's Travels to Beijing* (J. *Setsudō enyūsō,* C. *Xuetang yanyoucao*).[57]

In 1704, Tei Junsoku was appointed tutor to Crown Prince Shō Jun, who died before taking the throne, and Prince Shō Eki, who later became king. Two years later, he received the title Seigi Taifu and went back to China as the head of a tribute mission; en route to Beijing he worshiped at Confucius' birthplace. Before sailing for Ryukyu, he arranged for the printing of two works, *Amplification of the Six Maxims* (J. *Rikuyu engi,* C. *Liuyu yanyi*) and *Guide to Navigation* (J. *Shinan kōgi,* C. *Zhinan guangyi*), again at his own expense, for distribution upon his return.

Amplification of the Six Maxims was a basic moral primer written in semi-colloquial Chinese. This work originated with the first Ming emperor, who declared six maxims: (1) Be filial to your parents; (2) Respect your social superiors; (3) Live in harmony with fellow villagers; (4) Educate your children; (5) Work diligently at your occupations; and (6) Do no evil. Early in the seventeenth century, Fan Kuang of Zhejiang wrote an explanatory commentary on each maxim. The Shunqi emperor was so impressed with the work that in 1652 he promulgated it as an edict, sending a copy to each of the eight banners and to each province. According to the postscript Tei Junsoku wrote for the Ryukyuan edition, since Ryukyu benefited so heavily from trade and other interaction with China, it was essential that Ryukyuans going to China learn proper pronunciation. He regarded *Amplification of the Six Maxims,* written in Qing-era Chinese, a perfect text for this purpose. He also praised its value as a morality primer.[58]

Tei Junsoku went to Edo in 1714 as the official in charge of correspondence for a Ryukyuan embassy to congratulate the shōgun, Tokugawa Yoshimune. There, he presented *Amplification of the Six Maxims* to the shōgun as a gift from the daimyō of Satsuma. Yoshimune was most impressed with the work for its value as a moral primer and ordered Ogyū Sorai to punctuate it with Japanese reading marks and Muro Kyūso to translate it into Japanese, producing *General Meaning of the Amplification of the Six Maxims (Rikuyu engi tai'i)*. This and other editions of the text saw widespread use in elementary education throughout Japan well into the Meiji period.[59] Different versions of *Amplifications of the Six Maxims* also circulated in Ryukyu, where they served as basic reading texts.

Guide to Navigation was a detailed manual for pilots navigating between Fuzhou and Naha. Tei Junsoku wrote the book himself, primarily from two types of sources. First was pilots' lore that had been passed down through the generations in Kumemura. Second was his own experience studying navigational techniques under a Chinese ship's pilot. The book's contents include ocean maps, navigation by celestial bodies, methods of interpreting atmospheric phenomena, and even advice on invoking the divine protection of Tenpi (C. Mazu) and determining lucky days.[60] The major part of the work deals with compass techniques. Majikina Ankō points out that Tei Junsoku disseminated *Amplification of the Six Maxims* and *Guide to Navigation* for the same reason: to encourage Chinese studies in Ryukyu and increased interaction between Ryukyuans and Chinese.[61]

Aside from disseminating *Amplification of the Six Maxims,* Tei Junsoku's greatest contribution to education was establishing Meirindō (literally, Hall for the Illumination of Moral Principles), Ryukyu's first formal educational institution, in 1718. In 1719, Tei Junsoku revised the rites at the Confucian temple to accord more closely with Chinese practices. He made his final trip to China the following year at age fifty-eight. On that voyage, he brought back several tens of volumes of Chinese poetry, some of which he donated to the royal government, some to the Confucian temple library, and some to various acquaintances. He spent his last years in despair and semi-isolation after having lost all his sons to illness or accident.

Tei Junsoku tended to see China as a literary and aesthetic ideal that Ryukyuans and others should strive to emulate in the realm of culture. For him, the Chinese emperor and his capital were the center and source of culture and civilization. In 1697, at age thirty-five, Tei Junsoku traveled from Fuzhou to Beijing as a member of a Ryukyuan tribute embassy. He chronicled his trip to and from Beijing in verse, the following poem describing its start:

> In a ship adorned for paying respect to the Heavenly Court, we left the Qiong River.
>
> Turning north to face the Flowery Capital [Beijing], we were showered in rain and dew [imperial benevolence].
>
> We raised the sails from there and the wind carried us away.
>
> Pounding the gunwales we raised our voices to sing the Song of Great Peace.[62]

The poem expresses the joy and optimism of a literary man starting on a journey to the center and source of culture. Rain, no hindrance or inconvenience on this voyage, becomes imperial benevolence bathing the ship's crew. Of course, it would be expected that a Ryukyuan diplomat composing verse in Chinese would express such sentiments, but the content of this poem is consistent with the sentiment of all of Tei Junsoku's other writings.

A poem from the same voyage, *Crossing the Yellow River,* celebrates the vigor of the Qing dynasty as custodian of China's ancient cultural tradition while describing the power of the Yellow River:

The Yellow River abounds in the colors of autumn, joyous in this peaceful, prosperous time of the Great Qing.

Emerging from its source at Mt. Kunlun, it encounters the mountains and Mt.
Dizhu splits its flow.

Swirling, its waters lurch sideways like a hawk taking flight, rushing along, it is
like a dragon in the clouds.

Gazing at the shining glow of the Emperor's palace, we head up the river toward
the ancient foundation of Mt. Sanmen.

Where the river rushes into the sea with the combined force of all its branches,
the waves striking its banks make a strange sound that reverberates against
the sky.

It is as if the ship is crossing the sky, the stars flowing past on the surface of the
water.

The surging waves strike the ship's oars, and the leaves falling on the banks drop
into the mist.

The force of the river's flow seems strong enough to engulf the mountains
guarding the state of Qin, and now I truly realize the greatness of what is
carved on the memorial to Yu [legendary regulator of the flow of the
Yellow River].

We who have come from the eastern seas to demonstrate our loyal service to the
Emperor are uplifted in spirit but exhausted in body.[63]

Faced with the awesome physical and cultural power of China, Tei Junsoku is
both inspired and exhausted. Near the "shining glow" of the imperial palace,
the mighty river's roar reaches to the sky, yet the ancient, legendary sage
emperor Yu possessed power sufficient to control it. How could anyone not
strive to follow "Great Qing"?

In a similar vein, Tei Junsoku describes the uplifting and transformative
power of the Qing emperor during his visit to the Forbidden City:

The Forbidden City of the Divine Capital is surrounded by a long moat, and in
the clear sky wave brightly colored streamers.

Blooming yellow in the morning dew are many a chrysanthemum, as the imperial palace soars high, embraced by the purple of the autumn mountains.

Now I truly know the pleasure shared by the famous literati of old when they
ascended the tall platform [in the fall to drink, recite poems, etc.], and
even a lowly servant such as I can compose a poem and feel lofty.

> The transforming teachings of the sagely reign [of the Qing emperor] now extend far [to Ryukyu], so what need is there to seek the sublime by composing poems with titles like *"Gao"* [cakes]?[64]

Here, as in the previous poems, we see Tei Junsoku identifying himself with China's long and glorious literary tradition. He also identifies Ryukyu as part of this tradition, connected by the transforming teachings of the Qing emperors. He concludes another verse describing the sights and sounds of the imperial audience with the lines: "How can his followers in the eastern seas repay the imperial benevolence? We received the favor his Highness, offered up our tribute goods, and left the palace gate as if in a dream."[65] In his poetry and elsewhere (see below), Tei Junsoku spoke of China and its emperor in terms similar to the way Shō Shōken spoke of Satsuma and its daimyō.

Tei Junsoku was, of course, fully aware of Ryukyu's relationship with Japan, though his writings make no mention of it. A good example is the 1706 essay, *Brief Account of the Construction of the Confucian Temple and the Establishment of Learning* (J. *Kenbyō ritsugaku kiryaku* [often abbreviated as *Byōgaku kiryaku*], C. *Jianmiao lixue jilüe*), an essay narrating the development of Confucian studies in Ryukyu. The narrative begins by explaining the steps leading up to the construction of the Confucian temple. "During the Wanli period," we are told, "Murasaki Kintaifu Sai Ken [1585–1647] brought images of the sages back from China and venerated them in his household."[66] Later, the images were placed in the homes of leading Kumemura officials on a rotational basis until construction of the Confucian temple was finished. For Tei Junsoku and many of his peers in Kumemura, Confucianism was a system of literature and ritual, the mastery of which was essential for interacting effectively with Chinese officials. It did not become a blueprint for government until the eighteenth century.

After discussing Sai Ken, the narrative explains the origin of Confucian learning in Ryukyu. Its originators were four Chinese who came to Okinawa early in the seventeenth century, around the time of the Satsuma invasion: "To this day, the people of our country closely follow the way taught by the four teachers Mao Qingtai, Ceng Delu, Zhang Wuguan, and Yang Mingzhou. Their teaching was like the root of a tree." Regarding the origin of learning, "it was a radiance as bright as the sun and stars for the teachings of these four masters to have reached our country."[67] Although the study of Confucianism in Ryukyu did exist prior to the seventeenth century, Tei Junsoku regarded it as insignificant, saying, "Because nothing was written [about Confucian learning] prior to the arrival [of the four Chinese], it seems there was nobody to transmit it." Therefore, "It is not possible to know the situation prior to these four teachers."[68] By locating the temporal origins of Confucian learning in the early seventeenth century, Tei Junsoku can avoid mentioning that, prior to that time, Japanese Buddhist monks were the main transmitters of Confucian texts in Ryukyu. For him, the origins of Confucianism in Ryukyu and its subsequent development were a matter entirely connected with China. Japan is never mentioned, and we see nothing of, for example, Nanpo Bunshi, Tomari Jochiku, or Tomari's outstanding Ryukyuan student, Shō Shōken. In *Brief Account of the Construction of the Confucian Temple and the Establishment of Learning*, Confucianism came to Ryukyu only via China, and its custodians were the residents of Kumemura.

With its Chinese roots explained, the narrative moves on to a detailed listing of the Ryukyuan (Kumemura) Confucians. An official of high status served as Kumemura's education director. According to Tei Junsoku's narrative, the education director would lecture regularly, monitor students' progress, supervise trade and diplomacy with China, and participate in major ceremonies. There were no records of the activities of the education director prior to the seventeenth century, according to the account, which enabled Tei Junsoku to avoid mentioning that prior to the seventeenth century, monks from Japan conducted high-level education in Ryukyu, including tutoring of the royal family.

The first education director of record was Tei Dō, who returned from *kanshō* study in China about the same time as the four Chinese scholars came to Ryukyu. Upon his return, Tei Dō set up a corner of the Tenpi shrine as a makeshift school, where he began to teach. Tei Dō, of course, was the Ryukyuan official most openly opposed to Satsuma, but Tei Junsoku makes no mention of this matter or even of Satsuma. In Shō Shōken's history, Tei Dō was the evil minister Jana, who led the king astray and brought on the invasion. In Tei Junsoku's history, Tei Dō was a key founder of the Way in Ryukyu and a pioneer of Confucian education. After describing Tei Dō, the narrative lists successive generations of Ryukyuan heirs to the tradition—in effect a Ryukyuan *daotong* (succession of the Way). Here I mention only a few of the most important figures. In his narrative, Tei Junsoku simply listed them, so the biographical information below is derived from other sources.

When Kin Seishun (1618–1674) served as education director, he selected the scholar Shū Kokushun to lecture on the classics. Kin also served as lecturer to the king and was instrumental in securing royal support for construction of the Confucian temple. Kin was knowledgeable of conditions in China during the fall of the Ming, for although Tei Junsoku's account says nothing of it, Shimazu sent Kin to report to the bakufu on the Ming's demise.[69]

Following Kin Seishun was Ō Meisa (dates uncertain). We know that he was thoroughly familiar with the writings of Nanpo Bunshi. Indeed, in 1645 this Ryukyuan scholar even lectured on Nanpo Bunshi's writings to Satsuma's resident supervisor *(zaiban bugyō)*, Saruwatari Niisuke. Also, along with Kin Seishun and Tei Shizen, Ō Meisa was instrumental in handling Ryukyuan diplomacy in China during the difficult transition from Ming to Qing. He accompanied Kin Seishun to Edo to report to the Bakufu on conditions in China, and bakufu officials praised his fluent Japanese.[70]

Sai Kokki (1632–1702) comes next in Tei Junsoku's account. Having resided in China for eleven years at the peak of the fighting between Ming and Qing forces, he was particularly knowledgeable of conditions there. In 1674, when Ming loyalists sent an envoy to Ryukyu asking for assistance, the royal government called on Sai for advice. He advised rejecting the envoy's request but also suggested that Ryukyuan envoys on the next tribute mission bring two sets of official documents (one to Ming and one to Qing) to allow for an immediate response to changing conditions. The last major figure in the list of Ryukyuan inheritors of the Way was Tei Kōryō (dates unclear), Tei Junsoku's teacher prior to his first trip to China.[71]

The essay then explains the origin of the two official teaching posts in Kumemura, the teacher of reading and teacher of interpretation, and names the scholars who held them. Next we are told that since the *kanshō* system has been reinstated (after a hiatus of several decades following the invasion), the transmission of the Way could be expected to continue on its proper course. *Brief Account of the Construction of the Confucian Temple and the Establishment of Learning* concludes with an optimistic assessment of the present situation: "Now, the king reveres the sages and treats teachers well. The various *taifu* [high officials in Kumemura] all revere Confucianism and value the Way. I am delighted that the sincere will of the sagely Son of Heaven [the Kangxi emperor] to transform through learning has extended as far as Chūzan."[72] The construction of the Confucian temple and the establishment of formal education in Chinese studies, concludes Tei Junsoku, are specific manifestations of this desirable state of affairs and transformative imperial will.

Ryukyu's seventeenth-century connections with Japan in the realm of Confucian learning and Chinese affairs were numerous and directly involved the leading scholars of Kumemura, including Tei Junsoku himself. But *Brief Account of the Construction of the Confucian Temple and the Establishment of Learning* is silent on this point. Indeed, Satsuma and Japan are conspicuously present by their absence. Of course, the total absence of Satsuma/Japan may have been because Tei Junsoku intended that Chinese officials read his narrative. If so, silence about Japan would have been mandatory due to Satsuma's policy of concealing completely the Ryukyu-Japan relationship. Satsuma's power, in other words, would have been behind the absent "presence" of Satsuma/Japan in Tei Junsoku's lineage of the Way in Ryukyu.

Conclusions

Shō Shōken and Tei Junsoku were influential Ryukyuans of the late seventeenth century whose visions of an ideal "Ryukyu" differed in significant ways. Shō Shōken saw Ryukyu as vassal in a lord-vassal relationship with Satsuma, and he worked to improve the image of Ryukyu and its people in the eyes of its powerful overlord. Tei Junsoku saw Ryukyu, its king, and its officials as cultural vassals of the Qing emperor. Like Shō Shōken, he worked to improve Ryukyu's image in the eyes of Chinese literati, spending most of his career and personal resources promoting Chinese studies in Ryukyu. Both were correct in their different conceptions of Ryukyu. As Shō Shōken argued, it was indeed essential for Ryukyuan officials to accept Satsuma's control, to acknowledge the passing of Old-Ryukyu, and to formulate new policies for the new age. For these reasons, it was also necessary for Ryukyuan officials to master the high culture of Japan. But Ryukyu was valuable to both Satsuma and the bakufu as a separate country precisely because of its ties with China, all the more so after the Qing dynasty became a well-established power in East Asia. Because Ryukyu's foreign relations with China were based on the ritual assertion of a cultural relationship, thorough study of Chinese language, literature, and protocol was essential for at least some of Ryukyu's officials.

Looking ahead to the eighteenth and nineteenth centuries, Shō Shōken's major lasting legacy was the changes he made to Ryukyu's institutions and institutional culture. These changes helped improve Ryukyu's material standard of living and set the stage for further prosperity under Sai On's direction. Sai On's vision of Ryukyu differed greatly from that of Shō Shōken, but Sai On continued much of the process of institutional change that Shō Shōken initiated.

Tei Junsoku greatly aided the royal government's efforts to revive Kumemura as a viable center of Chinese studies and diplomacy. In the eighteenth century, scholars from Kumemura trained in Chinese studies came to dominate Ryukyu's domestic politics as well as diplomacy. In the generations after his death, Tei Junsoku became a symbol of personal virtue and excellence—a status that eluded Shō Shōken and Sai On, perhaps because their political power was inimical with an image of moral purity. An excellent example of Tei Junsoku's status in later Ryukyuan hagiography is an 1844 chronicle, *Record of the Good Deeds of Nago Ueekata (Nago Ueekata zenkō den)*.

According to the introduction, the work was written in Japanese to disseminate widely the knowledge of Tei Junsoku's virtuous accomplishments. As a
boy, "he exhibited benevolence and filial piety in his heavenly nature and his
face reflected a mild temperament and pleasant personality. He thoroughly
carried out the proper role of son, being ever mindful of the wishes of his
mother and father, and moreover, he excelled in academic pursuits never stop-
ping his reading day and night." As a teenager, "he despised viewing unright-
eous books and colors not in conformity with prescribed ritual forms. He
placed great value on ethics and behaved as a kind and filial brother."[73] As an
adult, his reputation for virtue was so great that even loud, rowdy drunks
would lower their voices out of heartfelt respect when passing by Tei Junsoku's
gate.[74] In short, Tei Junsoku came to symbolize moral authority and its transforming power. And it was precisely in the realm of moral authority, argued
Sai On, that Ryukyu could ascend to a par with its larger neighbors.

CHAPTER 3

Empowering Ryukyuans
The Theoretical Foundations of Sai On's Ryukyu

Sai On's vision of Ryukyu was more complex and nuanced than that of either Shō Shōken or Tei Junsoku. Although it faced opposition, Sai On's vision proved more successful by far than any other in reshaping the kingdom's institutions, political culture, intellectual landscape, and even physical appearance. Confucianism served as the theoretical underpinning of Sai On's vision of Ryukyu and the changes it produced in the realm of politics. Sai On faced a problem similar to that of Shō Shōken and Tei Junsoku: justifying the existence of the Ryukyuan state as a subordinate entity to China and Japan (Satsuma and the bakufu). But Sai On further sought to create the maximum subjectivity for Ryukyu itself. Whereas Shō Shōken saw Ryukyu's destiny as a vassal of Satsuma and Tei Junsoku saw it as a vassal of the Qing court, Sai On saw Ryukyu's destiny as being largely in the hands of Ryukyuans themselves. In many respects, Sai On was a sinophile like fellow Kumemura resident Tei Junsoku. On the other hand, being a pragmatic politician, he could not ignore the political power of Japan. He deployed Confucian ideology, sometimes in unique ways, in an attempt to minimize the impact of Satsuma's political power on Ryukyu while simultaneously empowering Ryukyuans to become masters of their destiny. This chapter deals with the theoretical aspects of Sai On's Confucian vision of Ryukyu; the next examines his vision as it moved from the realm of theory into the realm of political conflict and policy.

Early Career, Autobiography, Intellectual Orientation

The first Ryukyuan to write an autobiography, Sai On presented an idealized version of his life to subsequent generations as a model. Only the rudimentary facts in the autobiography such as date of birth, offices held, and official salary can be verified by other sources. The bulk of the text consists of unverifiable anecdotes that reinforce the main themes Sai On stressed in his other works. Much of the autobiography is probably fictitious, unreliable in the conventional sense of a record of the true facts of Sai On's life. That it is unreliable as a straightforward record of the events of Sai On's life, however, does not make the autobiography unimportant. Sai On could never be accused of excessive humility, and his autobiography is of great value as a window through which to view Sai On's image of an ideal person (himself). It also sheds light on his ideal vision of Ryukyu. This section contains an outline of Sai On's early life and career. For the major events of Sai On's life we rely mainly on *Sai-uji kafu,* the official record of the Sai lineage of Kumemura.[1] By analyzing key passages from his autobiography, portions of this section also serve as an intellectual biography, indicating Sai On's fundamental values and the core of his Confucian thought.

Sai On was the eleventh-generation Sai household heir, though he was not biologically related to the generations prior to his parents' because they both came to Kumemura from outside households. Sai On's father, Sai Taku (1644–1724), was a historian, a tribute envoy to China, and Kumemura's first elected magistrate. Sai Taku made significant contributions to the welfare of Kumemura. For example, he negotiated with Chinese officials to allow an increase in the size of Ryukyuan tribute embassies from 150 to 200 and to exempt from taxes the ship that would come to meet the embassy on its return from Beijing.[2]

Sai On had an older half-brother, the son of Sai Taku by a different mother. The *Sai-uji Kafu,* Sai On's autobiography, and the *Kyūyō* tell the same story of Sai On's mother asking her husband to take a mistress because of her concern over being unable to bear a male child. According to these accounts, Sai Taku was reluctant to do so, preferring instead to adopt sons. His wife insisted, however, and promised the family of the proposed mistress to treat any offspring as her own child. The mistress bore a child, later called Sai En. Later and unexpectedly, Sai Taku's wife bore the child who would later be called Sai On.[3] In the autobiography, we are told that Sai Taku wanted to install Sai On as household heir but that his wife insisted both children be given equal treatment and education. Furthermore, the two often quarreled over this matter and "their disagreement was not settled for a long time, and everyone else was able to hear of the matter."[4] Sai On's mother prevailed, and Sai En was designated household heir. Both children received similar educations, but while Sai En studied hard and made excellent progress, Sai On became upset over being passed over as heir and did not.[5] It is interesting that from this point, no further mention is made of Sai En in Sai On's autobiography. In the narrative, the half-brother serves to set up a situation in which the young Sai On is despondent over what he perceived to be bad luck or unfair treatment. As a result, he lacked motivation to excel in life and was a complete failure in his studies. This situation sets the stage for the first of two Zen-like awakenings that Sai On claimed as major turning points in his life.

The first awakening came at age sixteen. According to the autobiography, one cloudless night some young *yukatchu,* Sai On among them, gathered in front of the main gate to Kumemura to chat. Kobashigawa Niya, a boy from a family of the lowest rank within the *yukatchu,* said to Sai On, "This moonlit night is for *yukatchu* to enjoy together. You, however, are not a *yukatchu* and have pushed your way in here. You should go home immediately." Sai On angrily replied to Kobashigawa that it was he, not a real *yukatchu,* but one whose family had recently purchased aristocratic status, who should go home. Kobashigawa's alleged reply is nearly identical to exhortations Sai On included in some of his other writings:

> A *yukatchu* is one who is accomplished in calligraphy and scholarship, not one whose family is important. You cannot read or remember a single line or phrase. You have even forgotten the *Great Learning* and the *Mean.* Because you are fortunate enough to be a *ueekata*'s son, however, you can dress [like a high-status *yukatchu*], but all things considered, you are no different from a farmer's son. We have made much progress in reading and our teachers have praised us, but what praise have your teachers given you?

Kobashigawa then clapped his hands and laughed, and to Sai On's chagrin, the others chimed in in agreement with Kobashigawa.[6]

Here, Sai On uses the words of Kobashigawa to define what should set a *yukatchu* apart from a commoner. Heredity or, less frequently, purchase of a *kafu* defined the legal requirements for *yukatchu* status. But what really matters, Sai On claims, was accomplishment in scholarship. Even a Kobashigawa, with only a marginal hereditary claim to *yukatchu* status, had a strong claim based on his scholarly merit. Even the scion of as exalted a lineage as Sai On's household would be "no different from a farmer's son" without worthy goals and the resolve to carry them through.

According to the autobiography, Sai On returned home stunned. He brooded for two months and finally resolved to study in earnest. Despite slow initial progress, he rapidly made up lost ground and became teacher of interpretation at the remarkably young age of twenty-five.[7]

The incident at age sixteen stimulated Sai On's desire to learn, but even upon becoming teacher of interpretation, he lacked a clearly defined goal toward which to apply his learning. His second awakening came soon after Sai On's arrival in China as part of the entourage of a tribute embassy at age twenty-seven. According to the autobiography, Sai On visited the Lingyun Temple near the Ryukyuan trading compound in Fuzhou and got to know the head monk. This monk urged Sai On to talk with a scholarly recluse who was staying at the temple. The recluse initially acted impressed with Sai On's erudition, once asking him to compose a poem impromptu and lavishly praising the mediocre result. Unimpressed, Sai On wanted to stop seeing the recluse, but the head monk urged one final visit.

On this last visit, the recluse suddenly turned critical, accusing Sai On of having wasted his time and education and characterizing him as a disgrace to himself and useless to his country. He accused Sai On of spending all his time with "the dregs of learning" *(moji no kasu),* without ever having come to understand the real meaning of the classics he had spent so many hours memorizing. Shocked by this seemingly outrageous accusation, Sai On tried to defend himself.

"Are you familiar with the *Analects*?" the recluse asked. Sai On's reply, "Of course! I have carefully read all of the Four Books and Six Classics," initiated the following dialogue about *Analects* 1:5:

> *Recluse:* "What is the true meaning of this [passage]? Please explain the true meaning of the characters *jing shi* [reverent or mindful service]."
>
> *Sai On:* "With regard to the way of government, *jing shi* is concentration so as not to lack precision, that is, to be mindful while serving [in office]."
>
> *Recluse:* "Regarding procedures for such concentration, what specific steps would you take?"

The recluse burst out laughing at Sai On's answer and continued questioning.

> *Recluse:* "What sort of words are 'loving others'?"
>
> *Sai On:* "What I mean by 'loving others' is that in any case of putting the correct way into practice, one extends benevolence to a country's people."
>
> *Recluse:* "By what means would you endeavor to 'extend benevolence'?"[8]

Exasperated by these queries he could not answer in specific terms, Sai On was forced to agree with the recluse's assessment that "all things considered, you are inferior to a craftsman for you have forgotten yourself and your country." Sai On studied under the recluse for five months. He placed great importance on this encounter, devoting roughly one-third of the autobiography to it and saying of the above dialogue, "Hearing those words for the first time was like waking from a dream."[9]

The recluse should not be taken literally, and there is no concrete evidence of his existence in the flesh. By portraying his awakening in this way, Sai

On criticized those who considered themselves learned but merely parroted stock phrases and commentaries without any idea of how to translate those words into action in one's own set of circumstances. Such critiques of "empty" or "impractical" learning were, of course, common in the Confucian tradition. Sai On's explanation of *jing shi* and mention of "loving others" in the dialogue above bears a superficial resemblance to Zhu Xi's commentary on *Analects* 1:5.[10] The young Sai On's partial parroting of Zhu's interpretation, however, was but a parody of true understanding, for he had no idea how to express "loving others" in terms of specific policies that would benefit his society.

Another passage in the autobiography reveals a theme found in many of Sai On's other essays. The same recluse tells Sai On that "the Four Books, Six Classics, and other wise writings all deal with making the will sincere and governing the country. But you have disregarded the great function *(taiyō)* of making the will sincere and governing the country, and instead put your effort into reading books and writing compositions merely for your own amusement."[11] The only legitimate purpose of formal study, in other words, is to make the will sincere, which, according to the *Great Learning,* leads to the ultimate goal of properly governing the country.[12] In *Essential Discussion of Popular Customs* (C. *Suxi yaolun,* J. *Zokushū yōron*), Sai On explains this point in some detail. Effort in scholarship, he says, must start with the two characters "making the will sincere." To start with such training and bring one's effort to fruition results in clarification of appropriateness and the cosmic pattern *(yili)* and the manifestation of one's true talent. In this way, one joins the ranks of those who are of great use to society. "Why do vulgar scholars endeavor pointlessly to read books and write compositions? Even if one makes a name for himself in the literary arts, if he covets profit, loves fame, and the like [i.e. if his will is not sincere], he is no different from a common person. Could this be what it really means to cultivate learning?"[13] The similarity to the alleged words of the recluse in Fujian is obvious.

Sai On remained in China for two years, where he studied a variety of subjects. In the autobiography, he does not mention what may have been his most important intellectual training, geomancy. A *Kyūyō* entry for 1708 explains Sai On's study as follows: "When Sai On was a resident official in Fujian, he received an order to study geomancy in detail under Liu Ji. He received the secret books of that art and a large geomantic compass. He had already received silver coins from the government and used them to defray his expenses."[14] One indication of the degree of Sai On's mastery is that in 1717 the royal government ordered Kō Shiken of Kumemura to study geomancy under Sai On before going on the next year to study in Fujian.[15] In 1712, Sai

On, Mō Buntetsu, and others conducted a geomantic assessment of Shuri castle and other important sites. The lengthy *Kyūyō* passage describing the details begins with the statement, "There is nothing more important than geomancy for constructing a capital and establishing a country."[16] Geomancy informed Sai On's thought on a wide range of matters, including his forestry science and policies (see Chapter 4).

Soon after his return to Ryukyu in 1711 at the young age of thirty, leading officials of the royal government selected Sai On to serve as tutor to Crown Prince Shō Kei. This appointment launched Sai On's political career, for King Shō Eki died unexpectedly in 1712, and Shō Kei ascended the throne. Sai On continued in his post as Shō Kei's teacher, now with the newly created title *kokushi* (state instructor). The post of *kokushi* became a regular office of the royal government, held by Confucian scholars from Kumemura until the end of the kingdom. As part of his duties, Sai On compiled a Confucian anthology for the king's benefit, which the *Kyūyō* describes as follows:

> Seigi Taifu Sai On selected those items from the sages' classics, accounts of worthies, and a wide variety of other writings that contained inspiring words and [examples of] admirable conduct that would be particularly effective in [improving] personal conduct. He compiled them into a single volume, and called it *Yaowu huibian* [J. *Yōmu ihen*]. . . . He respectfully presented it to the king.[17]

The complete text of this work has recently been found. According to Tsuzuki's analysis, *Yaowu huibian* closely resembles Hu Guang's 1415 anthology, *Xingli daquan* (Compendium of human nature and the cosmic pattern), except that it contains none of the material on metaphysics from the Chinese text. Material in Sai On's anthology also came, directly or indirectly, from *Xiaoxue (Elementary Learning), Reflections of Things at Hand,* the Four Books, the Five Classics, and their commentaries, sets of household admonitions, and other sources.[18]

Sai On developed a close relationship with Shō Kei, which became political capital for later use in promoting Sai On's vision of Ryukyu. In 1716, he went to China for the second and final time to request Shō Kei's investiture as king. Although normally a pro forma request, this time officials at the Board of Rites became concerned about departures from normal procedure. Shō Tei had died in 1709, and Shō Eki in 1712, but Ryukyu had never requested Shō Eki's investiture and was requesting Shō Kei's investiture four years after he took the throne. Via the written word, Chinese officials first asked Sai On and his party about the delay in requesting Shō Eki's investiture. Sai On replied in writing that in 1711, Ryukyu sent an envoy to announce the death of Shō Tei and had planned to request investiture the next year in conjunction with the scheduled tribute mission. By then, however, Shō Eki had died. Ryukyu sent an envoy to report Shō Eki's death in 1714 and is now requesting investiture for Shō Kei.[19] The Chinese officials were not satisfied with this explanation. Why, they asked, if Shō Eki had died in 1712 and the mourning period was over in 1714, did not Ryukyu request investiture in 1715, instead of doing so a year later? Sai On replied that according to former precedents, investiture was always requested in conjunction with tribute missions. But because 1715 was an off year, the request was delayed until the present time to be submitted in conjunction with presenting tribute. This explanation seems to have satisfied the officials, because shortly thereafter the emperor formally granted investiture.[20]

Although the circumstances in this particular case are not clear, it is likely that financial problems were behind Ryukyu's delay in seeking investiture. Investiture was extremely costly for the post-invasion kingdom. As time went on, kings had to wait ever longer to receive investiture, while the royal government worked to scrape together the needed funds. According to the *Kyūyō,* Shō Kei's investiture completely depleted the treasury and required the imposition of an ad hoc tax on commoner residents of Shuri, Tomari, Naha, and Kumemura, which lasted until 1728.[21]

Upon his return from China, Sai On continued to instruct the king, while also assisting with preparations for the arrival of the Chinese investiture delegation. The *Sai-uji kafu* reports that by this time, silt had accumulated in Naha harbor to the point that it had become too shallow for large ships. In 1718, Sai On oversaw the dredging of the harbor.[22] As the date for the investiture drew closer in 1719, Sai On took charge of the king's practice sessions, as he and his officials prepared for the complex investiture rites.

The arrival of the Chinese envoys, along with several hundred merchants, soon brought on a major crisis. At considerable personal and financial risk, these merchants brought large quantities of goods to sell in Ryukyu. It was customary for the royal government to appoint a team of China specialists to negotiate with the merchants regarding the value of the goods and then purchase them once agreement had been reached. The problem this time was that the royal government was so short of cash that it simply could not purchase more than a fraction of the goods. The resulting dispute is known by its Okinawan name, the *Hangaa* (=J. *hyōka*) *jiken,* or Valuation Incident.[23]

A team of negotiators headed by Tei Junsoku went to deal with the Chinese merchants, who claimed that the total value of their goods came to 2,000 *kanme*[24] of silver. The royal government, however, had only 500 *kanme* on hand for purchases. When the Ryukyuan negotiators explained the situation, the merchants stated their disbelief that Ryukyu could really be so poor, arguing that even a small kingdom could afford 6,000 *kanme* of goods. They accused the Ryukyuans of being obstinate out of spite for the Chinese.

With negotiations at an impasse and tension increasing, Tei Junsoku and his group withdrew, and Sai On took over. He was able to convince the head investiture envoy of Ryukyu's situation with little difficulty, but the envoy lacked the courage to tell the merchants, fearing the trouble they might cause. Indeed, by this point in the dispute, the merchants began threatening to set fire to the investiture vessels, and thus remained in Ryukyu into the next year to trade with the Ōshima ship that would visit Naha in the meantime. The royal government, of course, was terrified of the possibility and closely guarded the ships around the clock.[25]

According to Sai On's self-aggrandizing account of the matter, the merchants began to demonstrate. Several hundred surrounded him as he was riding through the streets of Naha and demanded satisfaction of their claims. If we are to believe the account, while the other Ryukyuan officials panicked and fled, Sai On fearlessly faced the merchants and managed to convince them that Ryukyu could indeed afford only 500 *kanme* of goods. They released Sai On and the valuation of those goods Ryukyu could purchase continued. At the same time, Sai On organized a drive to collect silver and gold hairpins *(kanzashi)* from the residents of Shuri and Naha, which provided the equivalent of an additional 100 *kanme* of silver for the purchase of more goods.[26]

Whether events actually took place as Sai On later reported, it is clear that he was instrumental in defusing the crisis. Had the incident gotten out of hand, it would have marred Shō Kei's investiture and harmed relations between Ryukyu and China. Satsuma, of course, was quietly watching from a distance, and its officials were no doubt relieved that the Valuation Incident simmered down. The Valuation Incident was a boon for Sai On's political career, and the next year he was appointed to the status of *sanshikan zashiki* (roughly, "honorary member of the Council of Three"). Although typically honorary when awarded at the end of one's career, in Sai On's case this title was a signal that he was slated for appointment to the Council of Three in the near future. This appointment came eight years later in 1728. By then, if not earlier, Sai On had become the single most powerful person in the royal government. He had the support of both the king and Satsuma, and the formal status of a member of Ryukyu's highest governing body. On the other hand, Sai On faced opposition throughout his career, and we examine this opposition in subsequent sections and chapters.

Sai On's autobiography is more than simply an idealized account of one man's life recalled in old age. Read in the context of his other works, the autobiography reveals an emotive version of Sai On's vision of an ideal Ryukyu. Sai On the individual faced adversity from without, eventually acknowledged his shortcomings and strove mightily to overcome them, becoming a great man. Likewise, as we see in detail below, Sai On acknowledged Ryukyu's externally imposed limitations and internal shortcomings, while also urging Ryukyuans to take charge of their own destiny and create a prosperous society through hard, intelligent work despite past and present adversity.

Before examining this vision of Ryukyu in greater detail, we briefly address the question of early intellectual orientation. When writing, Sai On and his contemporaries from Kumemura rarely made explicit reference to the work of Chinese or Japanese scholars. In only one of Sai On's works, *Kadōkun* (Precepts for the household), does he appear to quote extensively from a wide variety of other sources. In fact, however, nearly the whole text of this work, including the references to other sources, is itself a copy or a close paraphrase of a 1711 essay of the same title by the Japanese Confucian scholar Kaibara Ekken (1630–1714). From this fact we may obviously conclude that Sai On received some influence from Kaibara,[27] but, it is otherwise difficult to trace Sai On's early reading and study with precision. Although his thought was clearly based on the metaphysics of Cheng-Zhu Neo-Confucianism, it was sufficiently distinctive to preclude facile classification of Sai On as a member of a specific school of Confucian thought or intellectual lineage.[28] The question of Sai On's intellectual affiliations requires further research. Here, I briefly examine a few possibilities that have thus far received little or no attention in the scholarly literature on Ryukyu.[29]

Confucian and other literature came into Ryukyu both from China and Japan. Ryukyuan envoys to both places were, of course, highly educated and typically interested in scholarly and technical developments. Although there are no extant, detailed records of books imported or the contents of libraries in Ryukyu, there are scattered references to bibliographic matters that indicate a high level of interest in books. Eighteenth-century Qing historian Zhang Xuecheng (1738–1801), for example, lamented the decline of libraries in Zhejiang province as follows: "Thirty years back, book buyers in Peking bought up many books from old families here, but in the last decade they have paid no attention to us. I've heard that foreign ships, for example from Japan and the Ryukyus, have come and bought many books for which they have paid high prices."[30] If indeed Ryukyuan book buying extended to Zhejiang, it indicates a particularly high demand for Chinese books. Ch'en points out that Chinese investiture envoys to Ryukyu noted the presence of Japanese books:

Another envoy pointed out that many editions of the Chinese classics that he had seen in Liu-ch'iu [Ryukyu] had been published in Japan. The texts were in Chinese but had Japanese reading marks at the side of each column of characters. There were also Japanese reign titles such as Hōreki, Eishō, and Genna. The Liu-ch'iuans said they got these books from Foochow, but the envoy was sure that there was no such thing in Foochow.[31]

In short, it is reasonable to assume that, by Sai On's time, Ryukyuan scholars had access to nearly the same literature as their contemporaries in China and Japan did.

Because Sai On resists easy classification, I see no need to force him into a particular category. Clearly he was a Confucian scholar, broadly defined. He drew on such a wide variety of intellectual traditions, however, as to render inappropriate attaching a label to him like "follower of Zhu Xi" or "follower of Wang Yangming," as many scholars of Ryukyuan history have done. A comprehensive examination of Sai On's Confucian thought is beyond the scope of this study, and interested readers should see the growing literature on this topic.[32] We now turn to the specific components of Sai On's vision of Ryukyu.

Satsuma's Metal and Ryukyu's Wood

In 1750, near the end of a long career in government, Sai On wrote *One Man's Views (Hitori monogatari),* in which he argued his views on key policy issues for the benefit of subsequent generations of Ryukyuan officials and *yukatchu*. A theme that integrates the various parts of the text is the status of Ryukyu and its connection with Satsuma. In *One Man's Views,* Sai On adumbrated a model that accounted for Ryukyu's dependence on Satsuma while also minimizing the extent of Satsuma's role in determining the direction of Ryukyuan society. It was ultimately up to Ryukyuans, he argued, to shape their own destiny. This theme of Ryukyuans taking responsibility for the destiny of their society runs through most of Sai On's writings as well as the "text" of his significant action during his career as a government official.[33]

One Man's Views can be divided into three main sections. In the first, Sai On stresses that (1) Satsuma's control has been beneficial for Ryukyu and (2) that even poor, small countries can achieve peace and prosperity if only they adhere closely to the "fundamental principles of the Way of Government" *(go-seidō no honpō)*. The middle section deals with how Ryukyuan officials should put these fundamental principles into practice via policies specific to Ryukyu's circumstances. In the final section, there is a return to the issues of Ryukyuan identity raised at the start of the essay.

"Our country has obligations to both China and Japan," begins *One Man's Views*, "which it lacks the means to fulfill."[34] In addition to its lack of material resources, Sai On claimed that Ryukyu had long been ignorant of the fundamental principles of the Way of Government. Nevertheless, Ryukyu had managed to exist as a kingdom since ancient times, a fact in need of explanation. One factor in Ryukyu's favor that helped compensate for its lack of material resources and proper methods of government was the favorable geomantic features of Okinawa. Its mountain ranges all connected to form a serpentine shape resembling a dragon. Because in geomantic theory dragons are associated with concentrations of the earth's material energies (C. *qi,* J. *ki*), large geographic features such as mountains forming the shape of a dragon would be particularly auspicious. In addition to the serpentine mountain ranges, Sai On claimed, the islands of Ryukyu are located under an area of particularly beneficial stars.

Knowledge of the principles of geomancy may have existed in Ryukyu since the fifteenth century, but it was not until the middle of the seventeenth century that significant numbers of Ryukyuans began to study this complex subject in a systematic fashion.[35] By Sai On's time a knowledge of geomancy had become widespread among educated Ryukyuans, and by the late eighteenth century, geomantic concepts had even spread to the countryside. Therefore, Sai On's geomantic explanation for Ryukyu's long existence as a state would have made sense to most *yukatchu* and local officials, the intended audience for *One Man's Views*. According to Sai On, even though Ryukyu had only recently begun to follow the fundamental principles of the Way of Government, it had managed to get by as a kingdom owing to a fortunate accident of geography.[36]

Because Sai On regarded Confucian principles as a universally applicable and essential foundation for government and society, he needed a plausible explanation for how Ryukyu could have gotten by without the Confucian Way for so long. Geography, having served as this explanation, never comes up again in the essay. Indeed, it goes on to explain that failure to adhere to the fundamental principles of the Way of Government will result in Ryukyu's decline.[37] We are not told why the favorable geomantic features and stars are no longer sufficient to ensure the kingdom's survival. Perhaps Satsuma's power was too great for them to overcome. In any case, it is to the Way of Government, not to topography or the stars, that Ryukyuans must now look to ensure the continued existence and prosperity of their country.

The discussion then turns to the inevitable question of Satsuma's role in the course of Ryukyu's history. Sai On went out of his way to stress the beneficial nature of Satsuma's domination. It was because of Satsuma, he said, that

Ryukyu finally took up the long-neglected fundamental principles of the Way of Government:

> The annual submission of tax rice to Satsuma can be viewed as a great harm to our country. All things considered, however, it is actually a great benefit that cannot be fully expressed in writing. In former times, the Way of Government was not at all established in our country. The peasants were negligent in their practice of agriculture, and the people were hard-pressed. Selfish customs gradually worsened, and from time to time there were rebellions. That the people were in extreme difficulty was inexcusable. Since coming under Satsuma's rule, however, customs have been rectified, and the peasants now compete to exert themselves in the pursuit of agriculture. Throughout the country things have become as we would like. This fortunate situation at this late date has come about because of Satsuma, and we should feel that it is difficult fully to express our indebtedness in writing. I have also written about this matter in *Articles of Instruction*.[38]

In Sai On's synopsis of Ryukyu's past, geography permitted an otherwise benighted kingdom to exist, and Satsuma's rule brought it the benefits of the Way of Government.

Interpreting Sai On's praise as a reflection of his and other Ryukyuans' fear of Satsuma is common in histories of Ryukyu. "This display of a fawning attitude toward Shimazu," state Shinzato Keiji et al., "was surely because of an acute cognizance of Satsuma's political pressure."[39] Satsuma's power, the conventional explanation goes, gave Sai On no choice but to include such flattering words in his writings intended for wide audiences, though he did not really believe them. This view is not unreasonable. That praising Satsuma was good politics is sufficient reason to explain Sai On's words. Although we can never be certain what motivated him to write what he did, here or anywhere else, it is possible—though not provable—that Sai On was sincere in his view that Satsuma brought about a beneficial transformation of Ryukyuan society. From Sai On's perspective as a Confucian, Ryukyu had been heading in the right direction during the first half of the eighteenth century. After 1609, Confucianism became an ever more powerful force in Ryukyu. At the level of the king, Shō Tei (r. 1669–1709) was the first Ryukyuan monarch to receive a systematic Confucian education. As discussed previously, it was in the early eighteenth century that ceremonial forms at the Ryukyuan court began to conform with Chinese practices. Sai On undoubtedly regarded such changes as signs of progress toward establishing the proper Way of Government.

The eighteenth century was also a period when a wide variety of cultural forms—literature, music, drama, fine arts, and technical studies—flourished as never before in Ryukyu. The introduction and widespread use in Ryukyu of so-called turtle shell tombs *(kikkōbaka or kamekōbaka)* from the Fujian area, the formation of formal lineage organizations (J. *monchū* O. *munchū*), and government registration of aristocratic lineages all took place in the interval between the careers of Shō Shōken and Sai On.[40] When Sai On wrote that since coming under Satsuma's rule "customs have been rectified," he may have had such developments in mind. The widespread composition of *ryūka* poems, the creation of Okinawa's distinctive form of musical drama, *kumiodori,* and the writing of official histories are but a few examples of cultural developments of the early eighteenth century.[41] Despite continuing financial problems, eighteenth-century Ryukyu was in much better material condition than during Shō Shōken's time. Furthermore, dealings with Satsuma had become routine. In short, as Sai On reflected on Ryukyu of the 1750s, it must have seemed vastly improved compared with the Ryukyu of previous centuries. Of course, it would have been natural for Sai On to portray the situation this way, since his policies had played a large role in the process.

Like virtually all Confucians, Sai On regarded well-ordered human relations as essential for a truly worthwhile existence, since the chaos of a disordered society blurs the distinction between humans and animals. The Ryukyu of former times, Sai On argued, was characterized by such a chaotic state of affairs:

> . . . Considering former times in our own country, the rulers were benighted and the ministers negligent, which destroyed methods of government and made behavior and customs deteriorate. Nowhere was free of evil and violence. At that time, there was someone called Kazui, of commoner status. He planned to murder the *aji* of Komeji[42] and wanted to take his wife. At that time, however, there was nobody who dared oppose Kazui. So the [*aji's*] wife made a plan herself and wreaked vengeance on Kazui. To this day, she has been called a wise woman. In those days, people could not be secure in their dwellings, they could not work at their occupations, and mothers, children, and siblings scattered and separated from each other. Truly, human misery could be no worse.[43]

A desirable society is one in which sagely rulers and diligent ministers exert a downward transformative effect on the customs and behavior of the common people. According to *One Man's Views* and *Articles of Instruction,* Satsuma's control was a key element in bringing about the conditions under which the proper Way of Government could flourish. All Ryukyuans, therefore, should be grateful.

Even if Sai On's praise of Satsuma reflected his honest assessment of Ryukyu's past and present situations, he did not find Satsuma's control unproblematic. His praise of Satsuma makes no mention of specifically how Satsuma transformed Ryukyuan government and customs, and any Ryukyuan able to read *One Man's Views* would have known of Satsuma's invasion and its continuing political power over Ryukyu. The rest of *One Man's Views* contains no more praise of Satsuma. Its focus is on how Ryukyuans can and must improve their country through their own effort. When toward the end of *One Man's Views* Sai On explains the precise role of Satsuma in sustaining Ryukyu, he makes it clear that it is Ryukyuans who play the greater role in determining the country's fate.

The second major point in the early section of *One Man's Views* is that even Ryukyu, though the poorest of the poor as far as countries go, is capable of becoming a peaceful and prosperous society. According to the text, there are nine grades of countries in the world. The nine grades are formed by subdividing each of the three categories superior, median, and inferior into three parts, high, middle, and low, to produce a range from high-superior to low-inferior.[44] The initial three-way division is a function of each country's resources. Some are naturally well endowed, while others are not. The high, middle, and low distinction within each resource level is a function of how heavily the country in question draws on its resources. A country, for example, with a medium level of resources that draws upon them heavily would be ranked low-median; one in the same resource category that draws upon them lightly would be high-median. At the highest end of the scale, "the superior countries with a high level of available resources, because they spend at a low level, should be regarded as high-superior countries."[45]

There is no explicit statement of Ryukyu's rank in this discussion, but the opening lines of *One Man's Views* about the kingdom's material inability to fulfill its obligations to both China and Japan leave little room for doubt about Ryukyu's status. Ryukyu had meager resources and heavy obligations and was therefore ranked low-inferior. Following this lengthy discussion of countries' rankings, Sai On asserts that "even countries ranked low-inferior, if they adhere to the fundamental principles of the Way of Government, can achieve peace and stability relative to that country's resource level."[46] In other words, even Ryukyu could be peaceful, stable, and prosperous.

In Sai On's usage, of course, "Way of Government" actually meant "my policies and views," and the middle section of *One Man's Views* contains a detailed discussion of them. Here, Sai On explains specifically what Ryukyuan officials should do to produce the stable and prosperous society Ryukyu could become. Several passages have an "I told you so" flavor as Sai On points out how subsequent developments proved he had been correct earlier in his career in advocating this or that policy. At the end of these discussions, the focus returns to Satsuma, which Sai On, like many Ryukyuan elites, called *o-kuni moto* (venerable foundation of the country), and Ryukyu's status.[47]

Sai On first defined a country *(kokudo)*. For a geographical entity to be a country, he argued, it must fulfill two conditions, the first being possession of a sufficient material foundation. More specifically, any place that does not contain all of the five elements (*gogyō,* here clearly meaning elements, not phases)—water, fire, earth, wood, and metal—cannot be called a country. Of the five, water, fire, and earth are ubiquitous, so the key elements are wood and metal. Ryukyu lacks metal. Ordinarily, therefore, it would not have the requisite material foundation to be a country. Being rich in timber resources, however, Ryukyu could export wood to Satsuma and import what metal it needed. By providing metal, Satsuma enabled Ryukyu to meet the first qualification for being a country.[48]

Certainly Ryukyu required metal goods such as agricultural tools and cooking pots in order to maintain a decent standard of living. Satsuma's "metal," however, involved much more than these obvious types of products. It was Satsuma's metal, in the form of silver coins, that funded Ryukyu's tribute trade with China and provided the kingdom with the means to send periodic embassies to the shōgun's court. In other words, Satsuma enabled Ryukyu to meet the obligations to both China and Japan that Sai On, in the opening lines of *One Man's Views,* stated were beyond the kingdom's means. As we have seen, it was Satsuma that obtained permission from the bakufu to mint special coins for Ryukyu's tribute trade and that obtained the tin and other metals that Ryukyu needed to present as tribute to the Qing court. Because Ryukyu's continued existence as a quasi-independent country depended on its maintaining formal ties with China, the small kingdom quite literally depended on Satsuma's metal. Conversely, the kingdom also depended on its timber resources. One of Sai On's most important accomplishments was the creation and implementation of a complex and effective forest management system throughout Ryukyu. He spent months in the field studying Ryukyu's forests first hand and wrote extensively on forest management. In Sai On's Ryukyu, timber was the kingdom's greatest resource.

The second condition required for a place to be a country was that it institute "the five ethical relationships and the four socio-occupational groups," shorthand for describing a well-ordered Confucian society. Satsuma supplied the metal that enabled Ryukyu to meet the first condition, but it was the task of Ryukyuans to construct the well-ordered Confucian society on this material foundation.[49] And it was the Ryukyuans' task that was more difficult and impressive.

To lend authority to this depiction of Ryukyu's status, Sai On distanced himself from it. His views were not merely personal opinions, he claimed, but a reflection of cosmic laws: "The Way of the five elements and the four socio-occupational groups may seem like an arbitrary human creation, but all things considered, it is the way of *ten* [heaven, the cosmos], deriving from yin and yang and the five elements in nature."[50] The Confucian society that Sai On described in *One Man's Views* and elsewhere, and promoted in his policies as a government official, was simply a reflection of the cosmic pattern and therefore unobjectionable. Portraying one's own views as "natural," of course, was and is a classic rhetorical strategy, hardly unique to Sai On.

One Man's Views is not the only place Sai On attempted to define what constitutes a country. In *Essentials of Governance* (C. *Tuzhi yaochuan*, J. *Toji yōden*), for example, he wrote: "Countries may be large or small, wealthy or impoverished. They may be able to rely on neighboring countries or have poor relations with neighboring countries. A country may be stable or peaceful or it may be imperiled by changing conditions. . . ."[51] The discussion in *One Man's Views,* however, is specific to Ryukyu and deals directly with the issue of the kingdom's subordination to Satsuma. Of course, Sai On was not consistent in his portrayal of the nature of the Ryukyu-Satsuma relationship. The early praise of Satsuma for bringing about an orderly society in which the Way of Government flourishes contrasts with the last section of the text, which relegates Satsuma to the essential but comparatively unimpressive role as supplier of Ryukyu's metal. Taken as a whole, however, Sai On's message to Ryukyuans is clear: Ryukyu's destiny is primarily in the hands of Ryukyuans, and this destiny could be great if all strive to create a Confucian society along the lines I have outlined.

Mastering Destiny

Sai On sought stability and prosperity for Ryukyu, but he also realized that "stability" makes sense only relative to an ever-changing cosmos. Although nothing in the physical world remains static for long, Sai On often lamented, the human mind easily slips into complacency. People tend to assume that the present situation will long continue unchanged, so they fail to make adequate long-term plans. "Unexpected expenses include things like sickness, death, loss to theft, bad harvests, and fire damage," Sai On wrote in regulations for the residents of Gushichan district. "Failing to take steps in advance to deal with such matters will certainly cause the household to be hard pressed, and ultimate decline will be unavoidable."[52] Knowing that such changes could occur at any time, people should be prepared to deal with them. For most, however, when their world does change, its forces seem beyond human control. Through study of the cosmic pattern (C. *li,* J. *ri*), long-term planning, and hard work, humans can achieve a large measure of control over their destiny (C. *ming,* J. *mei*), Sai On argued. By anticipating changes in the world and reacting to them accordingly, people in general, and Ryukyuans in particular, can maintain stability in their households and in their countries.

In many of his essays, Sai On discussed the idea of achieving stability through intelligent adaptation to change. At the level of the household, for example, he wrote:

> The general cycle of heavenly transformation makes a complete round every ten years. The prosperity or decline of humans also changes once every ten or twenty years, and all know that [a certain degree of prosperity] is not a fixed constant. Many are those who, though prospering, fail to make long-term plans, with the result that their households are destroyed and they have no legacy to pass down. For this reason, the superior person *(kunshi)* admonishes himself when he prospers, ponders long-term plans, and preserves his wealth. To have regrets after one has already declined is certainly of no value whatsoever.[53]

Expanding on this basic assertion, Sai On likened the human world to waves and human endeavors to boats. "Not even a sage," he said, "can avoid the world of waves." Ordinary, unenlightened people fail to cultivate their virtue when things appear to be going well. They "overturn the ship of their person, the ship of their household, the ship of their country, or the ship of the world."[54] In contrast, a sage keeps his boat afloat in changing, unpredictable seas, achieving stability amidst constant change.

The great enemy of an individual, a household, or a country, argued Sai On, is complacency. In *Conversations with a Rustic Old Man,* a lively philosophical essay in which Sai On speaks through the conversations of a fictional "old man," one passage begins with a description of several brothers from a prominent household. The brothers are wearing the finest clothes while riding a well-fed horse, "meandering around with a look of pride on their faces." The old man declares their actions "dangerous." A passerby remarks that he sees nothing particularly dangerous in the wealthy enjoying what they have. The old man then takes the passerby to task:

You! Shut up and listen! It is exceedingly difficult in this world to build up any of its myriad things and exceedingly easy to tear them down. Surely the founders of a prominent household put forth their fullest effort, gradually building up accomplishments and trust to create a prosperous household. Their effort was exceedingly great; their reputations extremely high. How in the world could their descendants borrow their ancestors' hard-earned wealth, take a liking to luxurious living, and "work" at amusing themselves? *Circumstances change easily with the passing of time, and that which the cosmos has decreed* (tianming) *is never constant.* If their amusing themselves is not dangerous, what is it? Yet you look upon them favorably. If your false views are not dangerous, what are they?[55]

The use of the term *tianming* here is significant. Often translated as "mandate of heaven," in classical Chinese political theory *tianming* explained the rise and fall of dynasties. Here, the household serves as a metaphor for the state, which is hardly surprising considering the typical Confucian view of the state as a family writ large.

The idea of *ming* (fate, destiny) was vexing for many Confucian thinkers, and it was not unusual for a single individual to make contradictory assertions concerning it.[56] Cynthia Brokaw summarizes some of the meanings inherent in the term *ming* as it was used in late imperial Chinese Confucian discourse:

> *Ming* . . . is the term that took on the widest range of meanings. It might refer to both the original, predetermined fate a person received at birth, at heaven's command, as it were, and to the mandate to govern conferred by heaven on rulers who earned it through their own virtuous achievements. Here *ming*, rather than the English word "fate," includes two potentially contradictory notions: a set, unchangeable destiny . . . and the success or failure earned through personal moral effort. . . . Thus, while Wang Chong concluded that "Fate is inescapable *(ming ze buke mian)*," Ge Hong stated, with equal conviction and lexical accuracy, "My fate rests with me, not with heaven *(wo ming zai wo, buzai tian)*."[57]

The fundamental issue connected with *ming*, therefore, was the extent to which humans could determine or change it. Discussions of *ming* often attempted to clarify the boundaries separating the realm of cosmic forces beyond human control and the realm of cosmic forces amenable to human control. Moral and ethical issues related to *ming* often centered around recognizing these boundaries and applying one's moral effort only in the realm where such effort could effect a change.

As in most aspects of his Confucian thought, Sai On relied heavily on the Cheng-Zhu writings as a theoretical starting point. It is useful, therefore, briefly to examine some representative statements on *ming* from Zhu Xi to highlight the distinctive qualities of Sai On's views. Zhu distinguished three varieties or aspects of *ming,* though he also asserted their ultimate unity. In the following passage from *Classified Conversations of Master Zhu (Zhuzi yulei),* we find a distinction between *ming* and *tianming* based on the difference between material force (C. *qi,* J. *ki*) and the cosmic pattern respectively:

> *Question:* The *"ming"* of *"Tianming* means human nature *(xing),"*[58] and the *"ming"* of "Life and death are a matter of *ming"* are not the same. What about this matter?
>
> *Answer:* We speak of the *"ming"* of "Life and death are a matter of *ming,"* as a function of material force. One's endowment of material force can be greater or lesser, thicker or thinner, and is not the same [for all]. We speak of the *"ming"* of *"Tianming* means human nature" as purely the cosmic pattern. But this *ming* of *tian* is, in the end, not removed from material force.[59]

Here, Zhu links the first variety of *ming* with the material force one receives at birth and the second variety of *ming* with the cosmos *(tian),* human nature, and the cosmic pattern. The caveat at the end indirectly links the second type of *ming* with the first via its embodiment in material force.

Zhu's differentiation between types or aspects of *ming* went a step further, specifying two varieties of material force–connected *ming.* One variety was connected with matters such as longevity and social status, the other with one's basic wisdom and moral worthiness. This second variety was a function of the turbidity or clarity of the material force one received at birth. In the following passage, a student ends up summarizing Zhu's view:

> *Question:* A teacher explained that there are two types of *ming.* One type is connected with wealth or poverty, high or low status. The other type is connected with clarity or turbidity, one-sidedness or correctness, wisdom or stupidity, worthiness or unworthiness. The first type belongs to [the realm of] material force and the second to the cosmic pattern. Upon examining this statement, I find that they both seem to belong to [the realm of] material force. It seems that wisdom or stupidity, worthiness or unworthiness, clarity or turbidity, and one-sidedness or correctness also belong to the realm of material force.
>
> *Zhu said:* Yes. It is only the *ming* that is our nature that is the cosmic pattern *(li).*[60]

Of Zhu's three varieties of *ming*, two were associated with material force and the third was associated with human nature–as–cosmic pattern.

Thomas Metzger describes the first of Zhu's two material force varieties of *ming* as follows:

> The first dimension consisted of the external circumstances of life: the individual's economic position, social status, and longevity. . . . These external circumstances were regarded as resulting from the particular portion of *ch'i* (ether of materialization) with which a thing had "been endowed." For instance, the unfortunate fact that so many evil rulers had failed to die young was due to their having "wholly obtained the kind of *ch'i* resulting in long life."[61]

Regarding the second material force variety of *ming:* "[The] given internal capacity or talent can be regarded as our second dimension of *ming*. If the first dimension already suggests a fatalistic outlook, the second does so even more."[62] Zhu's conception of *ming*, therefore, implies that both of the dimensions of *ming* connected with material force must be accepted as unchangeable fate.

Zhu's third dimension of *ming* was connected with the cosmic pattern. Metzger describes it as "purely metaphysical in character. . . . *Ming* in this sense was not something predetermined by one's external situation and the scope of one's moral efforts but something one 'reached' through moral efforts, that is, 'by exhaustively understanding true principle and realizing one's heaven-conferred nature.'"[63] It was this third dimension of *ming*, therefore, that should be the primary focus of moral effort.

Was it impossible to alter either of the dimensions of *ming* connected with material force? Metzger is correct in saying that in Zhu's thought, these two varieties of *ming* strongly suggest fatalism. Certainly one could argue that one's allotment of material force at birth was fated and unalterable. But Zhu and his followers thought that the material force dimension of human nature (C. *qizhi zhi xing*, J. *kishitsu no sei*) could be clarified and transformed through moral effort. If so, then material force–connected *ming* should be changeable in theory. On the other hand, it was apparent to Zhu and most Confucians that only a small number of people would be successful in such an endeavor. Zhu's follower Chen Chun wrote extensively on *ming* in *Beixi ziyi*. One rather lengthy passage contains the sentence, "If one makes an effort at learning, he may be able to transform his physical nature and turn darkness into light."[64] This single sentence certainly suggests that the material force–connected *ming* can be altered, but it is exceptional. The overall tone of the passage emphasizes the inequality of the allotments and thus the rarity and difficulty of such transformations.

Zhu and many other Confucians in late imperial China grappled with the issue of human effort versus uncontrollable cosmic forces, but none came to any clear, definitive conclusions. As Metzger explains:

> But how was [the cosmic pattern–connected] dimension of *ming* reconciled with the idea that the character of one's experience, morally and materially, was determined not by one's striving to "reach" something but by the nature of one's "given" constitution? The answer is that, at least with Chu Hsi, Confucians were easily satisfied with an imprecisely formulated concept of mixed causation. Although external circumstances like longevity were repeatedly regarded as determined by "heaven," Chu Hsi could still quote Chang Tsai's view that even this question of longevity might be affected by human efforts. Chu Hsi even said that one should try to "not accept" tendencies stemming from one's *ch'i-ping* [physical endowment].[65]

In short, Zhu was never able to clarify the boundary between the realm of *ming* as unchangeable fate and *ming* that human effort could alter.

Sai On's writings on *ming* are not entirely free of ambiguity and contradictory statements. In general, however, he appears to have been much more certain than Zhu about the nature of *ming*. For Sai On, the realm of uncontrollable fate was very small and the realm of things changeable through human effort was very large. He did not deny the existence of circumstances beyond human control, but he minimized their extent and importance.

Although Sai On generally assigned great power of change to humans, there were two rhetorical contexts in which he argued that *ming* is unchangeable destiny. First, he used the notion of unchangeable, inescapable *ming* to counter Buddhist notions of trans-generational karmic retribution.[66] In *Essential Views Upon Awakening,* Sai On argued this point first by explaining that people frequently confuse *ming* with the idea of *bao* (J. *mukui*), which in this context we may translate as "requitement" or "retribution." *Bao* explains why people sometimes get what they seem to deserve. An evil person dying early, for example, is often an example of *bao*. It is human society that generates *bao*, Sai On argued, not the cosmos. The way *bao* operates is simply that society generally respects those who do good deeds and behave properly. The more one deviates from what is socially desirable, on the other hand, the more others despise him. The good will of others in society tends to favor those who do good, helping them to advance socially and economically, and the reverse holds true for those who do evil. In neither instance, however, is there any connection with metaphysics or the good or evil deeds of ancestors.[67]

In contrast to *bao*, *ming* is part of the mysterious process of creation, Sai On argued, and not even a sage could escape its dictates. He mentioned several examples from ancient Chinese history and legend to illustrate the point. The great sage Yao, for instance, produced an incompetent son, Dan Zhu. Yao's sagely successor Shun was the son of the "Blind Man," a classic archetype of evil. The sagely King Wen suffered during much of his life, whereas "Bandit Zhi," a notorious brigand, lived an enjoyable life. Such personal circumstances, argued Sai On, could not have been the result of retribution within a single lifetime: "If such things should be called retribution [*bao*], could we say they were the result of crimes Yao and King Wen committed? Could we say they were the result of virtue on the part of the Blind Man and Bandit Zhi?"[68] In short, cases in which one encounters beneficial or adverse circumstances that he does not deserve are examples of *ming*, not *bao*.

Perhaps, however, Yao's having a son like Dan Zhu was the result of evil on the part of one of Yao's ancestors, not Yao himself. Not so, argued Sai On, again using historical examples: "If we call them cases of retribution from past generations, then Guan Shu[69] and the Duke of Zhou were both King Wen's children and grandsons of the great King Wang Li. How, then, could they be so different?"[70] Throughout the course of this argument in *Essential Views Upon Awakening*, Sai On attempts to distinguish *ming* from *bao* and to deny any metaphysical basis for the latter. *Bao* is entirely a social phenomenon, so cross-generational "*bao*" is impossible.[71] This line of argument required that Sai On stress the unchanging, inevitable, random character of *ming*.

The other context in which Sai On stressed these same characteristics of *ming* was in cautioning against fast and easy shortcuts in the process of self-cultivation. Although anyone could transform himself, doing so required a long and difficult process of moral effort aimed at "conquering material force." Some, however, neglected moral effort in favor of apparently easier ways of altering their personal circumstances. According to *Essential Views Upon Awakening*:

> The presence or absence of good or bad fortune, wealth or poverty is *ming*. Regardless of high or low status in this world, there is but one thing to do: vigorously conquer material force, control the mind, struggle and fight to eliminate any trace of selfish thoughts, eliminate disharmony, and entrust the cosmos *(tian)* with matters of good fortune or bad, wealth or poverty, and calmly await death.[72]

Arguing that there are no easy ways to get ahead in life required that Sai On present *ming* as unchanging, inevitable, and random. This passage suggests that it is *tian,* not human effort, that determines such things as one's social standing or degree of wealth. In other contexts, however, Sai On argued precisely the opposite point, declaring for example that "the power of humans is greater than that of the cosmos [*tian*]" and declaring that rise and fall, life and death are not dependent on destiny but on humans.[73]

The next section of the passage from *Essential Views Upon Awakening* cited above suggests a partial explanation for such contradictory statements: ". . . How is it that common people under the deception of material force seek madly after good fortune and wealth and seek desperately to escape poor fortune and poverty? They make countless plans and secret contrivances, trying to change what they cannot. This is not one's proper *ming.*"[74] The expression "proper *ming*" comes from Mencius[75] and means that as a result of moral effort, whatever fate one ends up with is the best he could have achieved. The person who has expended such effort, therefore, can die content, regardless of social or economic circumstances.

In fact, Sai On did argue that people could improve the socioeconomic status of their households. This process, however, could only be accomplished through the diligent moral effort of the household's members and might require more than a generation to come to fruition. The point of the passage in *Essential Views Upon Awakening,* therefore, is that the only effective way successfully to change one's material circumstances in the long run is moral effort. "Countless plans and secret contrivances" will be ineffective. Furthermore, moral effort is directed at conquering material force and eliminating selfish thoughts, not improving material circumstances per se. A lifetime of moral effort, therefore, might not eliminate the poverty of an individual or a household, but it will set the stage for further improvement in the next generation. In the short term, an individual's *ming* with respect to wealth and social status is unchangeable. In the long term, however, each individual's moral effort will contribute to a gradual improvement in the wealth and status of one's household, local community, and country.

Sai On generally used the term *ming* by itself when discussing that which human effort cannot change. He commonly spoke of something "appearing to be *ming,*" but actually being something humans can control or change. To describe a natural tendency or endowment that moral effort can influence, Sai On either used *ming* in a compound with a second term or used the term *tian.* The most common term was *tianming,* which in this case should not be translated "mandate of heaven." Almost as often, he used only the term *tian,* saying that something derived from *tian* or was the result of *tian.* Whether *tian* or *tianming,* the matter under discussion would typically be amenable to human control. As we have seen, Zhu Xi likewise distinguished between *tianming* and *ming.* For Zhu, the former was cosmic pattern–derived *ming,* the dimension of *ming* over which humans could exercise the greatest degree of control. Although neither man was entirely consistent in distinguishing between *tianming* and *ming,* Sai On's usage was in general accord with that of Zhu.

This association of *tian* with cosmic forces that humans can control, or at least influence, was common among Confucians. On the one hand, humans who have achieved a high degree of moral excellence possess awesome power, as the *Mean (Zhongyong)* explains:

> Only those who are absolutely sincere can fully develop their nature. If they can fully develop their nature, they can then fully develop the nature of others. If they can fully develop the nature of others, they can then fully develop the nature of things. If they can fully develop the nature of things, they can assist in the transforming and nourishing process of Heaven and Earth. If they can assist in the transforming and nourishing process of Heaven and Earth, they can thus form a trinity with Heaven and Earth.[76]

The term "sincere" *(cheng)* as used in the *Mean* encompasses a wide range of meanings and nuances.[77] Here, its basic meaning is full integration of one's self with the cosmos. Sai On's exhortation in *Essential Views Upon Awakening* to "struggle and fight to eliminate any trace of selfish thoughts," if successful, would result in such a state.

It is because the cosmic pattern inheres in the nature of all humans that the fully integrated person can act as a co-creator with *tian* to transform the world. Such a person is able, at least in part, to create his own destiny. Because of his integration with others, this destiny also affects the destiny of the larger human community in which he is enmeshed. Sai On did not discuss these points in even the detail presented here—they were so deeply rooted in the Confucian tradition as to need no explicit explanation. When Sai On spoke of the "sages'" teachings that human power is greater than that of the cosmos, it was almost certainly to this part of the Confucian tradition that he was referring.

For Sai On and most other Confucians, *tian* was immanent in humans. As Tu Wei-ming explains, "The relationship between Heaven and man is not an antinomic bi-unity but an indivisible single oneness."[78] For this reason, Sai On frequently criticized the tendency to speak of *tian* as a transcendent entity and then to assign causal power to its actions. Early in his career, he edited and revised his father's version of *Genealogy of Chūzan (Zhongshan shipu).* The discussion of Satto's son, King Bunei, overthrown by Shō Hashi, nicely illustrates Sai On's view of *tian:*

Bunei inherited the throne. He was wild with wine and women, luxury and extravagance. . . . Ah! The evil of vulgar customs is something we should fear! . . . Though it could be said that [Bunei's demise] was something *tian* carried out, in fact it was his own doing. Jie and Zhou, evil and oppressive, perished though they were descendants of sage kings. The founders of the Han and Tang dynasties rose though they were of commoner origin. It all depends on one's self. How could such things be called the inevitability of *tian*?[79]

Humans could act in accord with their heavenly nature and accomplish great things, or they could ignore it and do great evil. The choice and responsibility lies with each individual. Sai On decried extra-human, fatalistic explanations that had the effect of taking responsibility for Ryukyu's destiny out of Ryukyuans' own hands.

It is here that we see the most important difference between Sai On and Shō Shōken. Shō Shōken conceived of *tian* not in the Confucian terms discussed above, but in the tradition of Japanese *tentō* thought. In a section of commentary he appended to *Genealogy of Chūzan*, Sai On assessed Gihon's abdication, arriving at the opposite conclusion of Shō Shōken's *Mirror of Chūzan*:

Gihon relinquished the great enterprise [i.e., rulership] to a stranger because of famine and plague. How weak and lacking was his constitution in the extreme! Yao had his floods; Tang had his drought, which were both disasters. Not even a sage can escape such disasters, much less anyone else. At such times, if [a ruler] makes every effort to cultivate moral authority and to work at governing according to [correct moral] principle, the disaster can be overcome and the people's minds can be galvanized. Why on earth did a morning's grief cause him to give up the great enterprise of a hundred generations?[80]

This passage is clearly a critique of Shō Shōken and is a particularly good example of Sai On's view of *ming*, even though he did not specifically use the term. The ancient sages like Yao or King Tang (founder of the Shang dynasty) experienced the inevitable changes in nature that result in floods, droughts, and other difficulties. Such phenomena (in other contexts Sai On might have called them *ming*) are beyond even the control of sagely humans, much less anyone else. A drought, for example, cannot be prevented, but its impact would be much less severe for peasants with an adequate store of food and seed grain in reserve. In this sense, human effort can even affect the *ming* of a drought. To resign one's self to *tian* passively was, for Sai On, a sign of moral deficiency.

While he was critical of individuals who sought narrowly to increase their personal wealth and status, stating that such things were *ming* and thus impossible to change, at levels of social organization greater than the individual, the message was entirely different: that which appears to be *ming* is not really *ming* and can be changed if all the members of a family, household, lineage, or country set their resolve and work as hard as possible at their proper occupations.

Sai On repeated this message almost ad nauseam in his essays on household regulation. A typical simple example from *Expeditious Household Regulation* reads:

> All households either have fields but no stipend, have a stipend but no fields, have neither stipend nor fields, or have both a stipend and fields. All households differ, but any that make an effort will gain wealth. Thus when [its members] work hard and are not lazy, a household will gradually prosper. When they do not work hard and are lazy, the household will certainly decline. This is inevitable principle *(ri)*.[81]

A related point that Sai On made repeatedly was the need for each household to set aside a certain percentage of its wealth as "righteous savings" to be used only in the most dire emergency:

> A household is not a household of a single individual, but a household of all its members. If wealth is spent recklessly and not saved and one day something unexpected arises, the household will certainly be destroyed. This would destroy great righteousness, from shaming the ancestors above to harming one's descendants below. Therefore, with regard to household wealth, taking the yearly income, dividing it into ten parts, and setting three aside to provide for the unexpected is righteous savings. This righteous savings is the life *(inochi)* of the members of a household.[82]

The Japanese term *inochi* clearly means "life" in this case, but it is the same character as the Chinese *ming*. By planning ahead for unexpected circumstances—*ming*—a household could avoid some or all of the adverse consequences of those circumstances, thereby controlling its own destiny.

In his philosophical essays, Sai On also discussed household fortunes. Although some of the terminology was more explicitly Confucian, the message was identical. The following is the conclusion of a discussion between two commoners and the old man in *Conversations with a Rustic Old Man:* "Although wealth and poverty may seem to derive from *ming,* they are actually the result of diligence or laziness respectively. . . . Ah! Effort is the root of all good fortune; laziness is the root of all bad fortune. You should think about this matter well!"[83] Effort to increase the wealth of a larger group is morally correct and can modify *ming;* the quest to increase one's personal wealth without the arduous process of self-cultivation is morally incorrect and cannot modify *ming.*

"What about extreme cases of poverty in which it is impossible to set aside even one-tenth of the wealth?" an anonymous questioner asks in *Expeditious Household Regulation.* Sai On's answer is an impassioned appeal to reject fatalism:

> Even though such poverty may be regarded as extreme, if one-tenth of the wealth is not set aside, how could [household members] just give up and wait to die? When things reach such a point, if you redouble your efforts and work hard there will surely be a day's worth of wealth. This day's wealth should be set up, divided, and a small portion used as savings. This is righteous savings. From the Son of Heaven down to the common people, I have yet to hear of a case of a household managing to preserve itself after having thrown away its righteous savings.[84]

No matter how poor a household might be, it has some ability to control its destiny. One is reminded of Sai On's depiction of Ryukyu in *One Man's Views* as being the lowest, poorest category of country and his confidence that it could nevertheless become stable and prosperous.

Like nearly all Confucians, following the progression in the *Great Learning,* Sai On regarded the state as a natural extension of the family. A household can achieve stability amidst the inevitable fluctuations in circumstances by planning ahead and working hard. The same formula applies to the state. "Those who govern a country well," wrote Sai On, "must ascertain prosperity and decline before they become manifest. They must anticipate stability and danger before it arrives. This I call 'long-term planning' or 'planning without concrete form.'"[85] Those who have eliminated selfish thoughts and "conquered material force" would have the clarity of insight necessary to detect subtle tendencies that portend changing circumstances before these circumstances become apparent to ordinary people. As leaders of government, they would have the opportunity to take the necessary steps to prepare for those changes. In this way society could achieve stability in the midst of change and humans could at least partially control their own destiny.

"Generally, each affair and each thing necessarily has success or failure. This 'success or failure' pertains to people, not to *tian,*"[86] wrote Sai On. This basic assertion was the core of his view of circumstances, destiny, and human efficacy. Humans could not completely control the forces of the cosmos, but they bore ultimate responsibility for success or failure in any endeavor. Even the length of one's life span was largely one's own responsibility:

When someone who has carefully followed the way of nurturing himself and has thus lived a long life becomes sick and dies . . . it is *ming*. "It must be *ming*. Why else should such a man be stricken with such a disease?"[87] In the past, it was common practice for people carefully to follow the way of self-nurturing. Therefore, those who received a long life were numerous. In the present, popular customs are contrary to the way of self-nurturing. Therefore, those who receive a long life are extremely few. This being so, failure to receive a long life is something each person himself causes. How could it be something *tian* brings about?[88]

Conclusions

Sai On's Confucianism was closely connected with the question of Ryukyuan identity. Ryukyu's vague political status was the result, broadly speaking, of a tension between Japan and China. Shō Shōken and Tei Junsoku leaned to one side or the other of this tension. Sai On, by contrast, used the tension to produce a vision of Ryukyu different from those of his predecessors. Based on Confucian metaphysics, this vision placed Ryukyu on a moral par with its larger neighbors, with material stability and prosperity as the outward manifestations of an inward moral excellence. Sai On used the universal pretensions in the Confucian tradition to speak of Ryukyuan identity in a language that elided the original basis of Satsuma's domination of Ryukyu: military force.

One place to view this process of replacing the language of military force with that of Confucian virtue is the *Kyūyō*, an official history of Ryukyu edited by Sai On's Kumemura allies. Here, for example, Ryukyu's first official contact with China in the fourteenth century is characterized as "the basis for revamping cultural forms"[89] in Ryukyu. Military affairs do come up in the text, but military campaigns are typically portrayed as righteous means to moral ends, such as when Okinawa reconquered Ōshima in 1571, and "the king ordered that a different ruler be established [in Ōshima] and the peasants be put at ease."[90] Okinawa, in other words, conquered Ōshima to oust an oppressive ruler. The Satsuma invasion is given relatively little coverage, and, like *Mirror of Chūzan*, blames Tei Dō. The explanation of the king's return to Ryukyu from Satsuma reads:

> Already two years had passed with the king staying in Satsuma. The king said, "I serve the Chinese court, and it is a matter of righteousness that [my stay here] come to an end." [Satsuma's] daimyō was deeply impressed by such loyalty and righteousness and in the end had the king return. After that, our country returned to peace and tranquility.[91]

This passage in particular shows the rhetorical strategy of replacing relationships of coercion with those of Confucian moral authority—ground on which Ryukyu could compete with its larger neighbors. *Kyūyō* entries from the late eighteenth century on frequently describe acts of filial piety, loyalty, or other forms of righteousness by ordinary Ryukyuans.

Sai On's vision of an ideal Ryukyu was forged in the tension between Japan and China that enabled Ryukyu to continue its precarious existence as a quasi-independent country. This vision, however was not only focused on Ryukyu vis-à-vis its larger neighbors. It was equally focused on the various groups within Ryukyu. Naturally, in seeking to create an ideal Confucian society, Sai On and his allies had to effect major changes within Ryukyu itself. It is this aspect of Sai On's vision of Ryukyu, and the opposition it engendered, that we examine in the next chapter.

CHAPTER 4

Re-Creating Ryukyu
Sai On and His Critics

Sai On used Confucian ideology to forge a theoretical basis for Ryukyuan agency. Like many Japanese Confucians of the Tokugawa period, he worked to naturalize Confucian thought, adapting it to Ryukyu's particular circumstances. Unlike his Japanese counterparts, however, whose Confucianism played itself out mainly in the realm of discourse, Sai On's Confucianism was directly tied to the practice of politics and government administration. His vision of Ryukyu demanded that he try to re-create the island kingdom as an ideal Confucian society. This chapter examines the major elements of this re-creation and the opposition it engendered.

The major policies and programs Sai On promoted fall into three broad areas: (1) revision of ritual and ceremonial; (2) material prosperity; and (3) rectification of social life. It is important to note at the outset that in all of these areas Sai On's policies tended to add to and accelerate political trends already under way in Ryukyu. Our concern here is not a comprehensive analysis of seventeenth- and eighteenth-century Ryukyuan politics, which would require a separate book. It is sufficient simply to identify the larger political movements during or slightly preceding Sai On's tenure in office—trends that he had a direct hand in shaping. Understanding the main direction of politics in eighteenth-century Ryukyu is a prerequisite for understanding the resistance to and critique of those politics by other Ryukyuans.

Major Developments in Ryukyuan Politics

Maehira has argued that Ryukyu's early-modern period was characterized by a movement away from ceremonial *(girei)* toward realistic administration *(genjitsu seiji)*.[1] Such a view suggests that there was something unrealistic about rites and ceremony. On the contrary, however, the manipulation of symbols was a key element in creating and maintaining political authority, then and now. In early-modern Ryukyu, ceremonial was of the utmost importance for government, and Sai On and other officials devoted a great deal of energy to reconstructing and standardizing ceremonial forms.

In Old-Ryukyu the three main types of participants in important rites of state were Buddhist monks, the high priestess and other leading female religious officials, and the king, who often played a passive role. In the early-modern period, the king was the major actor in rites of state, while the high priestess, other female religious officials, and Buddhist monks performed secondary, supporting roles. In Old-Ryukyu, the high priestess communicated directly with "Heaven" (O. *teni,* roughly equivalent to O. *teda* or *tiida,* the sun) and Heaven "spoke" through her. In early-modern Ryukyu, the king became the central link between Ryukyuan society and Heaven, with Heaven taking on additional Chinese characteristics.[2]

Changes in the rites the king performed on the first day of the new year are indicative of the overall transformation in official ceremonial. In Old-Ryukyu, the king would perform these rites facing whichever direction the royal diviners deemed most auspicious for that year. As Tomiyama points out, this divination was based on Japanese *onmyōdō* (also *inyōdō,* "way of yin and yang") techniques. The royal government employed similar Japanese-style divination to select auspicious days for other purposes. Into the seventeenth century, Shingon monks from Japan exerted a strong influence on royal government ceremonial. During the eighteenth century, however, Ryukyuan officials made a conscious effort to replace Japanese-derived practices with Chinese practices. In 1719, for example, the practice of selecting an auspicious direction came to an end, and a rite called *Ne-no-hō* (roughly, "direction of the son [of heaven]") replaced the older new year's rites.[3] "The new year's rites . . . were revised so that they were conducted facing due north from the royal palace. In this way, the ceremony involved facing the Forbidden City and paying respects to the [Chinese] emperor," explained the *Kyūyō.*[4]

The turn away from Japan and toward China as a model for state ceremonial did not mean that the new Ryukyuan rites were a blind imitation of Chinese counterparts. In one phase of the new year's rites, the head of Kumemura would intone a felicitous supplication such as the following:

> Fifty-second year of Kangxi [1713], Mizunotomi, New Year's Day. The Chūzan King of Ryukyu, descendant of the royal line, your minister Shō Kei dares to report as follows to the Emperor of Heaven, God of Earth, and spirits of heaven and earth: We now encounter the three *yang* [lines of the *Yijing*], open up below [i.e., it is now the exact point of the new year], and the renewal of the myriad things. I reverently lead the ministers in this supplication that the winds be moderated, the rains fall on schedule, the country be at peace, the people be at ease, and that we forever comply with the Way of Heaven. . . .[5]

This Ryukyuan text is nearly identical with comparable Chinese supplications. The Chinese emperor offered prayers to the various deities of heaven and earth just as did the Ryukyuan king. There was, however, a significant difference. The emperor also offered prayers to the Lord-on-High *(shangdi)*, but the Ryukyuan king did not. This difference, of course, was a matter of propriety in a kingdom that formally recognized China as a cultural superior.[6]

The actual performance of the *Ne-no-hō* rite in Ryukyu also differed in a number of ways from the Chinese model. The Chinese utilized more elaborate props. Ryukyuans, for example, did not set up the special altar to *tian* that was central to the Chinese rite, and the temporary altar they did set up was not of Chinese design. Instead, it was similar to altars used for worship at sacred sites within Ryukyu.[7] There was an even more fundamental difference the nature of the Ryukyuan rite and its Chinese counterpart. Although the king did not worship the Lord-on-High, his worship of heaven and earth was still a ritual violation of the Chinese emperor's prerogative as the link between heaven, earth, and humans. Yi-dynasty Korean scholar-officials, for example, often objected to royal rites venerating heaven, which led to a substantial curtailment of such rites in Korea.[8] Some Ryukyuan Confucians similarly objected from time to time during the eighteenth and nineteenth centuries on the grounds that, in China, all but the emperor were forbidden to venerate heaven and earth. These objections, however, had little or no effect on Ryukyuan state ceremonial, and the king continued to venerate heaven and earth.[9]

Tomiyama argues that the king's worship of heaven and earth reflected a continuation of deeply rooted religious traditions from Old-Ryukyu. *Tian* in Old-Ryukyu was roughly synonymous with *teda,* the sun. The sun was the source of spiritual power, *seji,* which the high priestess transmitted to the king. The worship of *tian* by the king, therefore, was a continuation of this long Ryukyuan tradition. The new Ryukyuan rites, however, excluded women from participating in key roles, a significant departure from past practices. By facing Beijing and paying respects to the Chinese emperor, the Ryukyuans helped maintain an overall sense of propriety, partially offsetting the potential offense to propriety of their king's veneration of heaven and earth.[10]

There was another important change in ceremonial that also took place in 1719. Prior to that year, the head of Kumemura conducted Confucian temple rites on the first day of the new year, at the times of the traditional spring and autumn Confucian rites, and on other important occasions. These rites were conducted by and for the residents of Kumemura and had no broader significance. Starting in 1719, however, the king sent the Council of Three to preside over Kumemura's new year Confucian temple rites. This action brought the Confucian temple rites within the pale of official state ceremonial.[11]

This "nationalization" of the Confucian temple rites is an indication of the growing formal and informal influence of Confucianism within the royal government. Along with the pronounced sinification of state ceremonial, it also points to the growing power of Kumemura in Ryukyuan politics. In 1719, Shō Kei received investiture from the Chinese emperor. By that time, Sai On had been his tutor for nearly eight years and was rising fast in the royal government, particularly after his handling of the Valuation Incident. The exact role Sai On played in the above-mentioned changes is unclear, but it was probably substantial. In any case, the changes that did take place were precisely in line with his views.

Along with the sinification of state ceremonial, there was a gradual change in the status and image of the king. We have seen that Shō Shōken worked to distance the king from the female religious officials and elevate his status to a level clearly beyond theirs. Sai On and his supporters took Shō Shōken's measures several steps further by making the king into the image of a Confucian sage. After Shō Tei, Ryukyuan kings appeared in official histories without a deity name *(kamina)*. As Tasato points out, this change symbolizes a major shift in the basis of royal authority. In Old-Ryukyu, the king was a god; by the eighteenth century, he had been transformed into a Confucian sage.[12]

Sai On was much concerned with Ryukyu's material wealth and devoted a great deal of energy to scientific and technical matters. For him, the extension of knowledge through the investigation of things included investigating such "specific principles" *(ze)* as techniques for cultivating crops, forest management, and hydraulic engineering. Sai On took primary responsibility for developing Ryukyu's forestry and agricultural policies, spending months in the field in rugged areas of Okinawa. He personally led and supervised a team of workers in a major hydraulic engineering project. He also wrote or co-authored several volumes on agriculture and forestry. Here we examine Sai On's forest management policies as an example of his attempts to improve Ryukyu's material standard of living through applied technology.

Sai On was interested in a wide variety of agricultural matters, but he made his greatest contribution to the area of forestry. Considering the importance of timber resources in Sai On's conception of Ryukyu as a country, it should be no surprise that he devoted much of his time and energy to forest management. The products of forests were essential as the basis for Ryukyu's material well-being, as Sai On explained in *Secrets of Forestry* (C. *Sanlin zhenbi*, J. *Sanrin shinpi*): "The use of wood products is of great importance in people's lives, and the quality of human life has improved thanks to wood products.

Were we not able to rely on the power of wood products, we would become incapable of tilling fields, building houses, weaving clothes, making pottery, forging iron, and crossing the ocean."[13] Despite the importance of timber, Ryukyu had no system of forest management prior to Sai On's time, and most forests were in a state of deterioration.

By the time Sai On became a member of the Council of Three, timber resources were being depleted at an alarming rate, according to a number of sources. A 1735 *Kyūyō* entry, for example, states:

> There are not many in this country who have a good knowledge of the principles of forestry. So within the Nakagami region, the forests of Tanibaru are already used up, and those in the five districts of Chatan, Yomitanzan, Goeku, Mizato, and Gushikawa are nearly used up. In the Sanboku region, forests in the districts of Onna, Kin, Motobu, and Nakijin are steadily deteriorating, and good timber will soon be gone. Only in the four districts of Haneji, Ōgimi, Kushi, and Kunigami is there any good timber. After a few more years pass, the timber needed for the country's use will be insufficient. Sai On was ordered to lead officials on a tour of inspection of the various districts' forest lands and teach forestry methods. It was only after this time that the people of our country even knew that forestry principles existed.[14]

Similar conclusions about the state of forests throughout Ryukyu may be found elsewhere. For example, a 1738 report issued by the Forestry Commissioners' Office *(Yamabugyōsho), Somayama ni tsuite sōbakari jōjō* (General conclusions about forest lands) stated that a substantial increase in population since "former times" has resulted in the need for more houses, tools, boats, and so forth. The need to build ships to sail to China and for construction and repairs to the royal palace increased the demand for large trees. The report then stated that there had never been systematic planning and forest management; thus the problem had become so acute that the royal government finally appointed forestry commissioners.[15]

The report continued, emphasizing the need for careful long-range planning of forest lands since trees take much longer to mature than other agricultural products. It also pointed out the dire economic consequences of running short of timber: Ryukyu would then have to purchase lumber from Satsuma at high prices, resulting in a much higher tax burden. The second half of the report outlined a general policy for each region and island.[16]

Sai On pursued short- and long-term solutions to Ryukyu's forestry problems. He first established the Forestry Commissioners' Office and appointed three commissioners, each charged with overseeing a particular area of Okinawa.[17] Then, in 1736, Sai On personally led the three commissioners and several other high officials on a four-month study tour of each district in northern and central Okinawa. Even the *sessei* and other Council of Three members accompanied Sai On while his group was in the districts of Onna, Nago, and Haneji. Upon Sai On's return to the capital, the king left Shuri to meet him and his party in Urasoe. There, the king expressed his gratitude by personally preparing food and tea.[18]

The *Sai-uji kafu* describes some of the findings of the inspection team. For example, "In the five villages of Goga, Momobaru, Gabe, Matsuda, and Furikena in the timberlands of Haneji . . . there are ignorant people who clear out farmland by setting areas on fire." Fearing the principles of forestry would be forgotten, the *Kafu* also explains, Sai On wrote several handbooks on forestry and had the three commissioners disseminate their contents widely.[19]

Sai On wrote, co-authored, or participated in the writing of six handbooks on forestry.[20] These works provide valuable information on both forestry techniques and the organization of the forest management system. Briefly, supervision took place at three administrative levels: (1) the central government via the Forestry Commissioners' Office; (2) each district government office via an official with the title *sō-yama'atai;* and (3) each village via a functionary with the title *yama'atai.*[21] The burden of labor for forest upkeep, reforestation, and the creation of new forests fell on the districts, islands, and villages. The central government supplied the bulk of the capital and undertook most other financial burdens. Labor on forests was part of the peasants' corvée service. Just as the costs of forest management were divided among several levels, so too were any profits from the sale of timber and other proceeds from government forest land *(somayama).* With permission, local residents were able to use portions of government forest land for fuel and home construction.[22]

There was a system of fines for those caught cutting certain types of particularly valuable trees. According to *Yamabugyō kimochō,* the amount was 300 *kanmon* copper cash, of which half went to the person reporting the offense and half to the coffers of reforestation programs.[23] This forestry system involved close, informed supervision of forest lands at all administrative levels. Because local peasants shared in the profit from government forest lands and received cash rewards for reporting rule violators, they had a substantial incentive to cooperate with the government's policies. The use of material incentives here is one example of a general tendency in Sai On's thought and politics. Unlike some Confucian moralists, he recognized the importance and usefulness of profit (C. *li,* J. *ri*) as a means to motivate ordinary people to work hard in socially beneficial ways.

Although Sai On must have studied the large literature on forestry and agriculture then available in both China and Japan, we do not know which specific works he actually read. His approach to forest management was generally in accord with Miyazaki Yasusada (Antei)'s *Nōgyō zensho,* the most important book on agriculture in Japan at the time, but there were some significant departures. *Nōgyō zensho,* for example, placed a high priority on soil quality, as Conrad Totman points out: "Optimal forest planting is related to properties of the soil: if soil quality is not maintained, trees will not flourish no matter how hard one works."[24] For Sai On, however, soil quality was of little importance for silviculture: "For farming, soil quality *(tochi no sei)* is most important, but for forestry, soil quality is of no major consequence. The quality of trees depends on the configuration of the surrounding mountains. Therefore, for woodland cultivation, it is most important carefully to scrutinize the mountain topography."[25] Wind, not soil quality, was the major consideration in Ryukyu owing to the high frequency of severe storms: "Speaking of correct methods for constructing forests, [planting trees] to prevent wind from coming through places like the paths of mountain rivers, gaps between mountains, the boundaries of fields, and on mountain tops is most important."[26]

Wind created severe problems for Ryukyu's agriculture, causing trees to become bent and gnarled, thus reducing their value for lumber. Worse, strong winds blew precious topsoil from dry fields and sand into them. If accompanied by rain, strong winds might also wash topsoil away. During the worst storms, the wind blew salt water into low-lying fields near the ocean. Strong winds were also undesirable from the standpoint of geomancy.[27] It was in trying to solve these wind-related problems that Sai On developed forestry techniques distinctive to Ryukyu.[28]

The basic approach was to use suitable species of trees to form natural walls and windbreaks across virtually all of Okinawa and the other islands. Along roads, particularly high mountain roads, Sai On had Ryukyu pines *(Pinus luchuensis mayr)* planted at regular intervals. Some Okinawans still refer to these pines as "Sai On pines." Adan *(Pandanus odoratissimus)* was planted in the space between each pine. A thick, sturdy shrub, the adan and pines together formed natural walls that were both thick and tall. The same arrangement of trees also served to separate the boundaries of different fields, further protecting crops and soil from the ravages of wind, saltwater, and sand. *Nōmuchō,* Sai On's general handbook on agriculture, specifies that Ryukyuan farmers plant adan over wide areas as a defense against wind and waves. Other places for adan planting included both sides of any rivers or streams flowing through plains and alongside ditches.[29] Sai On's adan-based windbreaks were so effective that some are still in use today.[30]

The most distinctive contribution of Sai On and his commissioners to forestry management was an effective method for clearing out large quantities of old or gnarled trees. Owing to the need to protect against wind and erosion, eliminating gnarled trees was not always as simple as just cutting them down. If an area of trees were harvested and seedlings planted to replace the old growth, wind would rush through the cleared area. Even if the seedlings survived, they would grow up bent. Furthermore, the wind might also damage nearby agricultural fields. The solution to this problem was the *gyorinkei zōrinpō*, or "fish-scale pattern forest construction method," a technique unique to Ryukyu.

Under this method, old or bent trees would be harvested in numerous small, semicircular blocks within a given area of forest. A thin ring of old growth was left in place around each harvested block. The result was an interconnected network of semicircular old growth shells. This honeycomb-like network of old growth rings retained much of its ability to protect young trees and nearby fields from wind damage. When viewed from afar, the resulting pattern resembled the scales of a fish, with the boarder of each scale being the rings of old growth (see figure). Using this method, the majority of the total surface area could be replanted with only slight reduction of the ability of the stand of trees to block the wind. The old-growth shells would enable newly planted seedlings to grow straight. In describing how to use this technique, Sai On wrote:

> If trees that are in decline are cleared out using the fish-scale pattern, then the [new trees] will incorporate the material force of the mountain[31] [into themselves] and be able to flourish. Indeed, because the seeds will naturally be dispersed [throughout the cleared areas] and germinate, to the extent that bent trees are harvested [early], the remaining trees will flourish particularly well.[32]

This method of forest production and harvesting often required that no seedlings be planted because of the wind-assisted dispersion of seeds into the cleared areas within the network.

All indications are that Sai On's forest policies were successful in achieving their primary goal. The severe timber shortage he and others warned of never materialized. Iinuma Jirō points out that during their two sojourns in Ryukyu, members of Commodore Perry's crew were surprised at the overall productivity of Ryukyuan agriculture and the degree to which available land was put to effective use.[33] Writing in the 1950s, Kerr noted: "Here and there gnarled old trees arch the roads and line the mountains on 20th century Okinawa thanks to Sai

On's policies. A grove planted at Sai On's direction on Terama in distant Miyako still serves as a model for new windbreaks established to protect precious top-soil."[34] It was only after Ryukyu became part of Japan in the Meiji period that the forest management system Sai On established began to break down.

Sai On's forestry management system was part of a broader attempt by the central government to regulate the social, moral, and economic life of Ryukyu's peasants. A prerequisite for more effective regulation of the countryside was a

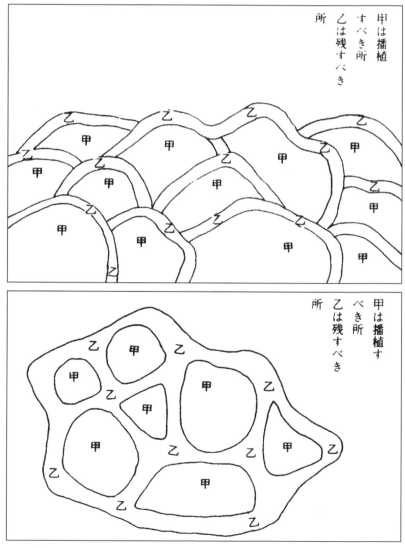

Top: fish-scale pattern of forest construction; bottom: an alternative method. Trees in the inner spaces should be harvested. From *OKS*, vol. 6, p. 198.

detailed knowledge of the actual conditions in each district. Satsuma surveyed all of Ryukyu immediately after its invasion, but by the 1730s, changed conditions had rendered that information obsolete. Shortly after Sai On's four-month survey of forest lands, he launched a more ambitious project: the Genbun Survey *(Genbun kenchi)* of 1737–1750. This survey established the basic economic framework for early-modern Ryukyu, and so important was it that Tasato has called its planning and execution Sai On's greatest achievement.[35] According to agricultural historian Nakama Yūei, the greatest change in peasant land use patterns in Ryukyu took place as a result of the survey.[36]

Historians of Ryukyu are in general agreement regarding the goals of the Genbun Survey. Nakama points out three major objectives. First was closing the gap between officially listed levels of production based on Satsuma's original survey and actual production, which had substantially increased in most areas. Second was to measure and assess the impact of geographical changes in villages and agricultural fields. The final goal was to tighten and systematize central government control over the districts.[37]

Tasato lists five objectives, the first being an attempt to eliminate the *jiwarisei,* the practice of rural villages periodically redistributing land among their members. Second was to increase production by establishing new villages and moving old ones, a process informed in part by Sai On's understanding of geomancy. A further goal was to create a program of forest self-sufficiency by implementing Sai On's forest management principles in each locality. A fourth objective was implementation of the so-called *yaadui* (J. *yadori*) program for putting unemployed *yukachu* to work as farmers.[38] Finally Sai On hoped substantially to increase government revenues as a result of tax assessments based on more accurate production figures.[39]

The *Kyūyō* describes the Genbun Survey as follows:

> Although there is a method for properly allocating fields in our country, boundaries have changed over the passage of many years. Council of Three member Sai On was ordered to teach this system for the first time, and Council of Three member Shō (Shikina Ueekata Chōei) was ordered to lead officials throughout the country on a tour of inspection. They went to the villages of the various districts correcting boundaries and allocating fields. They have already determined which lands are forest lands and which are fields, and the methods governing peasant production have largely been determined.[40]

One additional reason for the survey is suggested by the *Sai-uji kafu,* which states that agricultural officials did not understand the correct techniques for allocating fields. Their alleged lack of skill resulted in constant litigation over field boundaries, "causing the peasants unbearable grief."[41]

The survey, which required thirteen years to complete, was an attempt to standardize agricultural practices in the countryside. The ultimate purpose was to increase peasant production while simultaneously increasing the central government's ability to extract more of that production in the form of taxes. The survey projected the political authority of the royal government directly down to the level of each individual peasant household.[42] Six high-ranking officials actually conducted the survey. In the field, they split into several teams, each of which included a number of secretaries and other support staff. Sai On selected the six and personally trained them in techniques of hydraulic engineering, forest management, and surveying.[43] He directed the survey in person for the first few years until the teams gained sufficient experience. They used staves and compasses to measure the exact dimensions and position of each parcel of land. At the same time, they recorded information about the type of land and its quality. As they went from village to village, the survey teams also implemented Sai On's forest management system.[44] The teams compiled their results to form a four-volume register of all the usable land in Ryukyu, *Go-tōkoku go-kenchi no shidai* (Results of the survey of the country).

The Genbun Survey seems to have accomplished many of its objectives. The compiled data indicated a 250 percent overall increase in productivity since Satsuma's survey,[45] information that undoubtedly enabled the central government to take in more tax revenues. The survey clarified the boundaries between different types of land and specified the ground rules for the use of the these lands, eliminating most disputes over the boundaries of districts, villages, and lesser units of land.[46] It also functioned as a means to implement Sai On's forest management system throughout Ryukyu. One result of the survey was that the majority of forest lands became classified as *"somayama,"* putting them under the supervision of central government and local forestry officials.[47] The Genbun Survey was the royal government's first and last complete cadastral survey, and as Tasato points out, it laid Ryukyu's economic foundation for the remainder of the kingdom's existence.[48]

The Genbun Survey was but one of several steps Ryukyu's central government undertook to standardize social and economic activities in the countryside. In 1735, it began to issue *kujichō* (also, *kōjichō*) for each district. *Kujichō* were administrative handbooks containing detailed regulations for the conduct of local government. They also regulated local festivals and religious practices, local government ceremonial, and other *kuji* (roughly, "public affairs").

A sampling of passages from a reconstructed *kujichō* provides an indication of the degree of specificity to which the central government attempted to regulate life in the districts. Regarding, for example, the work schedule of local officials: "On work days and duty days every month, officials from the *jitōdai* on down to the *tikugu* shall go to the district office. Addendum: The *utchi* for each village will go to the district office on the first, tenth, fifteenth, and twenty-fifth day of each month."[49] The *kujichō* specified detailed procedures for routine cleaning of the district office. For example: "On the first and fifteenth of each month, the *tikugu* shall be ordered to clean and remove any insects from the [copy of the] *Ikokuhō go-jōgaki*, the registers of official notices, and so forth. The *jitōdai* is to inspect this work from start to finish and approve it."[50] On the training of *tikugu* (apprentice officials): "*Tikugu* and others taking lessons in arithmetic and penmanship shall be made to demonstrate their writing ability. The results are to be evaluated and graded. At year's end, all the writings shall be sent to the district's overseers in Shuri *(ryō-sōjitō),* who will grade them."[51] The *kujichō* were one of the tangible results of the royal government's attempt to standardize local administrative practices throughout Ryukyu.

One particularly important topic in the *kujichō* was the ceremonial obligations of district officials toward the royal government at certain times of the year. On the first day of the new year, for example, local officials from Okinawan districts gathered in the capital to participate in several rites with central government officials. In a ceremony that was an extension of the *Ne-no-hō* rite described previously, central government and local officials ritually venerated the king. On the offshore island of Kumejima, local officials gathered at the central storehouse, stood on a "Chinese platform" *(tōdai),* and bowed in the direction of Shuri castle. Later on the same day, approximately 840 local officials (twenty-four per district) made the rounds of various shrines and temples along with central government officials to pray for the country's prosperity.[52] These rites helped reaffirm the king in Shuri as the source of political authority. That both local and central government officials participated reinforced the idea that all officials work together in service to the king.[53] Because local officials in early-modern Ryukyu were technically commoners, their participation in important rites of state probably enhanced their sense of importance and their sense of connection with the central government.

Kujichō also regulated the details of local festivals and religious observances. The central government standardized yearly festivals in the districts, sometimes to the point of anomaly. Ie island, for example, had no wet fields, yet was still supposed to hold the Rice Ear Festival along with the other districts.[54] In general, the royal government's strategy regarding festivals was to prohibit those it regarded as morally or materially detrimental, modify others, and promote those that helped reinforce officially sanctioned values.

Some of Ryukyu's religious festivals combined notions of sexuality with those of agricultural fertility. *Shinugu ashibi* (J. *shinogu asobi,* also *uchihare asobi*) was a generic term for a common festival of this type.[55] The details of *shinugu ashibi* varied from place to place, but a common pattern was for the women of a village to gather at a secluded, sacred location. There, they would dance, often for several days. They often danced in the nude, and such dances typically suggested sexual activities with the deities.[56] This dancing typically had more than a religious function. Young men from the village often clandestinely went to watch the dancing and would later pursue those among the dancers who struck their fancy. The women dancing undoubtedly suspected that they were being watched.[57] In this way, *shinugu ashibi* was also an important part of relations between the young men and women of the villages.

A variety of other local festivals promoted more than simply religious enjoyment. A revised 1848 *kujichō* for Gushikawa district in Kumejima, for example, mentions an all-night *bon* dance in which "men and women mix with each other throughout the night, a hindrance to morality that is not good." It also mentions an event known as "Mushi no kuchi katame" that took place up to six times a year, in which all the men and women went down to the seashore and "made each other comfortable" *(ai-nagusame)* throughout the day.[58] A *kujichō* prohibited similar practices in Yaeyama, in part for "wreaking havoc on proper behavior" *(fūzoku no midare).*[59]

In *kujichō* and other official documents, the royal government prohibited *shinugu ashibi* and similar practices it regarded as morally improper. In 1730, it even restricted a deeply rooted practice in Kumemura, *tabi-odori,* a dancing celebration to send off crew members of ships bound for China. The traditional practice was for wives, lovers, sisters, and other female friends and relatives of the crew to dance and sing throughout the night before the ship was to sail. Connected with the ancient Ryukyuan belief that women had divine power to protect male relatives *(onarigami shinkō),* the stated purpose of the festivities was to ensure the crew's safety. Saying that it was inappropriate for women to behave in such a manner, the government limited the dancing to daylight hours.[60]

As the above examples indicate, conflict with Confucian morality was one reason the royal government prohibited or restricted certain festivals. Economic considerations, however, were even more important. Festivals were a diversion from agricultural activity. They required resources to carry out and entailed the additional cost of time lost to agriculture. A festival in Yaeyama, for example, was prohibited on the grounds that the head of each household had to provide rice cakes and ceremonial liquor *(miki)*, and Araki provides a wealth of similar examples from various *kujichō* fragments.[61]

Araki cites four reasons for the royal government's vigorous attempts to prohibit local festivals and religious practices. First is lost agricultural productivity. One mourning rite *(sakai)* for example, took place for forty-nine days, during which time none of the relatives of the deceased worked in the fields. Since nearly everyone was at least a distant relative of everyone else in remote agricultural villages, farming nearly stopped during such times. The second reason is closely related to the first: an attempt to increase the number of days per year the peasants spent working in the fields. Third was that the festivals themselves consumed needed resources. Yaeyama, for example, paid just over 2,600 *koku* a year to the royal government in taxes. Festivals in Yaeyama consumed approximately 15 percent of this amount in direct expenses. Finally, issues of morality were also a factor in many cases.[62]

In some cases, the government modified traditional festivals and observances to the point where they served a different purpose than originally intended. A good example was the practice of *"kama mawari."* Veneration of the hearth deity *(hi-no-kami)* was a fundamental part of household worship in Okinawan popular religion.[63] The *kama* was the kitchen hearth, and *kama mawari* was originally associated with *hi-no-kami* worship. By the eighteenth century, however, central authorities had secularized *kama mawari* and appropriated it for use in governing the peasants. Specifically, on the first and tenth days of the month, officials from the district office were to make rounds of each village to see that the kitchens *(kama)* were clean and that the villagers were well informed about fire safety.[64]

The eighteenth-century royal government clearly distinguished between those traditional festivals it sanctioned and those it regarded as improper, promoting the former and attempting to suppress or modify the latter. The four major festivals the royal government promoted in all the districts celebrated agricultural productivity.[65] This government revision and standardization of local festivals, religious observances, and other customary practices was part of a larger effort to reconstruct rural society to maximize its productivity in an age when agricultural production had become the material foundation of Ryukyuan society.

With the support of other officials, Sai On orchestrated a campaign against shamanism. Shō Shōken expressed a desire to combat this dimension of Ryukyuan folk religion, but he could not find support for such a project from other officials. That Sai On's campaign against shamanism received support from the central government as a whole is strong circumstantial evidence of the growing influence of his Confucianized vision of Ryukyu within the royal government. Confucianism, however, never took hold among the common people of Ryukyu. In the countryside, traditional religious practices remained deeply rooted throughout the early-modern period. Shamanism, particularly the employment of female shamans known as *yuta*, remained an integral part of Ryukyuan village life well into this century.[66] There is no evidence that the royal government's campaign against shamanism was ever successful.

An entry in the *Kyūyō* dated 1728, the year Sai On became a member of the Council of Three, reads:

> It has been common practice in our country to trust in the techniques of shamans *(yuta)* which has given rise to evil delusion. Moreover, this vulgar practice has been deeply rooted and has caused a great expenditure of wealth. Therefore, the king instructed the Prime Minister and Council of Three to make laws prohibiting and eliminating the practice of shamanism. This returned [society] to the correct Way.[67]

Sai On's colleagues from Kumemura wrote the *Kyūyō*, and its language clearly reflects a Confucian point of view. The prohibition mentioned in this passage was the 1728 *Toki, yuta togasadame,* the introduction of which reads:

> *Toki* [male diviners who select auspicious and inauspicious days] and *yuta* have existed in our society since ancient times. They have even been established within the royal government. But recently the number of *toki* and *yuta* has increased markedly, becoming a hindrance to society. Because they are employed in farming villages, the result has been the highly improper situation of cows, pigs, chickens, and the like being lost and expenses accumulating. This impoverishes the peasants.[68]

The primary justification for the prohibition, therefore, was that peasants tended to spend valuable resources to employ *toki* and *yuta,* thus causing themselves financial difficulties. Naturally, though unstated, peasant financial difficulties also caused difficulties to the royal government and its stipended officials who lived off the peasants' taxes. A harbinger of this 1728 prohibition was a Hyōjōsho ruling ten years previously. It declared shamanism a "base occupation" and stated that *yukatchu* who patronized the services of *yuta* should be made commoners.[69]

The 1728 prohibition is a logical extension of Sai On's critique, in his philosophical writings, of various practices and beliefs he regarded as superstitious.[70] Though Sai On's Confucianism undoubtedly informed the prohibition of shamanism, the official declaration of the new policy lacked any explicit

Confucian rationale. It is important to bear in mind that Confucianism was relatively new to the Ryukyu kingdom in 1728. Furthermore, for most of the previous century, its study was limited mainly to the residents of Kumemura. There, Confucianism functioned as a rhetorical tradition to be learned as part of the knowledge necessary to carry on successful trade and diplomacy with China. It was not until Sai On became Shō Kei's tutor that Confucianism began to function as a body of knowledge that might inform the practice of government in Ryukyu.

The activities of *toki* and *yuta* were clearly at odds with Sai On's Confucianism and also competed with the state. One of the major roles of *toki* was to set the dates for village festivals and other communal events. In the classical Confucian state, one of the ruler's functions as mediator between heaven and earth was creator of the calendar. Shō Shōken regarded the activities of *toki* improper, decreeing that "since former times, *toki no ōyako,* who are entirely illiterate, have been established among the peasants to select lucky and unlucky days, and are employed in connection with a variety of affairs. From this time on, however, affairs are to be settled using the Japanese or Chinese calendar."[71] By the time Sai On came to power, the royal government had its own calendrical officials and had distributed handbooks on the calendar to each local government office.[72] Extant *kujichō* contain such entries as, "When a communication from the Shunōza [a government department] setting the day for the Great Festival of the Rice Plants arrives [at the district office], it is to be sent immediately to each village."[73] The activities of the *toki,* therefore, were a direct threat to the authority of the central government in its capacity as the regulator of time.

Yuta, too, competed with the central government. In the late fifteenth century, King Shō Shin (r. 1477–1526) established a formal hierarchy of religious officials headed by his sister, who took the title *kikoe ōgimi.* This hierarchy of female officials corresponded closely to positions in the hierarchy of male government officials. In this way, the military power of the state and the religious authority of the female officials complemented each other, although even in Old-Ryukyu, the female religious hierarchy was subordinate to the king.

The *noro* (O. *nuru*) was the representative of this hierarchy at the local level. *Noro* were government officials and may have assisted in tax collection in some localities.[74] In early-modern Ryukyu, *noro* performed state-approved religious rites in their jurisdictions (usually one or two villages). Their close connection with the state, however, limited the range of activities in which they could legally participate. When illness or other bad fortune struck a household, its members did not turn to the local *noro* for help, but rather to a *yuta. Yuta,* therefore, competed with *noro,* undermining the latter's religious authority in the villages. The prohibition of shamanism, therefore, was a logical move on the part of the royal government. It made sense from the standpoint of Sai On's Confucianism, and it made sense from the standpoint of the state's desire to preserve and expand its authority.

All evidence indicates that the prohibition was ineffective. The values, attitudes, and beliefs of the common people that had supported the *yuta* prior to the prohibition continued undiminished after the prohibition.[75] An eighteenth-century handbook for officials in Miyako states that *toki* and *yuta* deceive the people and are a hindrance to productivity. It also states that the prohibition was not being enforced, since "*Toki* and *yuta* are numerous in each village."[76] Even when violators were prosecuted, the officially stipulated fines were impractically high. In practice, therefore, local government offices meted out lighter penalties, customarily exposing offenders in stocks for seven days. A 1788 *kujichō* for Kumejima states that the law was not being enforced at all, and an 1854 document states that "there are many who secretly employ *toki* and *yuta*."[77]

Documentary fragments in Kyoto University's collection of Ryukyuan materials indicate that at some point after 1728 (the date is unclear), there was a debate within the royal government over whether to repeal the prohibition on shamanism. Leading officials acknowledged a general failure in enforcing the ban but decided that the kingdom's political ideals would not permit repealing it.[78] We see in this example a widening gap between an increasingly Confucianized central government and a peasantry that continued steadfast in its traditional religious beliefs and practices—with local officials caught in the middle.

That basic Confucian concepts and terminology informed official thinking regarding the ban is clear from a post-1728 letter, the precise date of which is uncertain. The letter, most likely from a central government official to a district official, states that *toki* and *yuta* tried to get around the prohibition by cloaking their activities with *Yijing* divination (divination based on the *Yijing* would have been acceptable Confucian practice).[79] The author also laments that the prohibition of shamanism had no effect despite attempts at enforcement. In fact, he said, the situation had actually worsened. His description of the detrimental effects of shamanism and divination by *toki* is thoroughly Confucian:

> Because the cosmic pattern of the heavenly Way promotes good and dispels evil, when one encounters hard times, he should first engage in self-reflection and establish his determination to do away with evil and strive for what is good. If such an attitude is lacking, one will perversely think that [the hard times are because of] some insufficiency regarding the deities, and engage in *toki* divination.[80]

The letter also states that the deceptive words of shamans entice ignorant commoners to go beyond the bounds of proper religious activities such as venerating parents and ancestors.

Such evidence indicates that many eighteenth-century Ryukyuan officials supported the ban on shamanism and did so with an explicitly Confucian
rationale. The peasantry, however, saw the world in quite different terms. Both
Shō Shōken and Sai On, says Takara, prepared impressive scenarios for society.
They failed, however, to take due consideration of the tenacious strength of
traditional, popular religious beliefs and practices. The visions of these "great
men" *(ijin)* were powerless before such beliefs and practices.[81]

Sai On and his allies also attempted to regulate the social behavior of
Ryukyu's *yukatchu* and urban dwellers. A good example is prostitution. As the
following *Kyūyō* entry for 1725 indicates, the widespread practice of prostitution caused potential problems for the government in its attempts to regulate
households:

> Prostitutes wreak havoc on great ethics, [lying with] countless people in a
> single night. . . . A thousand seeds in one womb make it difficult to dis-
> cern [the father of any children]. Among customers who have taken such
> children as their own, many have been mistaken. This practice, therefore,
> has been forbidden. In recent years, the number of violators of this law
> has grown large. Those [offspring of prostitutes] who have disrupted the
> legitimate line of succession by having been entered into household reg-
> isters are to be expunged and made commoners. . . .[82]

The main concern of Sai On's government with respect to prostitution was its
potential to blur the distinction between *yukatchu* and commoners and the
formal hierarchy within elite households. A 1730 set of regulations for *yukatchu*
households, *Regulations of the Keitoza (Keitoza kimochō)*, contains a number of
articles regarding illegitimate offspring. Generally, only children of wives or
official mistresses were legitimate, and no illegitimate children were to be
entered into the household register. Regarding the specific case of prostitutes,
"Because entering children born of prostitutes into the official line of succession wreaks havoc on the foundation of ethics, it is never to be done."[83]

This brief survey of political developments in Ryukyu during Sai On's
time on the Council of Three is far from comprehensive. Nevertheless, certain
points should be clear. From the 1720s onward, Ryukyu's central government
became explicitly Confucian in ideology and increasingly desirous of expanding its control over the general population, from *yukatchu* to peasants in
remote areas. The result was a series of attempts to reconstruct Ryukyuan soci-

ety, eliminating popular customs and behaviors the state deemed undesirable. Although Confucian ethics undoubtedly informed these attempts to remake Ryukyu in the image of an ideal Confucian society, economic factors were of equal or greater importance. The central government sought to exert greater control over the produce of the land and thereby increase its revenues. As might be expected, the royal government's attempts at greater social control caused resistance.

Resisting Sai On's Ryukyu

We have already seen that attempts to prohibit the activities of *toki* and *yuta* were often unsuccessful in practice. There is indirect evidence, however, that the royal government had sufficient power to enforce even unpopular measures in at least some localities. The ban on *shinugu ashibi* and similar practices, for example, generated sufficient resentment to suggest vigor in enforcement. One critical voice was Onna Nabe (O. Onna Nabii, dates uncertain), poet, entertainer, and sometime critic of government authority. Her origins were humble, but her poems indicate contact with high government officials, probably as a courtesan. The following *ryūka* poem deals with *shinugu ashibi:*

> Yokatesame anebe
> How good it was in my older sister's day!
> Shinogu shichiasobi de.
> They could dance the *shinugu ashibi* to their heart's content.
> Wasuta yo ni nareba
> But in my day
> Otomesarete
> It has been prohibited.[84]

Another of Onna Nabe's *ryūka* more clearly indicates the power of the government's prohibition:

> Jitōdai shushi-tarimi[85] toritsugi shabera.
> Honorable *Jitōdai,* I present a petition from our youth.
> Shuri-ganashimi[86] yadairi yachū
> You who represents His Royal Highness day and night
> Aman yo no shinogu, O-yurushi-menshūre.
> Please allow the *shinugu* of ancient times.[87]

These poems suggest that local officials did enforce the prohibition of *shinugu ashibi,* at least in the central regions of Okinawa where Onna Nabe resided.

There is also evidence that the prohibition of *shinugu ashibi* and attempts to eliminate or modify local customs were unsuccessful, most apparently in regions remote from Shuri. Araki provides examples of festivals prohibited in the Miyako and Yaeyama islands that continued to be practiced in modern times.[88] There are also several cases of the royal government reversing itself regarding prohibited festivals. The prohibition of several festivals in the Yaeyama and Miyako island groups, for example, resulted in a drop in production, probably owing to popular resistance. The decline in production prompted the royal government to reinstate the festivals in 1793. Such passive resistance by local peasants, Araki points out, allowed many banned festivals to survive to the present day.[89]

Available evidence suggests that the royal government was better able to regulate the lives of peasants in the regions near the major urban areas of Okinawa than elsewhere. Still, it kept trying. Throughout the nineteenth century, the government in Shuri attempted to control the behavior of the residents of ever more remote areas. In the *kujichō* issued for Kumejima in 1735, for example, there was minimal mention of local festivals. In a revised *kujichō* for the same place in 1831, however, regulations concerning festivals were much more numerous and detailed, covering virtually every local practice.[90]

The passive resistance of Ryukyu's peasants was surely a hindrance to Sai On's ambition to remake the kingdom into his vision of an ideal Confucian society. This resistance limited the power of Sai On and the royal government, but it did not directly threaten or attack it. Opposition from within elite society, however, was another matter. By no means did all Ryukyuan elites support Sai On. Ryukyuan politics at the time tended to divide along several fault lines. Perhaps the most significant was that of the *yukatchu* of Shuri versus the *yukatchu* of Kumemura, who had only recently gained direct, large-scale access to political power within the central government. Another fault line divided the *yukatchu* of Kumemura, though this division has received relatively little attention from researchers.

The most serious challenge to Sai On's vision of Ryukyu, and to the political power of Sai On and his allies, came from a group of Shuri *yukatchu* literati, of whom Heshikiya Chōbin (1700–1734) is most famous. During his brief career, Heshikiya established himself as the foremost literary figure in early-modern Ryukyu. He was born to a middle-ranking *yukatchu* household, the eldest son of a father who died at age twenty-nine while in the midst of a promising political career. After executing him as a major criminal, the royal government confiscated and destroyed Heshikiya's household register *(kafu)* and similar records. Despite this attempt to suppress his legacy, most of Heshikiya's literary works survived and were widely read in his own time and thereafter.[91]

Heshikiya wrote mainly in classical Japanese *(gikobun)*, a form of writing that had become popular among the *yukatchu* of Shuri by the eighteenth century.[92] His major extant works consist of four novels and a *kumiodori* play. One of the novels, *Tale of Young Grass (Wakagusa monogatari)*, is set in Japan. The protagonist, a samurai and poet named Ozasa Tsuyunosuke (*tsuyu*, "dew," was a favorite metaphor for Heshikiya), meets and falls in love with a high-class prostitute named Wakagusa ("Young Grass"). The two must part, however, for the woman had been sold to a daimyō of another domain. In the end, they both commit suicide in their grief, the dew and young grass passing away after a brief flourishing. *Beneath the Moss (Koke no shita)* is set in Ryukyu, where an *aji* and a high-class prostitute, Yoshiya, fall deeply in love. Yoshiya's stepmother, however, arranges for her to marry someone else for financial reasons. In her grief, Yoshiya stops eating and starves to death, and the *aji* resolves to do the same to join his lover in the next world. In the autobiographical *Record of an Impoverished Household (Binkaki)*, a *yukatchu* who falls into poverty leaves Shuri to live in the countryside, in Heshikiya village in the district of Katsuren. There, he observes rural life for a year, putting his thoughts into poems. The tale ends with his return to the capital after receiving an official appointment. The protagonist in *Manzai* (Many talents) is Shirotarōgane, a handsome, learned man with great musical talent. He hears of a woman named Manabetarukane, falls in love with his image of her before they have ever met, and sets out to make contact with her. After traveling to her residence, he spies her washing her hair and manages to pass on some of his poetry to her through an intermediary. Although Manabetarukane's father thinks that she and Shirotarōgane would make a good match, he has already promised his daughter to be married into another household. As the day of Manabetarukane's wedding draws near, the despondent Shirotarōgane throws himself into the sea and drowns. Manabetarukane dreams of the event, rushes to the seashore, and finds his body. Just as she was about to join her lover in death, however, a deity in the form of an old man restores Shirotarōgane to life and has the couple marry. Heshikiya's most famous work is *Temizu no en*, a *kumiodori* drama about illicit love between a young couple, Yamado and Tamatsu.

The skeletal structure of each novel is a series of *waka* poems, fleshed out and connected by the plot. *Tale of Young Grass* clearly resembles *Ise Monogatari* in structure, and, argues Ikemiya Masaharu, all of Heshikiya's work indicates a strong influence of Heian-period Japanese literature. In effect, Heshikiya attempted to explore through his writing an ideal world in which people could pursue and fulfill their desires.[93]

Nearly all scholars of Ryukyuan literature agree that Heshikiya's works are, at least in part, a critique of the Ryukyu of his day. Tamae Seiryō sketches the steps of Heshikiya's literary and social development as follows: First, in *Tale of Young Grass,* Heshikiya discovered the rigid ethical duties and obligations *(giri)* of his "feudal society" and resisted their inhuman qualities *(hiningensei).* Heshikiya resisted the idea that humans are evil by nature, and in *Beneath the Moss,* he portrayed evil behavior as a result of the "contradictions" of feudal society. *Tale of Young Grass* and *Beneath the Moss* end in tragedy and failure. In *Manzai,* however, Heshikiya manages to transcend the tragic consequences of his society.[94] It is important to add that although Heshikiya may have overcome tragedy in *Manzai,* he did so by resorting to supernatural intervention. In *Manzai* and his other works, Heshikiya never proposed a realistic course of political action to promote his vision of Ryukyu, which we now examine.

Heshikiya's works often suggest a desirable possibility—typically happiness through the fulfillment of love—and portray the pain and suffering caused by the characters' inability to realize this possibility. Deeply religious, a Buddhist sense of pathos pervades much of Heshikiya's writing, as does a sense of compassion, aimed particularly at prostitutes. According to Tamae, one result of Heshikiya's religiosity is an elegant (as opposed to erotic) sensuality and the message that love is a great equalizer, dissolving distinctions in social status—between prostitute and *aji,* for example. In the case of prostitutes, argues Tamae, Heshikiya attacked the "contradictions" of Ryukyu's "feudal" society by stressing the goodness of those women at the bottom of it. One technique that Heshikiya uses in *Beneath the Moss,* for example, is to stress the oppressive nature of the day's dawning. At night, out of society's gaze, the *aji* and prostitute enjoy themselves as nature intended. In the oppressive light of day, however, the *aji* must sneak back to his residence.[95]

Heshikiya's ideal Ryukyu was a far cry from Sai On's hierarchical society, whose elites, ideally, strive to keep their emotions under control and where prostitutes and their offspring were excluded from membership in its system of elite households. In his philosophical writings, Sai On repeatedly stated that the primary duty of Ryukyu's elites is moral self-cultivation. The essence of success lies in conquering and preventing upwellings of material force, that is, improper thoughts, desires, and emotions. The following passage from *Essential Discussion of Popular Customs* (C. *Suxi yaolun,* J. *Zokushū yōron*) is a typical and thorough example of Sai On's understanding of the moral effort all should make:

> The *Great Learning* states, "When the mind is rectified, the personal life is cultivated." This mind is one of the five organs, and it is the place where the spiritual light of our heavenly nature resides. The pursuit of scholar-

ship, therefore, makes rectification of the mind its root. This rectification of the mind is like polishing a mirror. Thus Mencius' words about finding the lost mind[96] mean that it is not something to be found externally, but only by exhausting one's strength in polishing the mirror. Ordinary people always follow vulgar habits of behavior and become obscured by the attachment of material force, which sullies their minds. It is like the situation after a clear mirror has become covered with grime. This attached material force results from selfish desires. It is thus one's own grime. Therefore, if those with firm resolve in their minds endeavor with all their strength to defeat and eliminate attached material force in the midst of daily things and affairs, the mental impulses of selfish desires will fade and perish. When selfish thoughts have gone, the spiritual light of our heavenly nature clearly illuminates the self. And when the spiritual light is clearly manifest, though one may come right to the borderline of safety and danger, life and death, the mind will remain calm and unagitated. Then, how could it possibly be said that things like fame, fortune, sex, and liquor would be able to disturb our minds?[97]

For Heshikiya, one's mind would become calm and illuminated by allowing nature to take its course and human desires to be fulfilled, not by a strict regimen of moral effort backed up the laws and the coercive power of the state. In this sense, Sai On's vision of an ideal society and Heshikiya's were completely inimical.

For Heshikiya, society of his day was *"hakanai"* (empty, sad, unreal), like the morning dew. "Like the morning glory that knows nothing of its fleeting life," begins one of the many poems in *Beneath the Moss,* "I pray that I shall live as long as the pines and bamboo."[98] The concluding passage of this same work, in which the *aji* makes up his mind to follow Yoshiya into death, is also steeped in Buddhist imagery:

> . . . A monk seated at a temple practicing *zazen* at night was startled to hear the voice of a young woman say: "The mountain path I've entered leading to the world of the dead is dark and steep. May the lantern of the Law illuminate it with its light." But when he opened the window to look out, there was nobody. "Ah! It's someone lost in the dark," he thought. Taking pity on her, . . . he recited the sutras most respectfully and performed funeral rites.
>
> When the *aji* heard of this matter, he said, "Ah! It must have been Yoshiya. She must be so lost by herself. Well, shall I go now and show her the way? She's waiting." He then made up his mind to stop eating and die.[99]

Heshikiya celebrated freedom of love and the emotions but was keenly aware of the worldly constraints on that freedom. As the passage above exemplifies, much of Heshikiya's writing conveys a sense of fatalism and easy resignation to death as a way of escaping life's injustices. Again we see a view of society completely at odds with that of Sai On.

Higa Kazuo, in a trenchant analysis of the life, work, and significance of Heshikiya, points out that it was common in Heshikiya's works for characters to throw away their lives for love. Their motivation could best be characterized as "selfish" *(watakushi)*. Sai On stressed precisely the opposite: duty, sacrifice, and loyalty to the interests of the family and society.[100] For example, in his *Articles of Instruction,* a moral code with the force of law promulgated two years prior to Heshikiya's execution, Sai On exhorted Ryukyuans as follows under the heading "Morality Concerning Life":

> One should regard his life as being more valuable than any treasure and nourish and protect it. . . . High and low alike should treat their bodies with care.
>
> If there is some reason to sacrifice yourself on behalf of loyalty or filial piety, when this [act] is revealed, it will not be wasted effort. For all ages it will bring fame to your ancestors and descendants. But sacrificing yourself for any other reason is extremely foolish behavior. . . . [101]

Out of context, this passage sounds simplistic and obvious. In the Ryukyu of 1732, however, its message stood in opposition to the most popular writer of the day and Sai On's most powerful opponent.

Many scholars of Ryukyu regard *Temizu no en* as Heshikiya's sharpest critique of Sai On's Ryukyu. Matayoshi Hiroshi, following Ikemiya, points out that from the first days of *kumiodori* as a recognizable dramatic form, the royal government co-opted it to serve the state's ends. Although this dramatic form could potentially accommodate a wide variety of topics, nearly all *kumiodori* featured loyalty (usually avenging one's lord) or filial piety as their main themes.[102] In this form, *kumiodori* performances received formal recognition by the state and were shown with pride to visiting Chinese investiture envoys. *Temizu no en,* which highlights illicit love and the oppressive social structures that interfere with its fulfillment, is unique among *kumiodori.* The extant texts of *Temizu no en* contain a much wider range and number of variations than any other *kumiodori.* The reason, says Matayoshi, is that *Temizu no en* circulated underground, there being no officially authorized script, and therefore developed many local variations.[103]

In at least one instance, Heshikiya appears to have criticized Sai On directly in his work. Just before he joined the Council of Three, Sai On arranged for his oldest son to marry one of King Shō Kei's daughters, a most unusual marriage since Sai On's family was not of princely or even *aji*-level rank. Earlier in his career, Heshikiya was exiled to the countryside owing to a rumor that he was having an affair with this same daughter of the king (this exile became the basis of *Record of an Impoverished Household*). In a close reading of *Manzai*, Nishime Ikuwa analyzes the names and titles of the main characters. Leaving out the details of his argument, Nishime makes a good case that the novel is an allegory for the wedding of Sai On's son (male protagonist Shirotarōgane) and Shō Kei's daughter (female protagonist Manabetarukane). Shirotarōgane, for example, is the son of Asato Aji, who is the younger brother of the lord *(ōmori)* of Gushichan. Sai On's title at the time was Gushichan Ueekata.

On the surface, the novel seems to be nothing but praise for the couple. Toward the end, however, there is a subtle but significant change in the title of the "lord" of Gushichan, from the vague "*ōmori*" to "*aji*." Had Sai On really been of *aji* status, the marriage of his son to the king's daughter would not have been unusual, but because he was not, Heshikiya's use of "Gushichan Aji" was a subtle but effective attack on Sai On and the marriage of his son. Furthermore, Heshikiya's implicit likening of the royal family to a rural aristocratic household could not have gone unnoticed by Sai On and the royal government. It was after *Manzai* became public that pressure on Heshikiya from the royal government markedly increased.[104]

As a critic of Sai On's Ryukyu, Heshikiya was hardly alone. He was part of a sizable group of literati whose works circulated among the Shuri *yukatchu* and other literate Okinawans.[105] Other Ryukyuan popular writers celebrated love, romance, and sensuality, often associated with a critique of authority in general or the many new rules emanating from the royal government in particular. Onna Nabe, for example, wrote:

> Under the pine of [the] Onna [District government office],
> Stands a notice board full of prohibitions.
> But there is surely no rule prohibiting love.[106]

Heshikiya, Onna, and many others among the Shuri *yukatchu* did not share Sai On's vision of Ryukyu and worked to criticize it through their writing.

A struggle for power took place beneath the relatively prosperous surface of eighteenth-century Ryukyu. The vision and energy of Sai On and his supporters could not ultimately coexist with that of Heshikiya and his group. In *Jiayanlu* (J. *Kagenroku*), a record of his household affairs, Sai On wrote of "a certain person" who came to visit one day:

In the past, there was a certain person *(moushi)*. He appeared good on the outside but his mind was that of a wolf. Although he was from a local *(yukatchu)* household, his mind contained jealous thoughts, and everyone avoided him. This person ordinarily despised me and harbored plots to do me harm, which was known to everyone and to myself.

One day he unexpectedly paid me a visit, and the members of my household were quite alarmed. I made tea and received him as a guest. He laughed and talked, and as evening arrived he took his leave.

The household members admonished me saying, "He belongs among the carnivorous beasts and owls. Why didn't you avoid him?"[107] I said, "He did not intend any harm, so what harm could he have done?" Later, this person committed a treasonous crime and was executed.[108]

Most scholars have assumed that the "certain person" of this passage was Heshikiya Chōbin, but Higa points out that it could have been any of the persons executed in the so-called Heshikiya-Tomoyose Incident. He agrees, though, that the above passage was connected with the incident.[109] How could this unmentionable person have caused such concern among the powerful Sai On's household? Analysis of the Heshikiya-Tomoyose Incident suggests some answers.

Although many of the personal records of Heshikiya and his group were destroyed, the *kafu* of this father, Chōbun, describes the incident briefly:

. . . [Chōbin] conspired with Tomoyose [Anjō] and came up with an imprudent plot. They delivered a letter to the residence of the [Satsuma] inspector Kawanishi Hiraemon and, after that, mentioned various things about delivering another letter. They intended that the matter become a difficult problem for the country *(kokka)*. Because they were evil and reprehensible, they were executed at Ajiminato on the twenty-sixth day of the six month, 1734. The writings and emoluments of those involved in the incident were taken and are now gone.[110]

Tomoyose Anjō was the other major figure in the incident, and his father's *kafu* contains a strikingly similar account of Tomoyose's deeds: Heshikiya, Tomoyose, and the Satsuma inspector *(yokome)* Kawanishi conspired and sent a letter to the office of the Zaiban bugyō. These acts, too, resulted in a "difficult problem for the country," and the "evil and reprehensible" criminals were crucified at Ajiminato, their writings and emoluments taken by the state.[111] Higa points out that the two accounts are so similar in terms of content and language that it was as if their authors had been told what to write.[112]

Heshikiya, Tomoyose, and thirteen others were executed, and several tens of others were banished. The punishments did not stop there. Wives and children of those executed were made commoners or, in the case of sons, banished to the island of Yonaguni. A grandson of one of those executed was banished, making the punishments extend to three generations in at least one case. When Oyadomari Chokuzō was executed in connection with the incident, his younger brother Chokuryō took over as head of the household. Eleven years later he was accused of theft. Although laws in effect at the time specified banishment as the penalty, Chokuryō was executed.[113] It is clear from the severity and extent of the penalties meted out that something of the utmost gravity had taken place. Owing in large part to the royal government's attempt to cloak the incident in silence, however, the specific details of what happened are not clear.

Higa provides a clear summary of the major theories of the Heshikiya-Tomoyose Incident. The first Okinawan scholar to take up the subject was Majikina Ankō in the late Meiji period. He pointed out that, according to elderly informants who lived in the days of the kingdom, talking of the incident was taboo, and those who spoke of Heshikiya were regarded as wicked. Majikina explained the incident as a clash between "Japanese thought" (Nihon shisō) and "Chinese thought" (Shina shisō). The incident took place at a time when Sai On and his Chinese studies colleagues were in the ascendancy, and those who specialized in Japanese studies developed an intense hatred for Sai On. Heshikiya and his faction also resented what they regarded as Sai On's arrogance and royal pretensions because he had recently arranged for his son to marry the king's daughter and had allegedly referred to himself using insufficiently humble terms when in the king's presence. Heshikiya and his group turned to Satsuma, the only authority they thought could stop Sai On. Therefore, said Majikina, though the contents of the letter Heshikiya's group wrote are unknown, it was almost certainly a denunciation of Sai On and perhaps of Shō Kei as well.[114] As Higa and others have pointed out, this explanation is generally unconvincing. Although there was conflict between those who pursued Chinese studies and those who pursued Japanese studies, academic rivalry is insufficient to explain such a serious incident.[115]

The next to take up the topic was Iha Fuyū in the early Taishō period. Like Majikina, Iha based his explanation in part on oral accounts that had been passed down from the days of the kingdom. He, too, relied heavily on the idea that the marriage between Sai On's son and the king's daughter engendered enmity toward Sai On in some circles. Iha also pointed out that it was after Sai On eliminated his major opposition in the Heshikiya-Tomoyose Incident that he began in earnest to implement his various policies and plans.

Iha regarded the "certain person" in the *Jiayanlu* account to have been Heshikiya and interpreted Sai On's actions in that connection as a sign of his generosity and kindness. Higa, on the other hand, takes it as an example of Sai On's perversity. The lofty, moralistic rhetoric served only to mask a crafty politician ever on the lookout to advance himself.[116]

Heshikiya and Tomoyose carried out their activities in close cooperation with Satsuma's Kawanishi. The following description by Ikemiya includes many points on which most scholars of Ryukyu today would agree:

> Because a letter was sent to the Zaiban bugyō, the thinking is that it must have contained a critique of the nucleus of the royal government. The group who made the critique embraced the Satsuma official Kawanishi, and we may furthermore conclude that it was a group of people who felt close to Satsuma through Japanese literature and Japanese arts. It was probably the case that by delivering a letter critical of Sai On they hoped to have him removed from office. Because Satsuma supported Sai On's realistic *(jitsug-akuteki)* economic policies and his feudal *(hōkenteki)* ethics, however, it was shocked to find that even the Satsuma official Kawanishi had been drawn into the incident, and asked for decisive punishment. Sai On took this stance by Satsuma as an opportunity to silence a source of internal dissent and meted out even more severe punishment than was necessary.[117]

Ikemiya assumes that Heshikiya and his group felt a linguistic and cultural affinity with Kawanishi and others from Satsuma owing to the Ryukyuans' mastery of Japanese literature. It was, however, the classical Japanese literature of the Heian and Kamakura periods that Heshikiya and his group had mastered. Other than those Ryukyuans who had lived in Japan for some time, many would have had difficulty speaking any form of colloquial Japanese.[118] The peculiar form of Japanese spoken in Satsuma would have added to communication difficulties. It is difficult to specify the extent, if any, to which a perception by Heshikiya and his group of cultural commonality with Kawanishi may have influenced their actions.

Writing in 1974, Matayoshi Yōshi firmly rejected the conventional view that the letter Heshikiya and company delivered to the Zaiban bugyō was a critique of Sai On. Matayoshi argued that the letter was actually a critique of Satsuma's harsh rule and a request for the return of control over foreign trade to Ryukyu.[119] This interpretation better accounts for the severity of the royal government's reaction, since Heshikiya, Tomoyose, and the others were meddling in matters affecting the very foundation of the Ryukyuan state. The only additional evidence Matayoshi cites is the claim by Majikina Sachiko, one of

Tomoyose's descendants, that the letter contained an appeal for the return of trading rights to Ryukyu.[120]

Higa generally accepts Matayoshi's view with some modification. He likens the idealistic Heshikiya, Tomoyose, and others to the soldiers who took part in the February 26, 1936, military coup in Tokyo. None were willing to compromise (they were *"zettaisha"*).[121] Higa concludes that, in the main, the incident was a struggle between the royal government and a group that was working to undermine it or radically alter its policies. This struggle in turn exacerbated the divisions already present within society, such as those who advocated Confucian morality versus those who advocated the traditional freedoms of past ages or the scholars of Chinese literature versus the scholars of Japanese literature.[122]

Because the letter in question is not available, there are probably endless possibilities for speculating on its contents and the intentions behind it. Given the sparse evidence available, Higa's interpretation of the Heshikiya-Tomoyose Incident seems most reasonable. By the 1730s, the interests of Satsuma and Ryukyu's royal government under Sai On coincided so strongly that both were threatened by the activities of Heshikiya and Tomoyose. The incident contrasts markedly with the Chatan-Eso Affair, where, despite the vigor with which Satsuma prosecuted those involved, the royal government dragged its feet and ultimately meted out only minimal punishment. Because the activities of Heshikiya and Tomoyose were a direct challenge to the interests of both Satsuma and the royal government, not only were the punishments swift and severe, but the royal government was apparently successful in preventing Heshikiya, Tomoyose, and the others from becoming martyrs for a cause.

Sai On's praise of Satsuma in *Articles of Instruction* and his criticism of those "not familiar with the situation in former times" takes on new significance in light of the Heshikiya-Tomoyose Incident, particularly if Matayoshi and Higa are correct. Sai On's Ryukyu, about which he claimed "everything has become as we would want it to be," was anything but desirable for some Ryukyuans. Sai On encountered resistance to his vision of Ryukyu from peasants forbidden to practice their local festivals and employ shamans. Another, more urgent challenge came from dissatisfied elements within the traditional Shuri aristocracy. There was at least one other major challenge to Sai On's vision of Ryukyu, this one shrouded in an even thicker veil of silence than the Heshikiya-Tomoyose Incident. This challenge seems to have come from dissident elements in Kumemura, Sai On's base of power.

Near the Hinpun-gajumaru, a large, famous banyan tree in Nago, is a stone monument. The popular term for the monument is Hinpunshii, but it bears the official title Sanfu Longmai-bei (J. Sanpu Ryūmyaku-hi), roughly "Monument to the dragon vein connecting the three regions." In this context, "three regions" indicates the ancient divisions of Hokuzan, Chūzan, and Nanzan, covering the whole of Okinawa. Dragon vein is a geomantic term indicating a conduit of potent energy within the earth. The monument contains a lengthy inscription, revealing both by what it says and by what it suppresses.

According to the inscription, we can surmise that around 1740 a dispute either arose or became acute within the royal government. One faction claimed that Shuri was unsuitable as Ryukyu's capital owing to its complex topography and lack of flat land. Nago, on the other hand, had flat land in abundance and was thus more suitable as a capital. This faction advocated moving the capital to Nago, and we shall call it the "pro-Nago" faction. The pro-Nago faction further proposed that a transport canal be built to connect the harbor of Kogachi, in the northern part of the Motobu peninsula, with the harbor at Yabe in the southern part. This task could be accomplished with relative ease because almost all of the land between the two harbors was flat, though a single hill between them would have to be leveled.[123]

It was Sai On who most vigorously opposed the proposals and who wrote the text of the monument to explain to present and future generations why the pro-Nago faction was terribly mistaken. In an introductory statement, Sai On explains his reasons for erecting and inscribing the monument. Shuri, he begins, was the perfect site for the capital because of the topographical interconnections of Okinawa's various mountain ranges. Furthermore, the small hill separating the two harbors in the Motobu peninsula enabled this interconnectedness to extend as far north as Motobu and Nakijin and must therefore be left in place. Not everyone was aware of these "facts," we are told, and rumors still circulate to the effect that Nago would be a better site for the capital or that the two harbors should be connected. Therefore: "If such a thing were to be done, our country would lose its topographical interconnectedness. Because there would be terrible consequences for our country, I have expressed my desire to inscribe the above points on a monument to be set up in Nago."[124] One senses, of course, that there was much more at stake here than topographical interconnectedness, but Sai On provides no clue about what other political issues might be connected with the dispute over moving the capital and constructing the canal. The geomantic terms in which the argument is cast almost certainly obscure other issues entirely unconnected with the ways of wind and water (fengshui).

Sai On began his detailed arguments by criticizing those who would extol the superiority of either mountains or flatland, since both types of land are necessary and complementary:

In my own view, constellations delineate the heavens and rivers and mountains crisscross the earth, and there is nothing more poignant than the beauty of heaven and earth in complementary combination. Therefore, what forms the patterns in the earth is that which soars upward, forming mountains and hills. Mounds and hills dissipate and become flat plains and wet wastelands, which is all nothing but the combining and dissipating of the two physical forms of heaven and earth [yin and yang]. With this knowledge, when we observe places with mounds and hills, we know the origins of flatland and the so-called "unitary essence permeating the myriad mountains."[125]

Mesaki Shigekazu has pointed out that as geomantic knowledge spread to diverse groups in Ryukyu, it assumed varied forms. A quasi-science in one form, it blended into the native religion and popular superstitions in others.[126] Sai On's geomantic thought closely resembled Confucian metaphysics.

In the second half of the passage above, Sai On discusses the particular case of Ryukyu:

The three regions and forty-seven districts of our country are divided into, and united by, hills and flatland. The combination of these two produce the forces that are clearly manifest and those existing as potentialities. It allows us the benefit of having the same trunk with different branches and greatly reveals the potency of the land as expressed in the qualities of nature.[127]

Here, Sai On employs a common rhetorical strategy of aligning his point of view with the forces of the cosmos. It is still not clear, however, why these "facts" necessarily lead to the conclusion that Shuri would be the best site for the capital city.

The specific argument for Shuri as the capital employs an entirely different rhetorical strategy, an appeal to ancient authority. Sai On invoked the authority of the legendary sage Tenson, the alleged founder of Ryukyu as a political entity: "Tenson was the first to come to this land and found a country, establishing the royal castle at Shuri. As he based this selection on spiritual insight, how could it have anything to do with ordinary human understanding, and why is it that later generations have harbored such foolish views [regarding the ideal location for the capital]?"[128] This move from geomantic theory to an appeal to authority is a surprising turn in the argument. Shuri became the capital only after Shō Hashi unified Okinawa and well before there was any knowledge of geomancy in Ryukyu. It is quite probable that the pro-Nago faction had better arguments from a purely geomantic perspective and that Sai On felt unable to counter them directly. He therefore had to enlist the aid of the most venerable figure in Ryukyu's past, the mysterious Tenson.[129]

The text continues by summarizing the arguments of those who advocate connecting Kogachi and Yabe by canal to make boat travel more convenient. Sai On then links this issue, about which he seems to have better geomantic arguments, to that of moving the capital and criticizes both together:

> Ah! The royal castle and this hill are both mysteriously tapped into the dragon vein. How could one recklessly move the royal castle to another place? How could one recklessly level the hill and build a canal? The two districts of Nakijin and Motobu have but this one hill on which to rely to connect them and to make the three regions a single entity. The three regions, too, have but this single hill to connect them and thus preserve the vitality of Kyūyō [Okinawa]. If this hill is leveled and a canal built, then it is not only a matter of these two districts becoming disconnected, but of all Okinawa certainly losing the vitality of being a single entity.[130]

One wonders if the vitality subject to loss here was as much Sai On's political power as it was the *qi* coursing through the earth's veins.

In his conclusion, Sai On brings the authority of the king to bear on the issue:

> Recently, the king, with his heavenly nature and virtuous learning, has been worrying about this matter anew each day, and his deep concern has become most acute. In particular, he ordered his minister [Sai] On to have writing inscribed on a stone monument forever to inform subsequent generations of the connection between the destiny of the country and the potency of the earth, and of the unitary pattern *(li)* that permeates the myriad mountains.[131]

In this brief text, Sai On arrayed the cosmos, the potency of the earth, the founding sage of the country, and the king on his side. Beneath the one-sided surface of Sai On's inscription lies a major conflict that the monument seeks to suppress. It is unlikely that the creation of it brought an end to the conflict, because it was a full nine years after the monument was first erected that the names of Sai On and the other two members of the Council of Three were added to the end of the inscription. This addition of the names probably signaled Sai On's victory and official acceptance of his views.[132]

Who, then, were these opponents of Sai On, the pro-Nago faction? Their voices were so well suppressed that we do not know for sure. If indeed they advanced geomantic arguments for their proposals, then it is almost certain that the faction consisted of Okinawans from Kumemura. It is unlikely that anyone else would have had the requisite technical knowledge, and even if a few *yukatchu* outside Kumemura did have a deep knowledge of geomancy, it is unlikely that other Okinawans would have acknowledged their expertise.

If we assume that Sai On's opposition came from a group within Kumemura, we should ask who might have benefited from moving the capital to Nago and who might have had reason to oppose Sai On. Tei Junsoku, of course, was a famous Kumemura figure associated with Nago. Sai On upstaged Tei Junsoku on at least two occasions: when appointed as Shō Kei's tutor and in handling the Valuation Incident. Such circumstantial evidence has led a number of scholars to state that the monument was the result of a longstanding feud between Sai On and Tei Junsoku, which continued in the form of factional conflict after the latter's death.[133] This theory of a conflict between Sai On and Tei Junsoku has also been handed down to the present as a folk legend, and while it has merit, it is based largely on speculation, as Takara points out.[134] The precise identity, motivation, and circumstances of these opponents of Sai On remain unknown, a topic for further research. For now, traces of their suppressed voices exist only in the stone of the Sanfu Longmai-bei.

Conclusions

Sai On and his supporters attempted to re-create Ryukyu in their image of an ideal society, and they achieved a substantial measure of success. On the surface, the rise of Sai On's vision of Ryukyu may seem evolutionary, the inevitable result of reconciling Shō Shōken's pro-Japan vision and Tei Junsoku's pro-China vision based on Ryukyu's particular circumstances. As this chapter shows, however, Sai On's vision of Ryukyu encountered substantial opposition from diverse groups and individuals. It was a potentially unstable vision of Ryukyu that never achieved closure in practice. During his lifetime, Sai On was able to check or destroy opposition to his vision of Ryukyu, and it continued to dominate official policy until the end of the kingdom.

The fault lines that had divided Ryukyuan society in the eighteenth century—pro-Japan versus pro-China, Buddhism versus Confucianism, Shuri versus Kumemura, the Sai On faction versus the Tei Junsoku faction within Kumemura, peasant versus *yukatchu*—continued to divide it in the nineteenth century. The very success of Sai On's vision helped create further conflict among Ryukyuan elites during the decades following Sai On's death.

CHAPTER 5

Contested Visions
of Sai On's Ryukyu

Sai On spent the last decade of his life putting his view of Ryukyu into writing, and his legacy lasted long after his death in 1761. King Shō Kei died in 1751, and the next two kings took an active approach to ruling. The policies of Shō Boku (r. 1752–1795) further moved Ryukyu in the direction Sai On had advocated. The next king, Shō On (r. 1796–1802), whose name was no coincidence, continued the process of Confucianizing the kingdom by broadening Ryukyu's institutional base of formal Confucian learning. This move created a storm of controversy and fierce opposition from most residents of Kumemura. With some irony, it was the custodians of Chinese studies who opposed the logical extension of Sai On's vision of Ryukyu. After Shō On, Ryukyu suffered gradual economic decline. Owing to internal division within Ryukyu's *yukatchu* and economic decline caused by a number of factors, many beyond Ryukyu's control, Sai On's vision ultimately proved unsustainable in practice.

Shō Boku

Sai On retired from formal office when Shō Kei died, but he served Shō Boku as an advisor during the early years of his reign. During Shō Kei's reign, Sai On worked to enhance the prestige of the king and the royal line, the changes in state ceremonial discussed previously being but one example. Shō Boku took steps to enhance the prestige of the royal line even further. For example, he established a hall for the veneration of the royal ancestral tablets in 1753 and initiated a yearly feast before the royal ancestral graves. In Shō Boku's posthumous portrait *(ogoe)*, he is depicted with nearly twice the number of jewels on his crown than his predecessors.[1] Shō Boku actively supported Sai On's forest management system. In 1778, he traveled to Kunigami to inspect forest lands, and in 1791, upon hearing that forest lands were becoming depleted, he had the *sessei* and Council of Three make a tour of forest lands.[2]

Sai On lived at a time when Ryukyu had attained the peak of its post-invasion prosperity. The first indications of the severe economic problems that would steadily worsen during the nineteenth century appeared during Shō Boku's reign. By 1791, the royal government was 7,000 *kanme* of silver in debt to Satsuma owing in part to an increase in the number of embassies it was required to send to Edo. Crop failures and famine showed up in rural areas with increasing frequency. A devastating tidal wave hit the islands of Miyako and Yaeyama, literally washing away many of the resources Sai On had put into increasing the population of Yaeyama. In response, Shō Boku's government undertook surveys, dispatched *gechiyaku,* troubleshooters sent from Shuri to oversee the revival of badly declining areas, and forced wealthy households to make "loans" to the government. The percentage of *yukatchu* in the population increased dramatically during Shō Boku's reign, probably because many wealthy households were given *yukatchu* status in return for their loans.[3]

Perhaps the most important development during Shō Boku's reign was the promulgation of *Ryūkyū karitsu,* the kingdom's first comprehensive legal code. The project to create the code began in 1775 and reached completion in 1786. According to the *Kyūyō:*

> In our country, there has never been a fixed system of rewards and punishments. When confronted with a matter needing attention, it was decided on the basis of precedents. But many of the former precedents are unreasonable. Therefore, [Sessei] Shō Tenteki Ie Ueekata Chōkei and Baa Kokugi Peekumi Ryōtoku were ordered to gather together [edifying past examples], compile a book of noble deeds and legal sanctions, and use it for creating laws.[4]

The introduction of *Ryūkyū karitsu* reveals the Confucian ideology informing the code as a whole:

> Although the way of governing a country is based on virtuous teachings, we must also establish a code of laws. The basic purpose of these legal texts is to banish the evil the common people have acquired and resurrect their inherent goodness. They are written for the purpose of avoiding punishment. . . . Because the king had this law code compiled to aid widely in the transformation of customs, one should respectfully acknowledge his regal mind and enthusiastically read this text on a daily basis to investigate the limitless pattern of the Way, which is contained herein.[5]

The entire code consists of one volume of cases to serve as examples of exemplary conduct, and to encourage such conduct by specifying rewards, and eighteen volumes of laws, prohibitions, and specification of penalties, occasionally illustrated with past cases. Miyagi points out that the basic structure of the code, though not always the details of particular clauses, was virtually identical with the Qing legal code. Miyagi attributes this resemblance to Shō Boku's strong admiration of Qing China.[6]

Shō On

With the tremendous symbolic importance of names in East Asian cultures, there is perhaps no better evidence of Sai On's stature than that a king should be named after him, an official of *ueekata* status.[7] Shō On ascended the throne at age twelve and died at age nineteen—poisoned by his enemies, according to rumor. During his short reign, he promoted major changes to Ryukyuan scholarly and political institutions. In 1798, Shō On revised the *kanshō* system. For roughly the first century of the *kanshō* system, it was the nobility of Shuri who went to study in China. By the late fifteenth century, however, study in China had become the exclusive domain of the residents of Kumemura.[8] Shō On decreed that henceforth, instead of all four Ryukyuan students being selected from Kumemura, two would be selected from among the *yukatchu* of Shuri.

A year prior to this decision, Sai Scishō (1737?–1798), an outstanding, politically ambitious Confucian scholar and relative of Sai On, became the king's tutor. Although from Kumemura, Sai Seishō was a firm backer of the new policy and may have first proposed it to the king.[9] In 1797, the Council of Fifteen, a group of high-ranking officials just below the Council of Three, passed a resolution supporting the change to half of the *kanshō* coming from Shuri. The resolution begins by establishing historical precedent for the new policy, pointing out that for over fifty years following the establishment of Kumemura, princes and other high-ranking Shuri officials became *kanshō*. The resolution continues by pointing out that in recent decades the royal court at Shuri has become Confucianized:

> The educational transformation *(kyōka)* emanating from the Chinese court has spread widely, reaching distant countries . . . and has caused a deep moral transformation of our court. The *kanshō* set out to pursue study, and, upon returning, they transformed our law codes so that they promote the way of loyalty and filial piety. Throughout the country, all know to respect the ruler and their fathers.

The proposal also included a call for the establishment of a Confucian academy in Shuri. It ended with a reiteration of support for half of the *kanshō* coming from Shuri and expressed hope that this change, plus the academy, would aid in the transformation of even the common people.[10]

The view of the Council of Fifteen received wide approval in Shuri. The following year, the court sent a memo to Kumemura asking for a response from its ranked residents. Shocked, the officials of Kumemura were unable to come up with a speedy or effective rebuttal. Formulating a response took over four months, all the while the plan was being implemented in Shuri. Finally, when it came time to select *kanshō,* Kumemura officials sent a petition to the court protesting the new policy. Nearly all of Kumemura's leading residents signed on to the petition, but two prominent scholars, Sai Seishō and Tei Kōtoku (1735–?), refused to affix their seals.[11]

The petition began by stating, and frequently repeated, that the new policy was a threat to the livelihood of the residents of Kumemura. Like the text of the proposal of the Council of Fifteen, the petition also used history to bolster its case. Instead of stressing that the first *kanshō* were aristocrats from Shuri, of course, the Kumemura petition emphasized that, ever since the reign of Shō Shin, Kumemura residents exclusively had filled the ranks of *kanshō.* The protest then recounted that it was the first Ming emperor's sending of a group of Fujianese to Kumemura that first established proper ceremonial, music, and literary studies in Ryukyu. Following this narrative was a detailed accounting of the invaluable services that various residents of Kumemura have had rendered to Ryukyu as intermediaries between it and China.[12]

The Council of Three rejected the petition and ordered the magistrate of Kumemura to cease opposing the two and two policy on the grounds that the decision had already been made. The text of the order stated that since the purpose of the National Academy in China was to transform distant countries, study there should not be a monopoly of Kumemura but should be available to all Ryukyuan elites. Furthermore, the order stated, Kumemura was still guaranteed two students and the policy would not have a significant effect on the traditional occupations of its residents. In the face of the Council of Three's directives, the residents of Kumemura rioted. They directed most of their anger at Sai Seishō and Tei Kōtoku, attacking their residences and even hurling excrement at them. Reminiscent of Heshikiya Chōbin two generations earlier, the Kumemura leadership even sent a petition of protest to Satsuma's resident representative.[13]

Also reminiscent of Heshikiya's day, the royal government reacted with a strong show of force, arresting ringleaders and rioters over the course of several days. The penalties were stiff. Major instigators were banished to remote locations, often other islands. Other participants in the rioting were forced to retire from public life and become Buddhist monks. One of the ringleaders, Matsunaga Peekumi, was exiled to Kumejima. *Conversation of the Three Birds*

(Sanchō mondō), a strong critique of the present government, although ostensibly anonymous, was widely regarded as the product of his brush.[14]

Written in Japanese in a style intended for broad accessibility, *Conversation of the Three Birds* features a heron (familiar with wetlands and rice fields), a hawk (familiar with meadows and dry fields), and a crow (familiar with villages and urban areas) who have gathered to discuss the condition of Kumejima. They all agree that conditions in their habitats have declined significantly during their lifetimes. The heron initially states that the reason for this decline "must be because of the cumulative effect of natural disasters such as typhoons, floods, and droughts." Therefore, "There is nothing to be done but accept the destiny *(un)* of times."[15] The crow argues against such passive acceptance, saying "Heaven *(ten)* rewards goodness and punishes evil, and good fortune or bad, harm or benefit is something people bring upon themselves."[16] After describing the island's woes in great detail, the birds then discuss appropriate policies to rectify them. At one point, they discuss the king's responsibility, with the crow initially arguing that the king has so much to do that he could not possibly be responsible for the sorry state of Kumejima. The heron, however, strongly disagrees:

> Even though the ruler of the realm does not single-handedly administer its wide expanse, he appoints and directs the various officials, so it would be desirable that he himself establish fundamental principles. Although ours is a small island, because there are many official posts, were the ruler to appoint the right people to the right positions, fortify the law, clarify specific duties, encourage everyone in their duties, discuss what is good and evil, and clarify rewards and punishments, even were he to remain in his residence, [good government] could be accomplished.[17]

After this indirect rebuke of the king, the birds continue discussing the policies and other measures required to revive the moral and material life of the island's people. As this summary suggests, Confucian principles of government inform *Conversation of the Three Birds,* the birds usually coming to the conclusion that educational transformation from above is the key to reviving their island.

The month after the rioting in Kumemura ended, its residents experienced a second incursion into their traditional domains when the court enacted the other item in the original Council of Fifteen proposal: establishing a university in Shuri. Shō On announced the establishment of a national university *(kokugaku)* in Shuri and the government's intention to create a system of lesser schools branching out from it, eventually extending into the countryside. Scholars from

Kumemura would have benefited from the employment opportunities the new university would offer, at least in the short term, but the leadership of Kumemura opposed the prestigious title of the new educational institution:

> In Beijing there stands the National Academy, and it is called a university *(daigaku)*. A Confucian temple is situated in the left part of the campus, and entering students first pay their respects there. Also, on the first and fifteenth of each month, rites are conducted at the temple. . . . The school you are constructing has no Confucian temple, and even if you call it the national academy *(kokugaku)*, it is in fact more like the schools *(shoin)* in each district of China. . . . If you call it a *shoin*, it would correspond to the Chinese *shoin*, which we humbly think would be most appropriate.[18]

Perhaps realizing the futility of trying to block the university outright, the leadership of Kumemura at least hoped to have its status downgraded. The Meirindō academy in Kumemura, of course, had a Confucian temple, making it, in the logic of the petition, roughly comparable to China's National Academy. Shō On retained the name Kokugaku despite the petition.

The establishment of a university in Shuri seems to have been in accord with Sai On's vision of an ideal future. In *One Man's Views,* he called for the establishment of academies and for subjecting the students therein to periodic examinations. If, he argued, "they are placed according to their particular talents in suitable posts, we can expect an annual increase in the number of talented individuals." He called for the establishment of schools after such time that the greater part of the basis of the way of government has been established.[19] Although not a high priority, there is evidence that Sai On pursued the possibility of formal Confucian education for the *yukatchu* of Shuri. According to a 1741 diary entry of a Kumemura resident, Shō Kei communicated to Prince Motobu his desire that all young *yukatchu* in Shuri take up scholarship and that he hoped eventually to construct an academy. Not sure how best to proceed, Shō Kei suggested to the prince that a seminar be established in Shuri castle for all *yukatchu,* regardless of status, to be supervised by an instructor brought in from Kumemura. The king hoped that such a step would kindle sufficient enthusiasm for study among the elites of Shuri to pave the way for a successful school. He instructed the prince to sound out the opinion of leading members of the Shuri *yukatchu* regarding the matter. Majikina interprets Sai On's statement in *One Man's Views* as indicating doubt concerning the base of support in Shuri for the creation of a university at the time.[20]

The seminar that Shō Kei suggested started in the 1740s, and in 1751 lectures for the *yukatchu* of Shuri began on a regular schedule in each of the three districts *(hira)* of the capital. Three years later, the three-lecture series combined to form a single program, which later evolved into Shō On's National University.[21] Unlike Kumemura's Meirindō, whose purpose was to train diplomats for service in China, the school in Shuri was intended as a training center for government officials. Another development that presaged the Kokugaku was the establishment of a limited civil service examination system (O. *kō,* J. *ka* = *kakyo*), probably in 1760, but no later than 1763. The Ryukyuan exams were job-specific and were for lower and middle level specialist positions. There were exams, for example, for musicians, painters, secretarial and clerical posts in various government offices, the various grades of instructors in Kumemura, and for the selection of *kanshō*. According to Majikina, most exams were highly competitive, with only a small percentage of passers.[22]

In establishing the National University, Shō On sought to extend the connection between specific knowledge and government office to the higher ranks of officialdom. He made this intent explicit in a set of general principles promulgated at the time of the founding of the school, in which he declared unequivocally that henceforth, merit, not heredity, would be the most important criterion in the selection of officials:

> Without consideration of whether his lineage be exulted or base, if someone accumulates meritorious deeds, works hard at scholarship, and proposes plans that are beneficial to the country, then even if he be the son of a commoner, I will raise him up and make use of him. On the other hand, if someone fails his exams, indulges excessively in leisure, and fails to abide by wise teachings, then even if he be the son of a high-ranking *yukatchu,* I will have him dismissed and removed from office.[23]

These were strong words from an assertive king of but fifteen years. Had he not died four years later, it would have been interesting to see the extent to which he was prepared to carry out this stated attack on hereditary privilege.

By the start of the nineteenth century, Kumemura was losing its monopoly on Chinese studies and Confucian scholarship in nearly every area. Although the kingdom did not last long enough for Kumemura to lose its overall predominance in the academic realm, its position eroded steadily. Maeda Giken, following Higashionna, points out that from the reign of Shō Shin through that of Shō Ei (r. 1573–1586), Japanese monks inscribed all of Ryukyu's monuments. During the reigns of Shō Kei and Shō Boku, only Kumemura personnel performed this task. By contrast, from Shō On's time, residents of Shuri inscribed all of Ryukyu's official monuments.[24]

Sai On's ideal Ryukyu was a Confucian society, and in his day Kumemura residents were the custodians of the knowledge required to create it. Although Confucianism in any form never took hold among most of the peasants, it had, by the start of the nineteenth century, become the undisputed ideology of the state and its elite groups, including the *yukatchu* of Shuri. The dominance of Confucianism, however, did not lessen the intensity of political conflict within Ryukyu. The very success of the Confucianizing efforts of Sai On and his allies ended Kumemura's monopoly on Chinese and Confucian studies.

In part, Kumemura's loss was the result of the universalistic, totalizing claims common to nearly all varieties of Confucianism. Perhaps more important was the fusion of academic pursuits and political administration, one of Sai On's most significant accomplishments. Prior to the mid-eighteenth century, these two activities existed in separate realms. Of course, diplomacy with China was of great political importance for Ryukyu, but until Sai On, there had been a significant buffer between academics and domestic politics. Shō On's policies were, in many respects, the culmination of the work started by his namesake.

The developments of the last decade of the eighteenth century may shed light on the earlier, Kumemura-based opposition to Sai On that took the form of geomantic arguments about the proper location of the capital. Perhaps some elements within Kumemura realized that one of the results of Sai On's successful attempt to create a Confucian Ryukyu would be a loss of Kumemura's monopoly on Chinese and Confucian studies. Such a loss, of course, would have had severe economic consequences for this community of Ryukyuan elites. Iha interpreted the rioting in Kumemura similarly. In his view, the leadership of Kumemura was desperately trying to prevent the emergence of another Sai On (in the person of Sai Seishō), while Shuri was trying to encourage it.[25]

Ryukyu's Nineteenth-Century Decline

Japan's formal annexation of Ryukyu, a process that took place during the decade of the 1870s, brought Sai On's Ryukyu to a close. Throughout the previous six decades, however, Sai On's Ryukyu came under increasing stress. Unlike the eighteenth century, this stress was less because of opposing visions of Ryukyu and more because of the kingdom's steady economic decline. Shō Kō (r. 1804–1828) seems to have broken under the strain of Ryukyu's problems. He abdicated the throne in 1828 and sequestered himself at Urasoe castle. Owing to the numerous poignant poems he left behind, Dana characterizes Shō Kō as the most "human" of Ryukyu's kings.[26] A major blow to royal finances came from declining sugar prices. Much of Ryukyu's mid-eighteenth century prosperity derived from sugar production and sales. In 1706, the first Ryukyuan sugar appeared on the Osaka market, and by the 1720s, Satsuma's warehouse in Osaka sold only Ryukyuan sugar. By mid-century, the royal government had become dependent on sugar sales to finance its diplomacy and trade with China. At the same time, Satsuma's government had also come to depend heavily on sugar sales and sought to produce more from its own territories. In 1745, for example, it ordered that all tax "rice" from the northern Ryukyu islands be paid in sugar. Although Ryukyu and Satsuma depended on each other for cooperation in the sugar trade, and in the trade with China tied thereto, by the late eighteenth century, they also became competitors in the marketing of sugar. Through various regulations, Satsuma sought to prevent Ryukyu from putting its sugar on the market before the domain did, and Ryukyuans continually tried to circumvent these regulations.[27]

The increasing supply of sugar, the resulting drop in prices, and competition with Satsuma were by far the most important reasons for the kingdom's economic decline. Furthermore, Satsuma's relationship with Ryukyu grew more exploitative in general from 1830 onward owing to the domain's drive to reform its finances.[28] Other economic changes also contributed to Ryukyu's financial woes. For example, Britain's trade with the Qing empire in Guangzhou indirectly harmed the Ryukyu-Satsuma-China trade by siphoning off many of the best trade goods to the south. In 1751, only nine British ships sailed into Guangzhou to trade. By 1789, the number had increased to sixty-one, with an additional twenty-five ships from other countries. Because the China trade via Ryukyu became less profitable for Satsuma, the domain put less capital into it, which hurt both royal finances and the private income of Ryukyuan elites.[29]

As the state of royal finances declined, so did the economy in the countryside. Some agricultural villages simply died out. Outbreaks of disease were common, killing between 3,000 and 4,000 in each of the years 1825 and 1832. Neither Shō Kō nor his successor, Shō Iku (r. 1829–1848) were able to come up with any policies to deal with the worsening economic situation. What steps they took were limited to ad hoc, largely symbolic gestures. For example, Shō Iku skimped on his investiture ceremony and distributed the surplus funds to the districts for economic relief. By the time Ryukyu's last king, Shō Tai (r. 1849–1879), ascended the throne, the royal government was in such bad financial shape that his investiture was delayed eighteen years.

By the time of Ryukyu's formal annexation, the kingdom had long been in economic decline. Nevertheless, its formal and informal institutions continued to function in the sense that they helped prop up Ryukyu's social and economic hierarchy. Relations up and down that hierarchy, however, became increasingly exploitative as those above sought to extract more from those below. By the time of the kingdom's end, many of Ryukyu's peasants lived and worked in wretched conditions. Annexation by Japan had the potential to improve their lot, although, as we shall see, it did not have this effect in practice. In the 1870s, Sai On's ideal Confucian society was nowhere to be found.

Epilogue and Conclusions

The Ryukyu kingdom's protracted demise at the hands of Japan's Meiji state took place from 1872 until the mid-1880s. Its assimilation into the Japanese nation-state took much longer—the early 1920s in terms of institutions and administrative practices. Cultural assimilation is more difficult to assess, owing in part to the problems inherent in the idea of culture itself.[1] Still, a case can be made that the cultural assimilation of Ryukyu/Okinawa into Japan is not yet complete. As in the days of the kingdom, modern Okinawa saw a continuation of the process of constructing Okinawan identities in relation to both intra-Okinawa and extra-Okinawa Others and within a complex international environment. The particular issues and ideologies informing this process in Okinawa, however, differed significantly from those of the early-modern kingdom. This chapter examines some of these issues and ideologies within the framework of a brief narrative of modern Okinawa.

Narrowly speaking, the *Ryūkyū shobun* ("disposition of Ryukyu") took place between 1872 and 1879, but the precise nature and extent of Japanese sovereignty over the Ryukyu islands continued to be negotiated well into the 1880s. The term *Ryūkyū shobun* clearly indicates a desire on the part of the Meiji leaders to eliminate the ambiguity in Ryukyu's relationship with Japan and other countries. *Ryūkyū shobun* is difficult to translate because it has taken on many different meanings, and its precise significance continues to be debated. In its simplest sense, the creation of Okinawa Prefecture in 1879 ended the Domain of Ryukyu *(Ryūkyū han)*, formerly the Kingdom of Ryukyu, by making it part of Japan. But the *Ryūkyū shobun* was not simply an internal, administrative reorganization. The process of incorporating Ryukyu into the boundaries of the Japanese state called into question previous modes of East Asian interstate relations as Japan employed new notions of sovereignty based on European traditions and international law.[2] The *Ryūkyū shobun* was an international event that included complex negotiations involving China, Japan, Korea, the United States, France, and Ryukyuans resident in Tokyo, Okinawa, and China.[3] Historians from a variety of backgrounds have criticized the Meiji state's portrayal of the *Ryūkyū shobun* as simply an internal administrative change.[4] These critiques raise the question of whether Ryukyu/Okinawa was Japan's first colony, though typically by their refusal explicitly to mention or discuss it.[5]

From Kingdom to Colony: Ryūkyū Shobun and the Period of Preserving Old Customs

Shimazu Nariakira (1809–1858) became *daimyō* of Satsuma in 1851 and launched an ambitious program of reforms that included a plan to develop a trading relationship with France through Ryukyu. The plan required the active cooperation of leading Ryukyuan officials, who would negotiate a draft treaty between Ryukyu and France (Ryukyu already had a treaty with the United States). In the face of these developments, the leadership of Ryukyu split into a faction that opposed cooperating with Satsuma and a faction that supported cooperation. The latter faction included Makishi Peechin, Onga Ueekata, and Oroku Ueekata. This Ryukyuan factional split mirrored a similar split within Satsuma, with Nariakira's half-brother Shimazu Hisamitsu fiercely opposed to the ongoing reforms. Nariakira died suddenly of food poisoning in 1858, when negotiations with France were well under way, and Hisamitsu and his supporters took over. The effects were felt almost immediately in Ryukyu, where the faction opposed to cooperation with Satsuma suddenly became the favorites of Satsuma's new leaders. These Ryukyuans vigorously attacked Makishi and his supporters, ostensibly for crimes such as slander and bribery, but in actuality, for their previous cooperation with Nariakira. The punishments were severe. Makishi and Onga eventually paid with their lives. This bitter dispute had lasting repercussions for Ryukyu/Okinawa. Most important, it left the Okinawan nobility deeply divided into two factions. Japanese officials connected with the *Ryūkyū shobun* utilized this factional division to their advantage during the 1870s.

Late in 1871, a storm drove a Ryukyuan ship from Miyako Island into the southern coast of Taiwan, an area not under Chinese control. Local tribesmen killed fifty-four of the Ryukyuans, and twelve managed to escape through the jungle to a Chinese enclave. This incident became the first stepping stone for Meiji Japan's annexation of Ryukyu. The next year, Japan's ambassador to China made a formal complaint and asked the Qing government to punish the Taiwanese. China's response was to disclaim responsibility for large areas of Taiwan. Diplomatic activity continued for several years over the matter, the details of which need not concern us here. The result was that Japan eventually sent a force to Taiwan under the command of Saigō Tsugumichi in June 1874.

China's Zongli Yamen (the highest organ of state for foreign affairs) reacted to Japan's unilateral action with shock and disbelief. One reason for this reaction was the domination of China's foreign affairs by men who were convinced that Japan and China should cooperate, working together to resist European and American imperialism. Li Hongzhang, for example, described the incident as "Satsuma samurai, bearing resentment at the abolition of the domains in favor of prefectures, sought an excuse to take over Taiwan, and Japan's central government was unable to suppress them." When the Zongli Yamen met with Ōkubo Toshimichi, Ōkubo brandished international law, saying that the Taiwanese were not under Qing jurisdiction. Ultimately, with British mediation, China signed off on a treaty agreeing that Japan's action was correct and also agreeing to pay compensation money to the families of the Ryukyuan victims (little of which ever reached Okinawa, however).[6] What is particularly important is that the treaty referred to the Ryukyuans as Japanese subjects. In other words, an international treaty, with British blessing, stated that Ryukyuans were legally Japanese.

During the early stages of Japan's negotiations with China over the incident in Taiwan, the Meiji state took further action to control Ryukyu. In October 1872, Japan's foreign minister presented Ryukyuan envoys with an Imperial edict declaring the creation of the Domain of Ryukyu *(Ryūkyū han)*, and declaring King Shō Tai to be domain king *(hanō)*. Caught completely by surprise, the Ryukyuan envoys could do nothing but express gratitude. This change of names from kingdom to domain was intended in part to facilitate Japan's representing the slain Ryukyuans vis-à-vis China, and ultimately to facilitate annexation of Ryukyu. Strictly speaking, the establishment of the Domain of Ryukyu marked the start of the *Ryūkyū shobun*.

In 1875, the Meiji government dispatched Matsuda Michiyuki to Okinawa with orders to settle the Ryukyu issue. One of his first moves was to order a cessation of all ties with China. Several prominent Ryukyuans protested this order speaking in terms of Ryukyu's long history of dual obligations to China and Japan and describing the two countries as Ryukyu's father and mother. Having long existed in space between China and Japan within a framework of sovereignty and diplomatic relations based on Confucian ideals and ritual *(li)*, Ryukyu's history had abruptly collided with radically new conceptions of sovereignty based on international law and the nation-state. Internally, the Makishi-Onga Affair divisions were still in place. The side that had once opposed cooperation with Nariakira had continued in power and now stood for the status quo and noncooperation with the Meiji state and Matsuda. The once pro-Nariakira faction now became associated with support for Matsuda's plan to incorporate Ryukyu fully into Meiji Japan.[7]

Because the anti-Matsuda faction held sway in the royal government, Ryukyuan officials engaged in tactics of passive resistance and delay. By early

1879 Matsuda, who had brought in military forces from the mainland, moved to force the issue. On March 11, he announced that the domain would be abolished and made into a prefecture on the thirty-first day of the same month. On that day, he and a contingent of soldiers marched into Shuri castle. The king offered no resistance and soon left for Tokyo, a newly minted marquis in the Meiji peerage system.

The issue of Ryukyuan sovereignty, however, was not yet settled in the international arena. As with Japan's intervention in Taiwan, China protested the unilateral annexation of Ryukyu. Prominent Ryukyuans began setting sail for China, taking up residence in the Ryukyuan trading center at Fujian and frequently pleading with the Qing court to intervene on Ryukyu's behalf. Japan entered into negotiations with China in 1880, based in part on the prior mediation of former U.S. President Grant. Both sides proposed dividing the Ryukyu islands. China pushed for a three-way split, with Amami-Ōshima and surrounding islands going to Japan, Okinawa being restored to the control of the former Ryukyuan king, and Miyako and Yaeyama going to China. Japan proposed a two-way split. Essentially, Japan offered to give Yaeyama and Miyako to China in return for revising the Sino-Japanese treaty of 1873 to grant Japan the right to conduct business in China's interior and most-favored-nation status. In both scenarios, China intended to restore Miyako and Yaeyama to the control of the Ryukyuan king after it had acquired the territory.[8] Japan, although claiming that the *Ryūkyū shobun* was simply an internal affair, was willing to give up some of its territory in exchange for favorable treaty concessions. In this context, Japan's view of Ryukyu was that it was a conquered territory to be used as a bargaining chip in international negotiations. This same view reappeared in 1947, when the Shōwa emperor sacrificed Okinawa to U.S. control to accelerate the end of U.S. occupation of the mainland. By late 1880, both sides had come to an agreement along the lines of Japan's proposal, but China refused to ratify it. Negotiations continued for several more years off and on, but the press of more urgent matters eventually caused China to give up on attempting to resolve its differences with Japan over Ryukyu.

Japanese actions within the new prefecture similarly indicate a de facto status more like a colony or conquered territory than an integral part of the motherland. All prewar governors were central government appointees from the mainland with little authority to make major administrative changes without approval from Tokyo. The second governor, Uesugi Shigenori, was unusual in his concern for the plight of ordinary Okinawans. He made a personal tour of Okinawa and noted the misery of the peasants, who labored under former *yukachu* and local officials much as they had in the days of the kingdom. He went to Tokyo with a plan for a major reform in 1882, in which he proposed to streamline Okinawan administration, effecting an estimated savings in salaries of 90,916 yen out of a total budget of 158,177 yen. His plan called for spending the money thus saved on education and the promotion of industry, and it entailed no money from Tokyo and no new taxes on Okinawans. After receiving no reply, Uesugi appealed a second time, in the form of a lengthy essay on the plight of Okinawa's people and the urgency of reform. The governor's assistant wrote an impassioned plea to Treasury Minister Matsukata Masayoshi supporting the reforms. He pointed out that while the central government gave Hokkaidō over 1,000,000 yen annually, it gave nothing to Okinawa and extracted 200,000 yen in taxes from the impoverished islands. "Ah! why have only the people of this place been driven to the extreme of misfortune?" he wrote. This time, Tokyo gave an answer: no. Its stated reason was that Okinawa was not yet ready for such reforms.[9]

Indeed, Tokyo was preparing to implement an explicit policy in Okinawa of "preserving old customs" *(kyūkan hozon)*. In 1882, China was still pressing for concessions regarding Ryukyuan sovereignty and increasing numbers of former *yukatchu* were fleeing to Fujian. Uesugi's desire to remove most *yukatchu* and former local officials from power accelerated this flight to China. Soon after his reform proposal, Tokyo replaced Uesugi with Iwamura Michitoshi. Iwamura sought to use the former *yukatchu* and local officials to help govern the prefecture. He announced his strong support for the continuation of stipend payments for high-ranking *yukatchu* and continued formal recognition of the lower-ranking members of the aristocracy. His administration also provided economic aid to non-stipended *yukatchu,* such as seed money to start businesses. The lower strata of the *yukatchu* nevertheless encountered great difficulty in finding employment. Some worked as schoolteachers, some worked as interpreters for mainland Japanese officials, but most took up farming under arrangements similar to Sai On's *yaadui* system. Iwamura's support for the continuation of past practices brought many of the self-exiled *yukatchu* back from China.[10] Government stipends for high-ranking *yukatchu* continued until 1909.

The preservation of old customs policy affected four key aspects of Okinawa life: land tenure, taxes, local administration, and education. The *jiwari* system of land tenure continued from the days of the kingdom. In it, the village was the standard unit of agricultural production, and land was periodically redistributed among the villagers. Taxation continued as before, with levies on villages. It was up to local officials to distribute land and tax burdens, and they rarely did so equitably. Particularly oppressive was the sugar levy.

Although in 1882 it became permissible to pay salt and rice levies in cash, the sugar tax was not payable in cash until the general land reform of 1903 that did away with the former system. Individual sales of sugar were prohibited until the entire sugar tax had been paid, and all sales of sugar were to the government at a price set below that which the open market would bear. The prefectural government then sold the sugar on the open market at Osaka for a substantial profit. Like taxes and land distribution, the former administrative divisions of *magiri* and villages remained in place, as did the people who governed them. Local laws and customary practices also continued as before.

In the realm of education, Okinawa's first governor declared that reforming language customs was the highest priority in education. In its push to make the emperor's new subjects speak Japanese, the prefectural government built elementary schools at a rapid pace. By the start of the first Sino-Japanese war in 1894, 30 percent of the prefecture's children had completed elementary school. This school construction, however, was a serious burden on Okinawa's farmers. School funding came mainly from a special tax from former times used to support *gechiyaku,* the royal troubleshooters so common in the last decades of the kingdom. In the 1880s, the *gechiyaku* were gone, but the tax remained. Elementary education was intended to make Okinawans resemble mainland Japanese in terms of their basic cultural outlook. But it also served to instill in Okinawans an acute awareness of how different they were from their fellow citizens to the north under the preservation of old customs policy. During the 1890s, more and more Okinawans began to demand that the policy be scrapped and that they receive the same rights as other Japanese.[11]

While more and more ordinary Okinawans began to press for reforms and look forward to a future as Japanese, the lower-ranking former *yukatchu* tended to sink further into poverty. Many had little other than their status as *yukatchu,* and they often yearned for the past. The Kōdōkai (roughly, "Society for Public Unity") was founded in 1896 by former prince Shō En (Shō Tai's second son) and several other prominent Okinawans. It was the last gasp of the old order, and it received most of its support in Okinawa from the non-stipended *yukatchu.* The organization gave lip service to assimilation of Okinawa into Japan but stated that the cultural differences between Okinawa and the rest of Japan were too great for assimilation to be practical in the near future. The Kōdōkai sought to repair the spirit *(seishin)* of Okinawans, which had been rent by the kingdom's coming to an end. It proposed a "special arrangement" whereby the Shō family would assume the governorship of Okinawa Prefecture. The people would then rally around the Shō family, who would lead Okinawa into gradual cultural and institutional union with Japan's imperial government. Naturally, the Kōdōkai sought to restore the *yukatchu* to their former positions of authority.[12]

A petition of support for the Kōdōkai agenda garnered 72,767 signatures, and a delegation of nine went to Tokyo to present their proposal to Interior Minister Matsukata, who rejected it immediately. After its victory over China, the Meiji state had no need to compromise regarding Okinawa. Furthermore, it was clear to the majority of Okinawans that for better or worse, their future was with Japan. The Kōdōkai quickly faded, and no further proposals along the lines of its petition ever materialized.

Despite its title of "prefecture," did the Meiji state regard Okinawa of the late nineteenth and early twentieth centuries as an integral part of Japan or as a de facto colony? Constructing an argument for the latter would not be difficult. All prewar governors of Okinawa were mainlanders, as were most prewar education officials. The Meiji government was willing to sell part of Okinawa to China. Reforms in landholding and land taxes took place in 1873 on the mainland and in 1899 for Okinawa. Samurai stipends ended in 1876 on the mainland but continued in Okinawa through 1909. Universal conscription went into effect in 1873 in all prefectures except Okinawa, where it was not implemented until 1898. The first prefectural elections took place on the mainland in 1890, as did the first elections for the national assembly. In Okinawa, however, these elections took place in 1909 and 1912 respectively. Through the 1920s, Okinawa Prefecture consistently paid much more to the central government in taxes than the central government spent in Okinawa. In 1921, for example, the prefecture paid 7,430,000 yen in taxes compared with government spending in Okinawa of 1,910,000 yen. Although Japan's poorest prefecture, Okinawa bore the heaviest tax burden during the Meiji and Taishō periods.[13] In short, Alan Christy is correct to call for the inclusion of Okinawa in studies of Japanese colonialism.[14]

Becoming Japanese: Intellectual Strategies During the Period of Assimilation

As noted above, the spread of primary education in Okinawa led to demands to end the policy of preserving old customs. By the turn of the century, government officials and educated Okinawans embraced a new policy of assimilation *(dōka),* which Christy has analyzed.[15] This section focuses on a key dimension of the assimilation policy: intellectual strategies for portraying Okinawa as part of Japan. When Ryukyu became Okinawa Prefecture, its people and history became enmeshed with the emerging narrative of Japan as a nation-state. In 1903, at the Fifth Industrial Exhibition in Osaka, there was a display of ethnic groups from parts of Japan's empire. There, a Japanese man with a whip presided over Ainu, Koreans, Taiwanese, and two Okinawan women (depicted, at least by the Okinawa press, as prostitutes). The *Ryūkyū shinpō,* the major Okinawan daily newspaper of the time, protested the inclusion of Okinawans, saying "The inclusion of people from our prefecture alongside Taiwanese aborigines and Ainu from the northern seas makes us appear comparable to primitives and Ainu. What could possibly be a greater insult to us?" and "People of other prefectures and cities sometimes regard the people of our prefecture as a special ethnic [and/or racial] group within Japan, but we acknowledge not the slightest difference in our characteristics."[16] The Okinawan newspapers and other voices of protest found no problem with the concept of displaying "primitive" peoples. Their objection was that Okinawans, as "real Japanese," should not be regarded as similar to lesser groups such as Ainu or Taiwanese.

Okinawan constructions of Okinawan identity from the late nineteenth century onward must be understood within the context of colonialism and the modern concept of nation. The extent to which the modern Japanese discourses of nation intersected with concepts of race is debatable. In any case, Okinawan intellectuals often concerned themselves with questions of relatedness to Japanese in ways that nearly always addressed cultural ethnicity *(minzoku)* and sometimes addressed physical descent or biological relatedness *(jinshu).* We have seen that by the nineteenth century, most of Ryukyu's elites, whether residents of Kumemura or Shuri, saw Ryukyu as a Confucian society within the moral and cultural orbit of the Qing emperor. Even if some Okinawans were able to maintain this vision in the decades immediately following annexation by Japan, it became entirely untenable following the first Sino-Japanese war. By the twentieth century, national consciousness had permeated all levels of Japanese society. The only way out of colonial or semicolonial status for Okinawans was to convince both themselves and mainlanders that Okinawans were, and in important ways always had been, members of the Japanese national group.

Human communities on any scale larger than isolated villages are imagined, because the members of each will never meet, much less become familiar with, all or even most other community members. This point is perhaps the most important insight in Anderson's well-known study of nationalism.[17] Modern nations in their various flavors constitute one of many possible varieties of imagined communities. By the start of the twentieth century, Japan had become a nation by almost any definition, and Japanese of nearly all walks of life shared a consciousness of being Japanese. Duara, Anderson, and others have pointed out that spatially, nations are imagined to exist embodied in states.[18] In their temporal dimensions, nations are imagined to exist in the time of what Duara calls "History" (as opposed to "history"). The major characteristic of History is the advance of time in a linear and progressive fashion. The inevitable, evolutionary, forward movement of progress is the core of Historical narratives, a key component in national imagining, and an essential element of colonial ideology.[19] These spatial and temporal dimensions of national imagining were major components of Japanese nationalism in the early twentieth century.[20]

The issue of state boundaries was settled by Japan's annexation of Ryukyu in 1879 followed by victory over China in 1895. Spatially, therefore, Okinawa was indisputably part of the Japanese nation. The questions of temporal, cultural, and "racial" affiliation, however, were much less clear. Okinawan intellectual strategies for placing Okinawa and its people within Japan's national community, therefore, inevitably focused on questions of history, culture, and sometimes "race." Historian Higashionna Kanjun (1882–1963), for example, blamed the leaders of Satsuma *han* for the apparent cultural differences between Ryukyuans and Japanese. In pursuit of its own aggrandizement, Satsuma forced Ryukyuans to adopt Chinese cultural forms, preventing the kingdom's proper or natural cultural incorporation into Japan:

> Through its policies, Satsuma, vis-à-vis both the bakufu and China and other foreign countries, made a profit by preventing the Japanization *(Nihonka)* of Ryukyu. This was the fundamental policy and remained unchanged over the course of three centuries. It was on account of this policy that the Meiji government has had such a difficult time [assimilating Okinawa]. In other words, at the time Okinawa was made into a prefecture, breaking the ties with China caused [the Meiji state] terrible trouble—the result of three hundred years of well-established policy. My intent here today is that you kindly understand this policy [of Satsuma].[21]

Higashionna made these remarks in a lecture to a mainland Japanese academic society in 1914. One could argue that the sinicization of Ryukyu never extended to most of the population and assumed wide-scale proportions even among elites only during the nineteenth century, but the point here is to see one of the narrativizing strategies that Okinawan elites employed to minimize fundamental cultural differences with the mainland.

Linguist, folklorist, and all-around scholar of things Ryukyuan, Iha Fuyū (1876–1947) addressed the question of the ethnic and racial origins of Ryukyuans. In a chapter on the ancestors of the Ryukyuan people in his widely read book *Ko-Ryūkyū* (Old Ryūkyū), Iha starts with Shō Shōken's claim, taken entirely out of context, that the Japanese and Ryukyuan languages were once the same. After presenting a wealth of linguistic evidence to prove the truth of this assertion (unproblematic among contemporary linguists), Iha then made the linkage with race: "With the proof I have provided thus far, we can see that Japanese and Ryukyuan are sister languages, and, assuming language to be a perfect index of the inherent characteristics of a race *(jinshu)*, then Ryukyuans immediately become members of the same race as Japanese."[22] Iha was aware, however, that linguistic evidence alone might not carry the entire weight of making Japanese and Ryukyuans racially identical, so the essay continues with a variety of other historical evidence. It concludes in a celebratory tone, with Japanese and Ryukyuans finally reunited like long-lost members of the same family:

> That until the start of the Meiji era, Ryukyu's existence was one of misery should go without saying. So I shall end this essay by saying that the result of the uniting of our citizenry *(kokumin)* at the start of Meiji, while it did cause the demise of the already half-dead Ryukyu Kingdom, has revived the Ryukyuan people *(minzoku)*, unexpectedly reunited us with our brethren, and brought about a prosperous life for us under the same government.[23]

Like many intellectuals of his day, Iha regarded race as both a biological and a cultural category that served as a "natural" criterion for political and social organization. Iha's work in this area was not limited to academic discourse. He traveled throughout Okinawa giving talks in Okinawan for the benefit of ordinary people on the subject of "racial improvement" *(jinshu eisei*, eugenics) from the standpoint of evolution.[24]

Starting in the 1920s, cultural or lifestyle "improvement" *(kaizen)* became a prominent issue in Okinawa and among Okinawans elsewhere in Japan. Prejudice against Okinawans on the part of mainlanders had been a part of Okinawan life since the founding of the prefecture. In 1894, for example, Kodama Kihachi, head of Okinawa's education department, removed English from the list of middle-school subjects, declaring to the students of Okinawa's only middle school that it was pointless for students "who are not even fluent in ordinary language [*futsūgo*, i.e., Japanese] to study English."[25] Of the possible markers of Okinawan identity commonly criticized by mainlanders, language was most prominent. In the 1920s, discrimination against Okinawans became an acute issue owing to the economic disaster that struck the prefecture when sugar prices dropped steeply.[26] The desperate economic conditions that ensued caused many Okinawans to seek work in the factories of Osaka and other cities. In such circumstances, language became the primary marker of an allegedly backward Okinawan character and, therefore, also the key to any significant Okinawan lifestyle improvement. Despite abundant economic and structural explanations for Okinawan poverty, the common practice at the time was to blame it on alleged cultural deficiencies.[27] Above all, thought many Okinawans as well as mainlanders, Okinawans must become fluent at "standard" Japanese *(hyōjungo)* in order to prosper.

Language remained a major issue throughout the 1930s. Educational policy in Okinawa sought to eliminate all traces of Okinawan distinctiveness, because "when observing the children of this prefecture, their individual consciousness of being subjects of Great Imperial Japan *(Dainippon teikoku)* is lacking." This lack allegedly resulted from an insufficient "consciousness of self-sacrifice," and from other alleged deficiencies in Japaneseness.[28] Whenever officials criticized Okinawan culture, they inevitably assumed the existence of a homogeneous "mainland" or "Japanese" culture, despite the cultural diversity to be found within "Japan." Were a resident of Kumamoto Prefecture, for example, to have used his local dialect in Tokyo, he might be thought of as unsophisticated, and he might be hard to understand, but nobody would have questioned his qualifications as Japanese. An Okinawan exhibiting even minor characteristics of local speech, however, would call attention to the suspicious nature of his status as a full-fledged member of the national family. Many Okinawans supported the policy of prefectural education officials stamping out Okinawan speech by coercive means.

The policy of assimilation reached the peak of its intensity during the Pacific War. In 1939, Okinawan educational authorities instituted the Standard Japanese Enforcement Movement *(Hyōjungo reikō undō)* as part of Japan's broader spiritual mobilization campaign. Not all prominent Japanese and Okinawans, however, agreed that *forced* assimilation was desirable. Yanagi Muneyoshi and other folklore scholars of the Nihon Mingeikai (Japan folk arts society) frequently visited Okinawa for research. During a 1940 conference in Naha featuring society members and prefectural officials, Yanagi and his group criticized the Standard Japanese Enforcement Movement as misguided policy that "has instilled in the people of the prefecture a sense of inferiority, and is actually an impediment [to assimilation]."[29] This critique touched off a heated argument, the so-called Dialect Dispute *(hōgen ronsō),* that took place in the pages of newspapers, magazines, and journals. The governor countered Yanagi forcefully, saying that during the Sino-Japanese war, some Okinawans sided with China and that during this time of national crisis, unity was of the utmost importance. Lifestyle reform for Okinawans was therefore the urgent business of the day, and mastery of standard Japanese was the most important element in raising the material and spiritual lives of Okinawans.[30] The prefectural education board stated that "The greatest cause of poverty of the prefectural residents is insufficient ability in standard Japanese and the inability to express themselves. Their being misunderstood and unable to thrive outside of the prefecture is for this reason."[31] Such statements are a classic example of the process Christy describes in which Okinawan poverty was imagined to have stemmed from cultural causes.[32] Although prefectural authorities claimed they did not seek to disparage local speech, their actions and policies were in fact designed to eliminate Okinawan languages to the fullest extent possible.[33]

As with so many other issues involving Okinawan identity and its relationship to "Japanese" identities, the Dialect Dispute polarized educated Okinawans. On the surface, the debate was about teaching methodologies. In fact, however, it reflected a profound questioning of Japanese culture, ethnicity, nationhood, and the role of local cultures within the broader collectivity. The Nihon Mingeikai's journal devoted two special issues to this debate in 1940. In the end, however, prefectural policy remained unchanged. In the case of Okinawa, at least, the state would permit no difference from the imagined standard of "Japan," whatever that might have been.

Few "Japanese," however, were capable of accepting Okinawans as full-fledged members of the national family regardless of the degree of Okinawan "improvement." By the time the Pacific War reached Okinawa in the spring of 1945, the assimilation policy of the previous decades took a deadly turn. The fighting connected with the Battle of Okinawa itself, of course, took a terrible toll on the island's civilian population. Mass civilian suicides (*shūdan jiketsu;* *"gyokusai"* as a wartime euphemism) and murder of Okinawans at the hands of Japanese soldiers added greatly to the battle's brutality. Often the line between suicide and murder was unclear. Always in the background, and often in the foreground, were issues of identity. As one researcher, daughter of a survivor of one of the group suicides, explains:

> The villagers [of Zamami Island, near Okinawa] had received an education in not disgracing themselves as Japanese. That education centered on the Emperor and was pounded into them. "Do not use you own local dialect!" "Don't value Okinawan culture!" "Try to stand shoulder-to-shoulder with the Japanese!" This penetrated to the depths of their hearts.[34]

"Education for imperial subjects" *(kōmin kyōiku)* in the 1930s and 1940s, the actual events of the Battle of Okinawa (including frequent surrender of Japanese soldiers—a shocking sight for many Okinawans at the time), and the extended postwar U.S. occupation have created a dissonance with respect to identity that continues to linger beneath the surface of contemporary Okinawa.[35]

After the signing of the San Francisco Peace Treaty, Okinawa Prefecture remained under U.S. occupation. As had happened so many times before, Japan's leaders regarded Okinawa as not quite fully a member of the family, and therefore expendable in a pinch. U.S. military authority was absolute during this period, and it increasingly clashed with the wishes of the majority of Okinawans. Mass protests in the late sixties and early seventies bore fruit in the form of the reversion of Okinawa to Japan in 1972. But the U.S. military presence remained, and to this day, the prefecture has borne a disproportional burden of that presence in Japan. Prior to reversion, display of the Japanese flag (*hinomaru*) was prohibited. Flag waving thus became an ideal form of protest against the U.S. presence. By the 1980s, the Japanese flag had become a less popular, more ambivalent symbol. Ministry of Education attempts to force Okinawan schools to display it, for example, often met resistance. In 1987, at the National Athletic Meet, which was held in Okinawa that year, supermarket owner Chibana Shōichi tore down a Japanese flag and burnt it, causing an uproar throughout Japan.[36] Differing visions of Okinawa (and "Japan") have continued to clash in recent decades, and Okinawa remains a site of contestation over these visions.[37]

From the seventeenth through the twentieth centuries, Ryukyu/Okinawa has been a site of contestation in which conflicting visions of Ryukyu, Okinawa, Japan, and other imagined communities have played themselves out. The process continues in the present. This study has examined several of these visions during Ryukyu's early-modern period. From it we may draw conclusions with respect to four distinct yet overlapping topics: Ryukyuan history, Confucianism, Japanese history, and the construction of imagined communities.

Ryukyuan History

This study reveals a substantial degree of Ryukyuan autonomy and agency within a political and diplomatic matrix commonly described as "dual attachment to both Japan and China" (*Nitchū ryōzoku*). Economically, politically, and intellectually, Ryukyuans in early-modern times confronted a range of choices and possibilities. Ryukyu's precarious existence on the margins of Japan's *bakuhan* state and the Qing empire added urgency to those choices. In this connection, Sai On sometimes quoted the ancient Chinese maxim that a slight miscalculation at the start will lead to grave consequences later. Older studies of Ryukyu have tended to see it as an appendage of either China or, more commonly, Japan.[38] This tendency is not unreasonable considering that many early-modern Ryukyuans themselves tended to lean toward either China or Japan. Furthermore, Satsuma's power over the kingdom was substantial. If one wanted to make a case that early-modern Ryukyu was part of Japan, there is ample evidence to do so. Likewise, there is evidence to argue for subordination to China. In either case, however, one would have to overlook contradictory data, including evidence of de facto Ryukyuan autonomy.

Implicit in much of the present study is a rejection of choosing sides between China or Japan. Obviously, early-modern Ryukyu was closely tied to both places, and these ties affected nearly every aspect of Ryukyuan life. It was precisely because of Ryukyu's complex ties with the Qing empire and elements of Japan's *bakuhan* state, I would argue, that the kingdom was able to maintain a substantial measure of autonomy within the broader historical conditions of its time. The kingdom was unable, of course, to preserve its quasi-autonomous status when these conditions changed in the 1870s. One of the best indications of this early-modern autonomy was the existence of different views of Ryukyu among Ryukyuan intellectuals: Shō Shōken's view of Ryukyu as loyal vassal to Satsuma, Tei Junsoku's view of Ryukyu as having been transformed by the moral authority of the Qing emperor, Sai On's view of Ryukyu as an ideal Confucian society, and Heshikiya Chōbin's challenge to Sai On. Of course, Sai On's view eventually eclipsed the others, but it is significant that he envisioned a Ryukyu whose destiny was in the hands of Ryukyuans, not the Chinese or Japanese. In no case did any of the figures examined here see Ryukyu as *part of* China or Japan in the sense that we would typically conceive of sovereignty in modern terms. While this point may be obvious, it bears mentioning because many studies of Ryukyu's past tend to assume that modern conceptions of state and national sovereignty can be read back into the days of the kingdom unproblematically.

Early-modern Ryukyuans had no concept of the ideology of the modern nation-state. They constructed Ryukyuan identity on the basis of other ideologies, including Buddhism (Heshikiya), *tentō* thought (Shō Shōken), and Confucianism (Tei Junsoku and Sai On). Most important was Confucianism in the hands of Sai On, which eventually transformed Ryukyu's government and social elites. I am not suggesting that Ryukyu ever became the ideal Confucian society Sai On envisioned. Nevertheless, its official ideology of state, its laws, its major institutions, and its official ceremonial had all assumed Confucian form by the early nineteenth century.

An additional argument implicit in this study is that the Ryukyuan state and *yukatchu* became Confucianized relatively late in the kingdom's history and only after great struggle. Many older studies of Ryukyu have assumed that it was a thoroughly Confucian state since before the seventeenth century. Ta-tuan Ch'en, for example, says:

> After 1609 Liu-ch'iu [Ryukyu], as a powerless small country, had to accept Satsuma's will in every detail. But as the tributary relation with China was not disrupted and *Confucianism continued to be the state ideology*, the change does not seem to have altered the Liu-ch'iuan view that China was the center of the East Asian world and the source of cultural values.[39]

Not even Tei Junsoku was willing to push Ryukyu's Confucian past back into the sixteenth century. Buddhism and native forms of religion were the ideological basis of the Ryukyuan state until the eighteenth century. The eighteenth century was a time of transition, when Confucianism gradually supplanted older ideologies in Ryukyu's government. It was not until Shō On's reign, however, that Confucianism assumed its place as official, explicit state ideology, much to the dismay of the residents of Kumemura.

The rioting in Kumemura that resulted from changes in the *kanshō* system points to another important aspect of Ryukyuan history stressed in this study. Early-modern Ryukyu was a site of extensive political conflict. While this point, too, may be obvious, our understanding of early-modern Ryukyu would benefit greatly from greater clarification of the nature and configuration of this conflict. Here I have suggested the geological metaphor of fault lines running beneath the surface of Ryukyuan elite society—potential sources of disruption under certain conditions. The major "fault lines" included Pro-Chinese Ryukyuans versus Pro-Japanese Ryukyuans, Kumemura versus Shuri, a possible Tei Junsoku faction versus Sai On faction within Kumemura, and Confucianism versus Buddhism. Undoubtedly one major condition exacerbating this conflict in the eighteenth century was Kumemura's increasing power in domestic politics. In the late nineteenth century, Ryukyuan elite society continued to divide into opposing camps as seen in the Makishi-Onga Affair and in those Ryukyuans who favored cooperation with Matsuda and the Meiji state and those who sought aid from Qing China. Further research on the details of intra-Ryukyuan conflict would enhance our understanding of Ryukyuan history.

Confucianism

The case of Ryukyu provides an important angle from which to view Confucianism as it spread into non-Chinese contexts. The major figure, of course, was Sai On. He was a comparatively rare example of a serious Confucian thinker who also served at the highest levels of government for over thirty years. A close connection between theory and its application to the realm of politics and administration characterizes Sai On's Confucianism. In this connection, his greatest contribution to the Confucian tradition was his use of *quan* (J. *ken*), "situational expediency," as a means to bridge the gap between theory and practice. As I have argued elsewhere in detail, Sai On's uses of *quan* were unique among East Asian Confucians.[40] One of his uses of *quan* was a critique of Buddhism that simultaneously declared Sakyamuni to have been a sage, undermined the validity of Buddhism after Sakyamuni's time as misunderstood and inappropriate situational expediency, and affirmed the appropriateness of some of Sai On's own unconventional policies.[41] These distinctive features of Sai On's Confucianism were closely connected with Ryukyu's particular circumstances. Sai On modified and employed Confucianism in ways that made sense within the context of Ryukyu and supported his political agenda.

His Confucian counterparts in Japan also had to adapt Confucianism to suit their needs. One problem, of course, was reconciling the sinocentric tendencies in Confucian thought with an unwillingness on the part of most Japanese intellectuals to concede the moral or cultural superiority of China.[42] Regardless of the particular strategy employed in dealing with this or any other intellectual issue, however, the arguments of Japanese Confucians remained largely confined to the realm of discourse. One reason is that Confucian scholarship and statecraft generally occupied separate realms throughout most of the Tokugawa period.[43] As Tetsuo Najita points out:

> Lacking formal status, the jusha [Confucian scholars], for the most part, pursued scholarly careers detached from the administrative apparatuses of Edo and domainal rule. The majority did not receive stipends—which explains the large number of "physicians" among them. Some, of course, did gain access into political chambers as advisors of bakufu ministers, as in the cases of Ogyū Sorai and Arai Hakuseki. . . . By and large, however, the jusha were men without clear links to the centers of authority, even though the ideas they studied were closely linked to the problems of ordering and governing.[44]

A second reason for Japanese Confucianism remaining in the realm of discourse throughout most of the Tokugawa period was the relative stability of the *bakuhan* state under shogunal hegemony. It was not until the mid nineteenth century that intellectual discourse commonly demanded action in the political realm. During most of the Tokugawa period, Confucianism typically functioned as a personal creed for its followers, with strong religious overtones.

By contrast, Sai On's Confucianism was directly linked with the realm of politics and governing. Putting his vision of Ryukyu into practice required legal, ceremonial, and institutional reorganization of the kingdom. It even transformed the landscape of Ryukyu. Furthermore, Sai On's Confucianism spoke directly to the issue of Ryukyuan identity. It provided a theoretical basis for Ryukyuans to take charge of the kingdom's destiny and for Ryukyuan moral parity with its larger neighbors. Even if Confucianism played little direct role in Japan's governments, it carried great prestige among most learned Japanese, not to mention other East Asians. In other words, Sai On sought to empower Ryukyuans by employing a widely respected, prestigious ideology. Confucianism can serve and has served as the ideological basis of a totalizing subjectivity. Sai On's project may be unique, however, in its explicit employment of Confucianism to bolster the sovereignty (for want of a better term) of a country whose political status was ambiguous.

Japanese History

In the context of a critique of contemporary Japanese theories of civilization, Tessa Morris-Suzuki writes:

> Putting small societies back into the flow of time is the first step toward a non-Eurocentric (and non-Japanocentric) view of history. What differences would this make to the way we write history? It might, for example, mean that histories of Japan did not begin with the statement that "from the earliest known history to the present day we Japanese have been the same people living in the same territory, the territory of the present Japanese archipelago." Instead, they might begin by observing that "Japan as we know it today was formed in the mid-nineteenth century, when the country known as 'Nihon' imposed its political power over two neighboring countries, the Kingdom of the Ryūkyūs to the south and the land of the Ainu to the north." Each of the three parts of modern Japan, it would then be observed, had its own history, and these three parallel histories would become an essential part of the past of the modern state. Not only the past but also the present of Japan would then start to look subtly but distinctly different.[45]

Taking Ryukyu's early-modern history seriously as *Ryukyuan* history could prompt a reconsideration of the very idea of Japan itself.

Takara points out that it has been common for Japanese historians to regard even Old-Ryukyu as having been part of Japan. Their reasoning goes that Japanese and Ryukyuans, being members of the same ethnic group, must have been part of the same political entity *(tan'itsu minzoku = tan'itsu kokka).* Takara rightly criticizes this view as "ahistorical culturalism" *(hirekishitekina* "*bunka*"*ron*).[46] The view that members of the same ethnic group must share a basic culture and must therefore be (or ought to be) part of the same state is, of course, a basic premise of modern national thinking. Old-Ryukyu, however, was an independent state by any definition of the term, and the denial of its independent existence is an example of what Anderson calls "the subjective antiquity [of nations] in the eyes of nationalists," as opposed to their "objective modernity" in the eyes of those who have studied their historical development.[47] In other words, Ryukyu must always have been part of Japan, the thinking goes, because it is so today or because its people allegedly belong to the same ethnic group *(minzoku)* as "the Japanese."

Were the scholars whom Takara criticizes to take Ryukyu seriously as Ryukyu, their "Japan" would begin to look different. And one could take the critique further than Takara does. Looking at Japan from the vantage point of Ryukyu could, for example, stimulate questioning and rethinking of concepts like ethnic group and culture as they have commonly been appropriated in constructions of modern Japan.[48]

Early-modern Ryukyu can serve as a lens through which to view Tokugawa "Japan" in new ways. For example, what exactly was the "*bakuhan* state," of which Ryukyu was both a part and apart? Ravina has argued that it was a "compound state" in which various interdependent yet semiautonomous political entities, together, exercised all of the functions that today we typically associate with states.[49] The varieties of overlapping yet distinct sovereignty at work in early-modern Japan, the rhetorical strategies whereby daimyō or their apologists minimized shogunal authority within the context of their domains *(kuni* or *kokka),* and other aspects of political discourse and practice that Ravina describes help explain Ryukyu's relationship with Satsuma and the bakufu in ways that make it seem less of an anomaly and more typical of early-modern political practices. "Apologists for daimyō authority did not deny heaven's mandate passed through the shogunate. Yet in neglecting to explore this process, they made the shogunate's role incidental rather than critical."[50] Similarly, Sai On minimized Satsuma's role in Ryukyuan affairs. In many ways, the network of compound loyalties and obligations in which Ryukyu was enmeshed—and the substantial degree of autonomy it attained by playing one part of the network against another—was much like the situation of the large daimyō ("great country holders," *taishin kunimochi*) as described by Ravina. A major difference, of course, is that Ryukyu's network extended well into China. Deeply seated patterns of thought that regard the modern nation-state, with its centralized authority, as normative, combined with the lingering image of early-modern "Japan" as an isolated country, tend to make the question of what was part of Japan and what was not, what was inside and what was outside, seem terribly important. While this question certainly became important in the 1870s, the case of early-modern Ryukyu suggests that "Japan" was a much vaguer entity in Tokugawa times than we are normally accustomed to thinking of it today.

Imagined Communities

That early-modern Ryukyu was not a nation in the modern sense of the term as described by scholars such as Anderson and Gellner should be obvious at this point. Nevertheless, some early-modern Ryukyuans advanced visions of Ryukyu in which the kingdom became an imagined political and cultural community with the potential to subsume all Ryukyuans within its totalizing ideology. Sai On's vision of Ryukyu as ideal Confucian society was the most thoroughgoing of these imagined communities, and its consequences were felt to at least some degree in nearly all aspects of Ryukyuan life.

Early-modern visions of Ryukyu drew upon the ideologies available at the time: *tentō* thought, Confucianism, and Buddhism. Shō Shōken employed *tentō* thought to argue that Ryukyu accept its proper place as vassal of Satsuma and fulfill its duty in that capacity. Ryukyu, he argued, should accept its heaven *(tentō)*-ordained fate. Heshikiya Chōbin's Buddhist-inspired fatalism, by contrast, proved less productive and eventually took the form of a direct attack on Sai On and his policies. Tei Junsoku's Confucian vision of Ryukyu posited the kingdom as the cultural vassal of the Chinese emperor. By contrast, Sai On's Confucian vision of Ryukyu sought to confer on Ryukyuans the greatest possible degree of autonomy. He minimized the role of inevitable fate (Satsuma's power, lack of resources) and maximized the potential for Ryukyuan self-transformation. Ryukyu's ambiguous and precarious political status as a small kingdom with ties to China and Japan contributed to a creative tension from which developed a variety of imagined communities. These visions of Ryukyu all had political consequences and were all unstable. Even Sai On's vision was never able to achieve closure. Throughout the life of the kingdom, the imagined community of Ryukyu was a site of contestation.

Modern Okinawans continued to create imagined communities. Okinawa's political status remained vague through the 1880s. Even after the former kingdom had become part of Japan in the eyes of the international community, its de facto colonial treatment helped produce discourses on Ryukyu/Okinawa's relationship with the broader entity of Japan. Gone were the *tentō* thought, Buddhist, and Confucian ideologies, of course, their place taken by talk of culture, ancestry, ethnicity, "race," and modernity. Early-modern visions of Ryukyu made their way into modern Okinawa, however, transmitted and transformed by scholars like Iha and Higashionna. Iha, for example, quoted Shō Shōken's brief lines about the similar origins of certain Japanese and Ryukyuan names without mentioning the context of his arguing against the king's worship at Kudakajima. He then declared Shō Shōken to have been the first person to conclude that Japanese and Ryukyuans are of the same "race" *(Nichiryū jinshu dōkei ron)* based on comparative linguistic evidence—precisely Iha's favored approach in making the same argument.[51] Naturally, Iha had much to say about Sai On, whom he tended to portray as a visionary ahead of his time. For example, a declaration by Sai On in *Articles of Instruction* that all occupations are important to the welfare of society, intended to encourage unemployed *yukatchu* to take up commoner occupations, did not become the normative view in Japan until after the Meiji Restoration.[52] Ryukyu, in other words, was ahead of Japan in some areas of modern thinking according to Iha. Indeed, *Articles of Instruction* itself, Ryukyu's first "citizen's reader" *(kokumin dokuhon)* in Iha's view, also presaged later developments in Meiji Japanese education. Iha points out that Satsuma once sent a spy to Ryukyu because of rumors that Sai On was promoting "the worship of China" *(Shina sūhai no kibun)* among Ryukyuans. When the spy heard *Articles of Instructions* read aloud at a village gathering, he was fully satisfied that Sai On had Ryukyu following the proper course.[53] Implicit in Iha's portrayal was that Sai On was a figure in whom Ryukyuans should take pride and from whom they should take inspiration, for he was every bit as modern (or potentially modern) as his Japanese counterparts, if not more so.[54]

Iha and other modern intellectuals had at their disposal the texts of the major early-modern visions of Ryukyu, on which they drew selectively to augment their own visions of Okinawa. Therefore, to use Duara's terminology, modern Okinawan intellectuals served as agents of both transmittal and dispersion of older imagined communities. The process continues to this day as contemporary Okinawans and others put forth visions of Okinawa or Ryukyu that inevitably harken back to the early-modern past in search of support.

Ryukyuan Kings

Dates indicate reigns. Dates for some early kings are approximations.

Tenson Line:
Shunten 舜天 1187–1237

Shun Bajunki 舜馬順熙 1238–1248

Gihon 義本 1249–1259

Eiso Line:
Eiso 英祖 1260–1299

Taisei 大成 1300–1308

Eiji 英慈 1309–1313

Tamagusuku 玉城 1314–1336

Seii 西威 1337–1354

Kings of the Chūzan Region:
Satto 察度 1355–1395

Bunei 武寧 1396–1405

First Shō Dynasty:
Shō Shishō 尚思紹 1405–1421

Shō Hashi 尚巴志 1422–1439

Shō Chū 尚忠 1440–1442

Shō Shitatsu 尚思達 1443–1449

Shō Kinpuku 尚金福 1450–1453

Shō Taikyū 尚泰久 1454–1460

Shō Toku 尚德 1461–1469

Second Shō Dynasty:
Shō En 尚円 1470–1476

Shō Sen'i 尚宣威 1477

Shō Shin 尚真 1477–1526

Shō Sei 尚清 1527–1555

Shō Gen 尚元 1556–1572

Shō Ei 尚永 1573–1586

Shō Nei 尚寧 1587–1620

Shō Hō 尚豊 1621–1640

Shō Ken 尚賢 1641–1647

Shō Shitsu 尚質 1648–1668

Shō Tei 尚貞 1669–1709

Shō Eki 尚益 1710–1712

Shō Kei 尚敬 1713–1751

Shō Boku 尚穆 1752–1795

Shō On 尚温 1796–1802

Shō Sei 尚成 1803

Shō Kō 尚灝 1804–1828

Shō Iku 尚育 1829–1848

Shō Tai 尚泰 1849–1879

APPENDIX 2

Glossary of Selected Ryukyuan Terms

The following list includes Ryukyuan names, titles, offices, and other terms of importance in this study. The most common characters for each term are provided, but variations are common. In *kana* spellings, what is pronounced "yu" (and here written ゆ), often appears as "yo" in premodern documents.

Aji (or Anji) 安司: Local warlords in Old-Ryukyu; high status rank in *kinsei* Ryukyu, above *ueekata* and below prince.

Atai (J. Atari) 当: Local officials who served as specialized inspectors (e.g., *yama-atai* supervised forests; *kōsaku-atai* supervised farmlands).

Chūzan 中山: One of three divisions of Okinawa, whose ruler eventually united the whole island under his command in the early fifteenth century. As the kings of Okinawa expanded their territory, Chūzan became synonymous with the Ryukyu Kingdom, much like Yamato became synonymous with Japan.

Council of Fifteen (Omote jūgonin) 表十五人: An influential group of officials comprised of the heads of major government divisions. It ranked immediately below the Council of Three.

Council of Three 三司官: Ryukyu's highest governing council, which, together with the *sessei*, comprised the Hyōjōsho.

Edo nobori 江戸上り: The practice of the Ryukyuan king sending periodic embassies to the shōgun's court in Edo.

Funshii (C. Fengshui) 風水: Literally, "wind and water." Geomancy. The science of ideal spacial arrangement to take fullest advantage of the flow of energy through the earth.

Gechiyaku 下知役: Officials from the central government appointed as troubleshooters to temporarily take over and revive districts in severe economic decline. *Gechiyaku* appointments were common during the nineteenth century.

Hi-no-kami (O. Fii-nu-kan) 火の神: A hearth or fire deity, with a likely historical connection to the solar deity *teda*. There were two distinct varieties, the official deity, or *seiji hi-no-kami*, and the household hearth deity, or *minzoku hi-no-kami*.

Hyōjōsho 評定所: The highest lawmaking body in the royal government. It consisted of the Council of Three plus the *sessei*.

Jimoku 耳目: Another term for *mōshikuchi*. See *Mōshikuchihō*.

Jitō 地頭: District administrators in early-modern Ryukyu who resided in the capital. There were several classifications of *jitō*, including *waki-jitō* and *aji-jitō*, distinguished by the person's social status rank and the size of the area he administered.

Jitōdai 地頭代: Highest local officials. *Jitōdai* were not *yukatchu*.

Kanshō 官生: Ryukyuan students sent to study at China's National Academy at the expense of the Chinese government.

Kikoe ōgimi 聞得大君: Highest rank in the official religious hierarchy, typically held by the wife or a close blood relative of the king.

Kokushi 国師: Literally, "state instructor." The official title of the king's tutor, an office first held by Sai On.

Kujichō 公事帳: Administrative handbooks.

Kumemura 久米村: An area adjacent to Shuri that became Ryukyu's center for Chinese studies and diplomacy with China. During the eighteenth century, Kumemura also became influential in domestic politics, but its power declined during the nineteenth century.

Kumiodori 組踊: A distinctive Ryukyuan dramatic form featuring music and dance, created by Tamagusuku Chōkun (1684–1734).

Kyūyō 球陽: An official history of the Ryukyu Kingdom that was periodically updated for each reign. Kyūyō is also another name for Okinawa.

Monobugyō 物奉行: The division of the royal government charged with the administration of finances and economic productivity.

Mōshikuchihō 申口方: The counterpart of the Monobugyō, charged with police and judicial affairs, education, and royal household affairs.

Ne-no-hō 子の方: The most important state ceremony of the new year, during which the king prayed to heaven and earth while facing the direction of Beijing. Ne-nō-hō was part of the sinicization of state ceremonial that began early in the eighteenth century. It was modeled on Chinese imperial veneration of heaven.

Niya (also, Niyaa) 仁屋: The lowest *yukatchu* rank, automatically bestowed upon coming of age.

Noro (O. Nuru) 巫女: The lowest level of the official religious hierarchy. *Noro* typically oversaw one village or several nearby villages.

Okazugaki (O. Ukazigachi) 上申書: A formal petition of support or recommendation, usually for an official appointment, presented from those lower in rank to those higher in rank.

Old-Ryukyu *(ko-Ryūkyū)* 古琉球: The Ryukyu kingdom prior to 1609.

Onarigami おなり神: A woman serving as a protective deity for a close male relative, typically her brother.

Peechin 親雲上: A status rank indicating roughly the middle range of the *yukatchu*.

Peekumi 親雲上: Similar to *peechin* (and written with identical characters) but indicating a higher rank. *Peekumi* were *peechin* who held the post of *jitō* (or any of its variants).

Sanshikan 三司官: The most common Chinese-style appellation for the Council of Three.

Seji せじ: In Old-Ryukyu, and to a much lesser extent in *kinsei* Ryukyu, spiritual power derived from the sun and transmitted to the king via the High Priestess *(kikoe ōgimi)*.

Sessei (O. Shisshii) 摂政: Roughly, "prime minister." A royal relative and the highest government official who typically worked in conjunction with the Council of Three.

Shiakechi 仕明地: Lands brought into cultivation for the first time under Shō Shōken's program to increase the amount of agricultural land.

Shinugu Ashibi (also J. Uchiharare asobi) しぬぐ遊び: Sacred dancing by the women of rural villages, often performed nude and with sexual overtones. The royal government banned the practice in eighteenth century.

Shuri ōyako 首里大屋子: A high-ranking local official immediately below the *jitōdai*.

Shuri tenganashiime 首里天がなしいめ: An honorific, literary appellation for the king.

Tabi odori 旅踊: In Kumemura, prior to the departure of a ship for China, female friends and relatives of the sailors would dance all day and night to help ensure the safety of the crew.

Taifu 大夫: High Kumemura status rank.

Teda (O. Tiida) 太陽: The sun, typically conceived of as a deity.

Toki 時: Diviners in the native religion, usually male, who predicted lucky and unlucky days.

Ueekata (J. Oyakata) 親方: The highest status rank a non-royal relative could attain. Corresponded roughly to government posts of *sanshikan zashiki* or higher.

Yukatchu 良人: Members of Ryukyu's aristocratic class. Formal creation of the *yukatchu* took place in the seventeenth century, and the class was divided into a range of status titles such as *ueekata, peekumi, satonushi,* et cetera.

Yuta ゆた: Unofficial female shamans of great importance and influence in native Ryukyuan religion. *Yuta* were thought to be capable of curing illness, improving household fortunes, and providing protection against malevolent spirits. Though banned in the eighteenth century by the royal government, *yuta* continued to flourish well into this century.

List of Abbreviations

ODJ	*Okinawa daihyakka jiten*
OKS	*Okinawa-ken shiryō*
ROHM	*Ryūkyū ōkoku hyōjōshō monjo*
RSS	*Ryūkyū shiryō sōsho*
SOZS	*Sai On zenshū*

Notes

Introduction

1. Toguchi Masakiyo, *Kinsei no Ryūkyū* (Hōsei daigaku shuppankyoku, 1975), p. 2.

2. One tendency in the study of Ryukyu has been to view it either as a part of China (via its tributary relations), or, more commonly, as part of Japan. Mitsugu Sakihara, for example, argues that early-modern Ryukyu was essentially part of Japan, via Satsuma, from the early seventeenth century onward, for example: "But in the area that made substantial differences, Ryukyu's autonomy was probably closer to that of other vassals [in Japan's *bakuhan* state] than to that of an independent state. In economic aspects, its economy was tied to that of Japan, through Satsuma. . . ." (p. 12). See "The Significance of Ryukyu in Satsuma Finances During the Tokugawa Period" (Ph.D. diss., University of Hawai'i, 1971), esp. pp. 10–17. Toguchi, whose detailed study of early-modern Ryukyu provides a wealth of useful information, argues that studies of Ryukyu should be regarded as belonging to the genre of local Japanese history *(chihōshi)* because bakufu policy thoroughly influenced the kingdom (*Kinsei no Ryūkyū,* pp. 480–481). The trend in studies of Ryukyuan history since the early 1980s has been to examine Ryukyu not only with respect to China or Japan, but in a broader Asian context. The present study reflects this trend, and argues for a substantial measure of Ryukyuan subjectivity, without, however, denying the important influence of bakufu and Satsuma power in shaping Ryukyuan subjectivity.

3. There is a vast and rapidly growing literature on nationalism. Some of the best works include Anderson, *Imagined Communities: Reflections on the Origin and Spread of Nationalism,* rev. ed. (London: Verso, 1991); Ernest Gellner, *Nations and Nationalism* (Ithaca, NY: Cornell University Press, 1983); E. J. Hobsbawm, *Nations and Nationalism Since 1780: Programme, Myth, Reality,* 2d ed. (Cambridge: Cambridge University Press, 1992); Walker Connor, *Ethnonationalism: The Quest for Understanding* (Princeton: Princeton University Press, 1994); and Homi K. Bhabha, ed., *Nation and Narration* (London, Routledge, 1990). The work of Gellner and Anderson is especially well known, and my discussion of nations here assumes a basic familiarity with it.

4. Prasenjit Duara, *Rescuing History from the Nation: Questioning Narratives of Modern China* (Chicago: The University of Chicago Press, 1995), p. 54.

5. Ibid., pp. 51–55.

6. Ibid., pp. 55 (quoted passages), and 56–69 for the empirical evidence.

7. Ibid., pp. 73–74.

8. *Okinawa daihyakka jiten,* ed. Okinawa daihyakka jiten kankō jimukyoku (Naha: Okinawa taimususha, 1983), 4 vols.

(HAPTER 1   **The Status of Ryukyu and Its Relations with Japan and China**

1. Quoted in George H. Kerr, *Okinawa: The History of an Island People* (Rutland, VT: Charles E. Tuttle Company, 1958), p. 160.

2. This document took on great importance at the time of Japan's annexation of Ryukyu in 1879. When China protested, the Meiji government presented this and other documents to the international community as "proof" of Ryukyu's having been an integral part of Japan since "ancient" times.

3. Kerr, *Okinawa,* p. 161.

4. Ibid.

5. Ibid., p. 162.

6. Ibid., pp. 162–163.

7. "Hanzai to keibatsu," in *Shin Ryūkyūshi, kinsei hen,* vol. 1 (Naha: Ryūkyū shinpōsha, 1989), pp. 262–263.

8. Quoted in Kamiya Nobuyuki, *Bakuhansei kokka no Ryūkyū shihai* (Azekura shobō, 1990), p. 25. Chūzan originally indicated the central portions of the island of Okinawa, from where the line of kings that eventually unified all of Okinawa emerged. When the kings of Okinawa had extended their control over all of the Ryukyu islands in the late fifteenth century, Chūzan became synonymous with Ryukyu.

9. Ibid., p. 26; Kamiya Nobuyuki, "Satsuma no Ryūkyū shinnyū," in *Shin Ryūkyūshi, kinsei hen,* vol. 1 (Naha: Ryūkyū shinpōsha, 1989), p. 66.

10. Higashionna (Higaonna) Kanjun, "Shimazu-shi no Ryūkyū tōji kikan," *Higashionna Kanjun zenshū,* vol. 1 (Daiichi shobō, 1978), p. 68. Higashionna cites the following passage from the *Kyan nikki,* a diary recording the political events of the time: "When Jana [Tei Dō] was a child, he went to Nanjing to study, and perhaps because he did not return to his country for a long time, being ignorant of the ways of Yamato, he caused a cataclysmic event in the realm [i.e., the invasion]." In Ryukyu's later official histories, Tei Dō's mistaken poli-

cies and advice become the sole cause of the invasion, though recent historians of Ryukyu are nearly unanimous in the view that Satsuma had intended to conquer Ryukyu since before Hideyoshi's time. Furthermore, Tei Dō's policies would have little or no effect regarding the invasion at the late date (1605) that he became a member of the Council of Three.

11. Ibid.

12. Kamiya, *Ryūkyū shihai,* pp. 27–29; Kamiya, "Ryūkyū shinnyū," p. 66. Ta-tuan Ch'en provides a specific example of this policy in practice during the later years of the kingdom: "[The royal government, acting on orders from Satsuma] demanded in 1866 that during the sojourn of the [Chinese] investiture mission all men around Naha must wear long trousers. According to Iha Fuyū, the government issued this order because it feared that when Chinese envoys took excursions in the suburbs they might see Liu-ch'iuan [Ryukyuan] farmers wearing *shitaobi* (Japanese-style loin cloths), which might reveal the Liu-ch'iu–Japan relationship. See Ch'en, "Investiture of Liu-ch'iu Kings in the Ch'ing Period," *The Chinese World Order: Traditional China's Foreign Relations,* ed. John King Fairbank (Cambridge, MA: Harvard University Press, 1968), p. 145.

13. Quoted in Kamiya, *Ryūkyū shihai,* p. 30.

14. *ROHM,* vol. 1, p. 130.

15. *Ryūkyū shihai,* p. 34; Kamiya, "Edo nobori," in *Shin Ryūkyūshi, kinsei hen,* vol. 2 (Naha: Ryūkyū shinpōsha, 1990), pp. 14–15.

16. *Ryūkyū shihai,* pp. 34–37.

17. Gotō Yōichi and Tomoeda Ryūtarō, eds., *Kumazawa Banzan,* Nihon shisō taikei 30 (Iwanami shoten, 1971), p. 425. See also pp. 426–431.

18. "Kinsei Nihon ni okeru kaigai johō to Ryūkyū no ichi," *Shisō* 796 (October 1990):71–72. Arai's two essays are *Ryūkyūkoku jiryaku* and *Nantōshi.*

19. *ROHM,* vol. 1, p. 132. See also pp. 139–140; and Maehira, "Kaigai jōhō," pp. 71–72.

20. Uehara Kenzen, *Sakoku to han bōeki: Satsuma-han no Ryūkyū mitsubōeki* (Yaetake shobō, 1981), pp. 68–69.

21. Kamiya, "Edo nobori," pp. 16–17.

22. Uehara, *Han bōeki,* pp. 70–71.

23. Kamiya, "Edo nobori," pp. 16–17.

24. Ibid., p. 21.

25. Uehara, *Han bōeki,* pp. 80–81.

26. Ibid., pp. 83–84.

27. Ibid., p. 85.

28. Ibid.

29. Quoted in *Higashionna Kanjun zenshū,* vol. 1, p. 70.

30. Quoted in ibid., vol. 5, p. 238.

31. Ibid., p. 239.

32. Uehara Kenzen, "Bōeki no tenkai," in *Shin Ryūkyūshi, kinsei hen,* vol. 1 (Naha: Ryūkyū shinpōsha, 1989), pp. 133–135.

33. Uehara, *Han bōeki,* pp. 72–75.

34. A number of descriptions of the incident are available. See, for example, Uehara, *Han bōeki,* pp. 75–77.

35. Quoted in ibid., pp. 78–79.

36. Ibid.

37. A *shō* was 1.8 liters, a *gō* was one-tenth of a *shō,* or 0.18 liters and a *koku* was roughly 180 liters.

38. Uehara, *Han bōeki,* pp. 85–87.

39. Ibid., pp. 89–90.

40. Kamiya, "Edo nobori," pp. 18–19. For additional discussion of bakufu reactions to the Qing conquest of China, see Ronald Toby, *State and Diplomacy in Early Modern Japan: Asia in the Development of the Tokugawa Bakufu* (Princeton: Princeton University Press, 1984), pp. 118–140.

41. Quoted in *Higashionna Kanjun zenshū,* vol. 5, p. 232.

42. For details, see Sakihara, "The Significance of Ryukyu," pp. 193–196.

43. Toby, *Diplomacy,* especially pp. 45–52, 182–183, 188–189; and Kamiya, "Edo nobori."

44. See Manabe Takahiko's articles in *Kagoshima daihyakka jiten,* ed. Minami Nihon shinbunsha, Kagoshima daihyakka jiten hensanshitsu (Kagoshima: Minami Nihon shinbunsha, 1983), p. 1034; and *ODJ,* 3, p. 884. An additional extant *Ryūkyūjin odori* has been discovered since these articles were written.

45. In 1704, when Ienobu was formally designated as shogunal heir, the bakufu also declined to accept a Ryukyuan embassy. See Uehara, *Han bōeki,* pp. 103–104; and Kamiya, "Edo nobori," pp. 15–17.

46. An entry for 1709 in the *Kyūyō,* an eighteenth-century official history, describes the food shortages and resulting famine as follows:

   Poor harvests have continued for several years in our country. This year, several typhoons arose followed by drought. The fields were parched and the rice withered. As a result, there was no new grain, and old grain had already been consumed. The people lost their source of food. For their daily subsistence they ate wild vegetables and peeled the bark off of trees. By the winter, mountain plants and seaweed had all been exhausted, and those who starved to death by the road totaled 3,199. In the spring of the following year, bands of robbers appeared and the upper classes lost their discipline. They secretly broke into people's houses and stole useful goods. They stole food and clothing along the roadways (no. 654).

   Kyūyō, ed. Kyūyō kenkyūkai (Kadokawa shoten, 1974).

47. *Han bōeki,* p. 104.

48. Ibid., pp. 103–104; and Kamiya, "Edo nobori," pp. 16–18.

49. Kamiya, "Edo nobori," p. 18; and Uehara, *Han bōeki,* pp. 107–108.

50. Uehara, *Han bōeki,* pp. 107–108. My analysis here in particular and throughout this chapter differs from the image of Ryukyu and its relationship with Japan presented by Jurgis Elisonas. See "The Inseparable Trinity: Japan's Relations with China and Korea," in *The Cambridge History of Japan: Volume 4, Early Modern Japan,* ed. John Whitney Hall (New York: Cambridge University Press, 1991), p. 300.

51. Ibid., pp. 105–107.

52. Ibid.

53. For a detailed discussion of Ryukyu's total productivity, see Mitsugu Matsuda, "The Government of the Kingdom of Ryukyu, 1600–1872" (Ph.D. diss., University of Hawai'i, 1967), pp. 22–25; and Sakihara, "The Significance of Ryukyu," pp. 18–40.

54. See Toby, *Diplomacy,* pp. 140–167, for a general discussion of these information routes.

55. "Kaigai jōhō," p. 86.

56. Ibid., pp. 75–76.

57. Ibid., pp. 70, 73–74, 85.

58. Ibid., p. 77.

59. "The Satsuma-Ryukyu Trade and the Tokugawa Seclusion Policy," *Journal of Asian Studies* 23.3 (May 1964):107.

60. *Han bōeki,* pp. 90–103.

61. Ibid., pp. 94–95; and Sakai, "The Satsuma-Ryukyu Trade," pp. 396–397.

62. Uehara, *Han bōeki*, pp. 96–97.

63. Ibid., pp. 97–99.

64. Ibid., p. 99; and Mori Toshihiko, "Satsuma-han to Ryūkyū ōkoku," *Nihongaku* 11 (March 1988):88–89.

65. Uehara, *Han bōeki*, pp. 99–102.

66. Ibid., pp. 109–111.

67. Ibid., pp. 111–133.

68. *Ryūkyū, Shinkoku no kōekishi: nishū* Rekidai hōan *no kenkyū* (Daiichi shobō, 1984), pp. 12–21 and throughout chapters 2 and 3.

69. See Sakihara Mitsugu, "Totōgin to Satsu-Ryū-Chū bōeki," *Nihon rekishi* 323 (April 1975); Araki Moriaki, *Shin Okinawashi ron* (Naha: Okinawa taimususha, 1980), pp. 121–129; Tasato Osamu, "Sangyō no imeeji," in *Kinsei shomondai shiriizu 5: kinsei no sangyō* (Urasoe: Urasoe-shi kyōiku iinkai, 1987), pp. 13–14; and Kamiya, "Edo nobori," p. 24.

70. A *kan* (or *kamne*) was the equivalent of 8.72 pounds or 3.75 kilograms.

71. Araki, *Shin Okinawashi ron*, pp. 126–127; Tasato, "Sangyō," p. 14. Sugar was a royal government monopoly and became a significant source of revenue by the late seventeenth century.

72. "Satsuma-Ryukyu Trade," p. 394.

73. Araki, *Shin Okinawashi ron*, p. 128; Uehara, *Han bōeki*, p. 134.

74. *Shin Okinawashi ron*, p. 128. The question of the degree to which Satsuma profited from the tribute trade is debatable, and even Araki is not entirely consistent on this point. Certainly the trade was not profitable for Satsuma in the seventeenth century (see also Sydney Crawcour, "Notes on Shipping and Trade in Japan and the Ryukyus," *Journal of Asian Studies* 23.3 [May 1964]:379). Both Araki and Uehara point out that Satsuma sought to reduce the scale of the tribute trade throughout the latter half of the eighteenth century (Araki, *Shin Okinawashi ron*, pp. 127–128; Uehara, *Han bōeki*, p. 139). There is no doubt that, overall, Satsuma profited from trade with China in the late eighteenth century. It is likely, however, that most of this profit came not from the tribute trade but from unauthorized trade *(mitsu bōeki)*. As in Ryukyu's case, it may have been that Satsuma's government found its support for Ryukyu's tribute trade to be a burden, while individual merchants and officials within Satsuma enriched themselves either through the tribute trade itself or through the opportunities for private trade connected with it.

75. The classic study on various aspects of premodern China's foreign relations is Fairbank, *The Chinese World Order.*

76. Miyata, *Ryūkyū, Shinkoku no kōekishi,* pp. 7–15.

77. The relevant excerpts are quoted in ibid., pp. 30–33.

78. Xu Gongsheng, *Chūgoku-Ryūkyū kōryūshi,* trans. Nishizato Kikō and Uezato Ken'ichi (Naha: Hirugisha, 1991), pp. 185–186. See pp. 179–200 for a general discussion of Ryukyuan students in China.

79. Ibid., p. 189.

80. Ibid.

81. Dana Masayuki, "Kinsei Kumemura no seiritsu to tenkai," in *Shin Ryūkyūshi, kinsei hen,* vol. 1 (Naha: Ryūkyū shinpōsha, 1989), pp. 21–30.

82. Xu, *Kōryūshi,* p. 192.

83. According to the *Kyūyō:* "When Sai On was an official residing in Fujian, he received an order to study geomancy from Li Ji [Xikai]. He carefully studied secret texts and compass techniques. He had already received silver from the royal government to defray his expenses" (no. 649).

84. See *Kyūyō,* nos. 388, 469, 488; Takara Kurayoshi, *Ryūkyū ōkokushi no kadai* (Naha: Hirugisha, 1990), p. 218; and Xu, *Kōryūshi,* pp. 192–193.

85. Xu, *Kōryūshi,* pp. 193–194. Also *Kyūyō,* no. 273.

86. Xu, *Kōryūshi,* pp. 193–194; *Kyūyō,* no. 349.

87. Xu, *Kōryūshi,* p. 193.

88. A *Kyūyō* entry dated 1679 reads: "We have heard of no previous instance of people in our country with a knowledge of physiognomy *(xiangfa).* Vice Interpreter Tei Meiryō was sent to Fujian as a resident official. There he studied the *Huangu* method and brought it back to our country, where it spread widely" (no. 493). *Huangu* is a term of Daoist origin indicating reform and change of one's character and disposition to become an immortal.

89. For an excellent discussion of immigrant Chinese in Old-Ryukyu, see Tomiyama Kazuyuki, "Tōitsu ōkoku keiseiki no taigai kankei," in *Shin Ryūkyūshi, ko-Ryūkyū hen* (Naha: Ryūkyū shinpōsha, 1991), pp. 141–162.

90. Quoted in Shimajiri Katsutarō, *Kinsei Okinawa no shakai to shūkyō* (San'ichi shobō, 1980), pp. 85–86.

91. Ibid., p. 85. For other accounts of Kumemura's decline, see Tomishima Sōei, "Minmatsu ni okeru Kumemura no suitai to shinkōsaku ni tsuite," in *Diijiai*

Zhong-Liu lishi guanxi guoji xueshu huiyi lunwenji, ed. Chū-Ryū bunka keizai kyōkai (Taibei: Lianhebao wenhua jijinhui guoxue wenxianguan, 1987), pp. 476–477.

92. Dana, "Kumemura," pp. 209–210. See also Shimajiri, *Shūkyō,* p. 86.

93. Dana, "Kumemura," p. 212. See also Tomishima, "Minmatsu ni okeru Kumemura," p. 478.

94. See Tomishima, "Minmatsu ni okeru Kumemura," pp. 483–487, for a detailed discussion of Kumemura titles and salaries.

95. Throughout this study I use *yukatchu* to refer to the Ryukyuan upper class. The two morphemes comprising the word would be *yoi hito* in Japanese. The Japanese loan word *samuree* was also in common use in the early-modern period to refer to this class, but because the Ryukyuan *samuree* had no connection with military affairs, the term is potentially misleading. In contemporary publications, the Sino-Japanese *shi* or *shizoku* is the preferred term, but it would have been rare in the speech of early-modern Ryukyuans. English terms such as noble or aristocrat are rough approximations of *yukatchu* but suggest connotations not appropriate to the Ryukyuan situation.

96. Dana, "Kumemura," p. 213.

97. Tomiyama Kazuyuki, "Tōitsu ōkoku keiseiki," pp. 150–156.

98. "Sappō no yōsō," *Shin Ryūkyūshi, kinsei hen,* vol. 1 (Naha: Ryūkyū shinpōsha, 1989), pp. 79–81.

99. Maehira Fusaaki, "Ryūkyū ōkoku ni sappō girei no tsuite," *Okinawa no shūkyō to minzoku,* ed. Kubo Noritada sensei Okinawa chōsa nijūnen kinen ronbunshū kankō iinkai (Daiichi shobō, 1988), pp. 193–194.

100. Tomiyama Kazuyuki, "Kannin seido no issokumen," in *Shin Ryūkyūshi, kinsei hen,* vol. 2 (Naha: Ryūkyū shinpōsha, 1990), pp. 63–83.

101. Ibid., pp. 71–73. Matsuda points out that the first known election of a high official in Ryukyu was in 1690, in Kumemura. The practice soon spread to selection of members of the Council of Three. See Matsuda, "Government," pp. 149–150.

102. Tomiyama Kazuyuki, "Kannin seido," pp. 80–83. Satsuma's approval, of course, was also required, and there is no indication that Satsuma ever objected to a king's selection.

103. Old-Ryukyu is a literal translation of *Ko-Ryūkyū,* which indicates a period from roughly the thirteenth century until 1609.

104. The ceremony was known in Ryukyu by various names, including *ten no mihai* and *ne no hō.*

105. Tomiyama Kazuyuki, "Ryūkyū no ōken girei—saiten girei to sūbyō saishi o chūshin ni," in *Ōken no kiso e,* ed. Akasaka Norio (Shinyōsha, 1992), pp. 203–215.

106. As Tomiyama and others have pointed out, "It is a well-known fact that the residents of Kumemura, descendants of Fujianese immigrants, played an extremely important role in introducing Chinese culture to Ryukyuan society. But it was only from the second half of the seventeenth century that the Shuri royal government began actively to adopt and expand Confucianism and Chinese standards nationally, and this change became fundamental policy only in the early eighteenth century." See ibid., pp. 216–217.

107. Ibid.

108. Ibid, p. 218.

109. The written language of Ryukyuan officialdom was Japanese *(sōrōbun),* except, of course, when conducting diplomacy with China. Well-educated Ryukyuans also wrote essays and poetry in classical Chinese. Significantly more Ryukyuans were literate in Japanese than in classical Chinese.

110. Naha-shi kikakubu bunkaka, eds., *Naha-shi shi,* shiryō-hen daiichi kan jūichi, Ryūkyū shiryō, vol. 2 (Naha: Naha-shi yakusho, 1991), pp. 37–38.

111. For an excellent analysis of this process, see Alan Christy, "The Making of Imperial Subjects in Okinawa," *Positions* 1.3 (winter 1993).

112. Maehira, "Kaigai jōhō," p. 73; Kamiya, *Ryūkyū shihai,* pp. 199–200.

113. Kamiya, *Ryūkyū shihai,* p. 200.

114. Several small islands in the Satsunan chain to the west of Tanegashima and Yakushima.

115. No. 261.

116. Quoted in Higashionna, "Shimazu-shi," p. 71.

117. Ibid.

118. Ibid., p. 70.

119. See Itokazu Kaneharu, "Hyōchaku kankei no torishime kitei ni tsuite," in *ROHM,* vol. 1, p. 22.

120. Higashionna, "Shimazu-shi," p. 71.

121. Anderson, *Imagined Communities,* esp. p. 5.

122. Quoted in *Kagoshima daihyakka jiten,* p. 1032. The distinction between *Nihon no kotoba* and *Satsuma kotoba* in this passage is a good example of the relatively loose consciousness of Japan held by many Japanese of the early and middle Tokugawa period.

123. Maeda Giken, *Nago Ueekata Tei Junsoku hyōden* (Haebaru-chō: Okinawa insatsu danchi shuppanbu, 1982), pp. 127–131.

124. Even after the rise of nations such gaps continued to exist, of course. The idea of the nation, however, went a long way toward suppressing awareness of these gaps.

125. Takara, *Ōkokushi*, p. 392.

126. Gotō and Tomoeda, eds., *Kumazawa Banzan*, pp. 148–149.

127. Toby, *State and Diplomacy in Early Modern Japan*, pp. 45–52.

128. Mark Ravina, "State-building and Political Economy in Early-Modern Japan," *The Journal of Asian Studies*, 54.4 (November 1995):997–1022.

CHAPTER 2 Looking North and Looking West

1. Takara, *Ōkokushi*, p. 214.

2. Ibid.

3. Ibid.

4. Also known as Shō Jōken, Shō Zōken, and Haneji Chōshū.

5. Nanpo Bunshi was the major figure in the so-called *Satsunan gakuha*. The only substantial study of this group of Satsuma-based Confucians is Ijichi Sueyasu's nineteenth-century work, *Kangaku kigen*. It is available in *Zoku-zoku gunsho ruijū*, vol. 10 (Kokusho kankōkai, 1907), pp. 558–746. Regarding prominent members of the *Satsunan gakuha*, see pp. 581–599 and 612–649. For a summary in English, see Gregory Smits, "Sai On (1682–1761) and Confucianism in the Early-Modern Ryukyu Kingdom," vol. 1 (Ph.D. diss., University of Southern California, 1992), pp. 168–171.

6. Known at the time as *"Bunshi ten,"* Nanpo Bunshi's system for reading classical Chinese has continued in use with only slight modification to this day.

7. *RSS*, vol. 1, p. 14.

8. Umeki Tetsuto, "Kinsei nōson no seiritsu," in *Shin Ryūkyūshi, kinsei hen*, vol. 1 (Naha: Ryūkyū shinpōsha, 1989), pp. 190–191.

9. The characters for this office would be read *"sesshō"* in Japanese contexts.

10. Umeki, "Nōson," p. 189.

11. *OKS*, vol. 1, pp. 3–4; and Takara Kurayoshi, "Shō Shōken no ronri," in *Shin Ryūkyūshi, kinsei hen*, vol. 1 (Naha: Ryūkyū shinpōsha, 1989), pp. 161–162.

12. Takara, "Shō Shōken," pp. 165–166; Takara, *Ōkokushi*, pp. 226–227.

13. *OKS,* vol. 1, pp. 4–5; Takara, "Shō Shōken," pp. 164–165.

14. In this instance, the term Shō Shōken employs is *karō,* the name of Satsuma's body of senior officials.

15. *OKS,* vol. 1, p. 5; Takara, "Shō Shōken," p. 165.

16. Umeki, " Nōson," pp. 190–191.

17. *Kyūyō,* no. 382. In the context of Ryukyuan government posts, *zashiki* meant "quasi" or "assistant," and indicated lesser or second-class status.

18. For relevant passages in *Directives of Haneji,* see *OKS,* vol. 1, pp. 19, 21–23, 26–28. See also *Kyūyō,* no. 402.

19. "Nōson," pp. 193–194.

20. Smits, "Sai On," pp. 188–189.

21. "Shō Shōken," pp. 168, 171–172.

22. *Haneji shioki, OKS,* vol. 1, pp. 51–52.

23. See ibid., pp. 13–16.

24. Ibid., p. 15.

25. *Okokushi,* p. 215.

26. Maehira Fusaaki, "Kōkai to shinkō," p. 10.

27. Ibid.

28. On the connection between Satsuma's invasion and native religion, see Itokazu Kaneharu, "Sai On to Shushigaku: kinsei Ryūkyū ni okeru sono shisōshijō no ichizuke," *Kyūyō ronsō,* ed. Shimajiri Katsutarō et al. (Naha: Hirugisha, 1986), pp. 263–265.

29. No. 464.

30. The practice was stopped in 1673, after which time the king sent a representative.

31. *Haneji shioki, OKS,* vol. 1, pp. 43–45.

32. Ibid., pp. 44–45.

33. Ibid., p. 45.

34. "Shō Shōken," pp. 172–177; *Okinawa rekishi monogatari* (Naha: Hirugisha, 1984), pp. 107–112; and *Ōkokushi,* pp. 219–223. For an example of the type of use of Shō Shōken's *"Nichiryū dōso ron"* that Takara criticizes, Matsuda states that "Haneji pointed out in one of his instructions that the Ryukyuans were of

the same ancestry of the Japanese, even in things such as landscape, the five human relationships, the five grains, and the names of animals and plants. He thus placed emphasis on the physical and cultural similarity between Ryukyu and Japan, and by this means he tried to show his countrymen the need to follow Japanese ways" ("Government," p. 83).

35. Takara, *Ōkokushi,* p. 221.

36. *Haneji shioki, OKS,* vol. 1, p. 48.

37. Ibid., p. 48.

38. Ibid., p. 55.

39. *Jochiku-ō den,* which is part of Ijichi Sueyasu's nineteenth-century work, *Kangaku kigen,* p. 627.

40. *Haneji shioki, OKS,* vol. 1, p. 24.

41. "Wabungaku no nagare," in *Shin Ryūkyūshi, kinsei hen,* vol. 2 (Naha: Ryūkyū shinpōsha, 1990), p. 219.

42. Ōshiro Tatsuhiro, *Ryūkyū no eiketsutachi* (Purejidentosha, 1992), pp. 220–221.

43. *RSS,* vol. 5, p. 12.

44. Ibid.

45. Dana Masayuki, *Okinawa kinseishi no shosō* (Naha: Hirugisha, 1992), pp. 3–4.

46. Additionally, although kings prior to the first Shō dynasty appear with the honorific *kō,* the kings of the first Shō dynasty appear without any honorific suffix. Because the first dynasty's founder came to the throne by military force and most of his successors were warlike, Dana interprets this omission as a Confucian distinction between *wangdao* (J. *ōdō,* "kingly way") and *badao* (J. *hadō,* "way of the hegemon"). See ibid., p. 4.

47. Ibid., p. 7.

48. A typical description of *tentō* is found in the opening sentences of *Shingaku gorinsho:* "*Tentō* is the ruler *(shujin)* of heaven and earth. Because it has no physical form it is invisible" (Ishida Ichirō and Kanaya Osamu, eds., *Fujiwara Seika, Hayashi Razan,* Nihon shisō taikei 28 [Iwanami shoten, 1975, 1982], p. 257). *Tentō* texts typically exhorted present-day rulers to rectify their minds, pointing out that *tentō* grants rulers a mandate to govern but will remove such a mandate should the ruler prove morally deficient, either during the wicked ruler's own reign or, more typically, during that of a descendant.

49. For example, Sakima Toshikatsu, *"Omoro" no shisō* (Yonabaru-chō: Ryūkyū bunka rekishi kenkyūjo, 1991), pp. 65–68.

50. The secondary literature on *tentō* thought is relatively sparse, and the topic deserves fuller study. See Ishige Tadashi, "*Shingaku gorinsho* no seiritsu jijō to sono tokishitsu: *Kana shōri, Honsaroku* rikai no zentei toshite," in *Fujiwara Seika, Hayashi Razan,* ed. Ishida and Kanaya, pp. 490–504; Ishige Tadashi, "Sengoku, Azuchi-Momoyama jidai no shisō," *Shisōshi,* ed. Ishida Ichirō, vol. 2 (Tokyo: Yamakawa shuppansha, 1976, 1984), pp. 1–61. In English, Herman Ooms provides a brief survey of some major themes in *tentō* texts. See *Tokugawa Ideology: Early Constructs, 1570–1680* (Princeton: Princeton University Press, 1985), pp. 80–96.

51. *RSS,* vol. 5, pp. 35–36.

52. Ibid., p. 48. Jie and Zhou were archetypical evil rulers in the Chinese classics.

53. Ibid., p. 54.

54. Ibid., p. 25. Yao and Shun, of course, were legendary Chinese sage kings.

55. For example, he was in charge of a team of Ryukyuan officials who supervised the purchase of Chinese goods during Shō Kei's investiture in 1719. Owing in part to the Ryukyuan officials' clumsy handling of the matter, the Chinese merchants rioted and Tei Junsoku and the other officials were forced to flee to a nearby temple.

56. Biographic details of Tei Junsoku's life are available in several sources, the two most thorough being Maeda, *Tei Junsoku;* and Iha Fuyū and Majikina Ankō, *Ryūkyū no go-ijin* (Naha: Okinawa Sankei shinbunsha shuppan jigyōbu, 1965), pp. 209–290.

57. Setsudō was Tei Junsoku's literary name. He produced several other collections of poetry and served as the editor and compiler of the first kingdom-wide collection of Chinese poems, *Chūzan shibunshū* (C. *Zhongshan shiwenji*).

58. Iha and Majikina, *Go-ijin,* pp. 230–231.

59. For details on the text's dissemination in Japan, see ibid., pp. 234–238. See also *ODJ,* vol. 3, pp. 839–840. By the end of the Meiji period, there were at least sixty-one different published varieties of works dealing with the Six Maxims throughout Japan.

60. Ōshiro, "Eiketsutachi," pp. 238–239.

61. Iha and Majikina, *Go-ijin,* pp. 223–225.

62. Shimajiri Katsutarō, comp., *Ryūkyū kanshi sen,* trans. Uezato Ken'ichi (Naha: Hirugisha, 1990), p. 37.

63. Ibid., pp. 43–44.

64. Ibid., p. 51. The final line of the poem is apparently a sarcastic reference to another's verse.

65. Ibid., p. 53.

66. Maeda, *Tei Junsoku,* p. 249. For a discussion of this text, see Maeda Giken, *Okinawa, yogawari no shisō: hito to gakumon no keifu* (Naha: Daiichi kyōiku tosho, 1972), pp. 156–163; and *Tei Junsoku,* pp. 92–98. The original text is available in Maeda, *Tei Junsoku,* pp. 249–258.

67. Maeda, *Tei Junsoku,* p. 250. There is little information on these figures. One household biography, *Itomine kaden,* says the following of Ceng: "There is a memorial tablet for Ceng Delu in the Shū household. Nobody knows why this person came here from China and there are many theories. Brilliant and widely learned, he became a teacher to others. He loved scholarship, served his teacher, and became Seigi Taifu" (quoted in Maeda, *Yogawari no shisō,* p. 159).

68. Maeda, *Tei Junsoku,* p. 250.

69. *ODJ,* vol. 1, p. 920.

70. Maeda, *Yogawari no shisō,* p. 161.

71. Ibid., pp. 161–162.

72. Maeda, *Tei Junsoku,* p. 253.

73. Naha-shi kikakubu bunka shinkōka, eds., *Naha-shi shi, shiryō-hen, dai ichi kan jū, Ryūkyū shiryō,* vol. 1 (Naha: Naha-shi yakusho, 1989), p. 708.

74. Ibid., p. 709.

(CHAPTER 3 Empowering Ryukyuans

1. There is one book-length biography of Sai On in Japanese, Maeda Giken, *Sai On: denki to shisō* (Naha: Gekkan Okinawasha, 1976). An English account that relies mainly on Maeda can be found in Edward E. Bollinger, *Saion, Okinawa's Sage Reformer: An Introduction to His Life and Selected Works* (Naha: Ryukyu Shinpō Newspaper, 1975), pp. 13–102.

2. *ODJ,* vol. 2, p. 179.

3. *Kyūyō,* no. 516; *Sai-uji kafu,* ed. Naha-shi kikakubu bunkaka, *Naha-shi shi, shiryō hen,* vol. 6 (Naha: Naha-shi yakusho, 1966), p. 365; and *SOZS,* pp. 103–104.

4. *SOZS,* p. 104.

5. Ibid.

6. Ibid., p. 105.

7. Ibid.

8. Ibid., p. 107.

9. Ibid., pp. 107–108.

10. *Shisho shūchū,* ed. supervised by Yasuoka Masahiro and Morohashi Tetsuji, *Shushigaku taikei,* vol. 7 (Meitoku shuppansha, 1974), pp. 38–39.

11. *SOZS,* p. 107.

12. The relevant passage, in Wing-tsit Chan's translation, reads: "The ancients who wished to manifest their clear characters to the world would first bring order to their states. Those who wished to bring order to their states would first regulate their families. Those who wished to regulate their families would first cultivate their personal lives. Those who wished to cultivate their personal lives would first rectify their minds. Those who wished to rectify their minds would first make their wills sincere. Those who wished to make their wills sincere would first extend their knowledge. The extension of knowledge consists in the investigation of things." (*A Source Book in Chinese Philosophy* [Princeton: Princeton University Press, 1963], p. 86.)

13. *SOZS,* pp. 155–156.

14. No. 649. For a discussion of the possible identity of Liu Ji, see Tsuzuki Akiko, "Kinsei Okinawa ni okeru fūsui no juyō to sono tenkai," in *Okinawa no fūsui,* ed. Kubo Noritada (Hirakawa shuppansha, 1990), p. 29. Her conclusion is that we cannot be certain of Liu Ji's identity.

15. Tsuzuki, "Kinsei Okinawa ni okeru fūsui," p. 19.

16. *Kyūyō,* no. 688.

17. Ibid., no. 702.

18. Tsuzuki Akiko, "Sai On no juka shisō ni tsuite: *Yōmu ihen* o megutte," *Ryūkoku daigaku ronshū* 445 (February 1995):296–304.

19. Both the *Kyūyō* (no. 713) and the *Sai-uji kafu* (p. 367) contain similar accounts of this incident. Sai On's "conversation" with the Chinese officials took place in writing to avoid possible misunderstandings arising from the Ryukyuans' lack of fluency in spoken Chinese.

20. Ibid.

21. *Kyūyō,* no. 780.

22. *Sai-uji kafu,* p. 367.

23. For a description of the royal government's procedures for purchasing Chinese goods, as well as this particular incident, see Ch'en, "Investiture of Liu-Ch'iu Kings," pp. 143–145, 150–152.

24. One *kanme* or *kan* is 8.72 pounds.

25. Shimajiri, *Shūkyō*, p. 129.

26. *SOZS*, pp. 110–111.

27. To my knowledge, only one scholar of Ryukyu has ever pointed out this obvious connection with Kaibara Ekken. Uehara Nario says, in reference to Sai On's views as expressed in *Kadōkun*, "It is obvious that he took these views verbatim from the thought expressed in Kaibara Ekken's *Kadōkun* (1711), and we may say that Kaibara influenced [Sai On]." See "Sai On ron," *Shin Okinawa bungaku* 66 (winter 1985):161. Indeed, simply referring to Kaibara's text enables the reader to fill in a number of lacunae in the text of *Kadōkun* in the *Sai On zenshū*. Recently, Tsuzuki Akiko has pointed out that Sai On may not have written *Kadōkun* (private communication).

28. For a detailed analysis of those aspects of Sai On's thought that derive from Cheng-Zhu Neo-Confucianism, see Itokazu, "Sai On to Shushigaku," pp. 263–292. Here, Itokazu argues against the view of Iha Fuyū that Sai On was a follower of Wang Yangming.

29. Prewar studies of Sai On's intellectual affiliations were based less on a careful reading of his works than on attempts to identify the elusive Fujian recluse of Sai On's autobiography. See, for example, Higashionna, "Sai On no gakutō," pp. 78–81. The more recent work of Itokazu has explored the similarities between the thought of Sai On and that of Cheng Yi and Zhu Xi in considerable depth. For a summary of the debates over Sai On's intellectual affiliation and new proposals for dealing with this issue, see Gregory Smits, "Sai On no gakutō to shisō: toku ni bukkyō/Shaka ron o chūshin to shite," *Okinawa bunka kenkyū* 23 (March 1997):1–38.

30. Quoted in David S. Nivison, *The Life and Thought of Chang Hsüeh-ch'eng* (Stanford, CA: Stanford University Press, 1966), p. 251.

31. "Investiture of Liu-Ch'iu Kings," p. 163.

32. In addition to essays by Itokazu, Tsuzuki, and Smits cited above, see also Gregory Smits, "The Intersection of Politics and Thought in Ryukyuan Confucianism: Sai On's Uses of *Quan*," *Harvard Journal of Asiatic Studies* 56.2 (December 1996):443–477; and Gregory Smits, "Unspeakable Things: Ryukyuan Confucian Sai On's Ambivalent Critique of Language and Buddhism," *Japanese Journal of Religious Studies* 24.1–2 (spring 1997):163–178.

33. The idea of meaningful action as text, of course, comes from Paul Ricoeur. Ricoeur defines meaningful action as "an action the importance of which goes 'beyond' its *relevance* to its initial situation." Such action is in effect inscribed in the course of events, and it "leaves a 'trace', it makes a 'mark' when it contributes to the emergence of . . . [social] patterns which become the *documents* of human action." See *Hermeneutics and the Human Sciences,* trans. and ed. John B. Thompson (New York: Cambridge University Press, 1981), pp. 206–207.

34. *SOZS,* p. 76.

35. For an excellent overview of the development and significance of geomancy in Ryukyu, see Tsuzuki, "Kinsei Okinawa ni okeru fūsui," pp. 15–58.

36. *SOZS,* p. 76.

37. Ibid.

38. Ibid. For the relevant passage from the *Articles,* which closely resembles that cited here, see *SOZS,* p. 16.

39. Shinzato Keiji, Taminato Tomoasa, and Kinjō Seitoku, *Okinawa-ken no rekishi* (Tokyo: Yamakawa shuppansha, 1972), p. 115.

40. Takara Kurayoshi, "Kinsei Ryūkyū e no sasoi," in *Shin Ryūkyūshi, kinsei hen,* vol. 1 (Naha: Ryūkyū shinpōsha, 1989), p. 26.

41. Ibid.

42. Present-day Komesu in the city of Itoman.

43. From *Conversations with a Rustic Old Man (Saō hengen)* in *SOZS,* p. 66.

44. This classification scheme seems to be of Sai On's own creation, but there were numerous models of nine levels of gradations of which Sai On may have been conscious. For example, the well-known Buddhist notion of nine grades of aspirants to Amida's Pure Land (J. *kuhon* or *kubon*) closely resembles Sai On's classification of countries.

45. *SOZS,* p. 78.

46. Ibid.

47. Although Sai On clearly regarded Ryukyu as a country, he never applied the terms *kokudo* or *kuni* to Satsuma. Whether he regarded Satsuma as a *kuni* like Ryukyu or a unit of the *kuni* Yamato, as most Ryukyuans called Japan as a whole, is difficult to say. In any case, it was the status of Ryukyu, not Satsuma, that he found problematic.

48. *SOZS,* p. 88.

49. Ibid.

50. Ibid.

51. Ibid., p. 132.

52. Ibid., p. 15.

53. Ibid., p. 194.

54. Ibid.

55. Ibid., p. 32, italics added.

56. Some of the better discussions of the concepts of *ming* and *tianming* include, for classical Confucianism, David L. Hall and Roger T. Ames, *Thinking Through Confucius* (Albany: State University of New York Press, 1987), pp. 204–249. For Confucianism in late imperial China, see Wing-tsit Chan, *Chu Hsi: New Studies* (Honolulu: University of Hawaiʻi Press, 1989), pp. 212–221; Cynthia J. Brokaw, *The Ledgers of Merit and Demerit: Social Change and Moral Order in Late Imperial China* (Princeton: Princeton University Press, 1991), pp. 52–60, 153–156; and Thomas A. Metzger, *Escape from Predicament: Neo-Confucianism and China's Evolving Political Culture* (New York: Columbia University Press, 1977), pp. 113–134.

57. Brokaw, *Ledgers,* p. 53.

58. This is a famous opening sentence of the *Mean,* which I have rendered here rather literally for ease of comparison with the rest of the passage.

59. *Zhuzi yulei,* ed. Li Jingde, vol. 1 (Beijing: Zhonghua shuju, 1986), p. 77.

60. Ibid.

61. Metzger, *Escape from Predicament,* p. 129.

62. Ibid., p. 130.

63. Ibid.

64. Wing-tsit Chan, trans., ed., *Neo-Confucian Terms Explained* (*The* Pei-hsi tzu-i) *by Ch'en Ch'un, 1159–1223* (New York: Columbia University Press, 1986), p. 41.

65. *Escape from Predicament,* p. 131.

66. Trans-generational karmic retribution was a major tenet in most Japanese *tentō* texts. Its function was to explain how the retribution due evil rulers might be delayed, affecting the rulers' sons or grandsons.

67. *SOZS,* p. 96.

68. Ibid.

69. The sagely Duke of Zhou's evil younger brother.

70. *SOZS,* p. 96.

71. For another example of this argument, see ibid., pp. 45–46.

72. Ibid., p. 101.

73. Ibid., p. 128.

74. Ibid., p. 101.

75. In *Mencius,* 8-A:1, for example: ". . . By retaining his heart and nurturing his nature he is serving heaven. Whether he is going to die young or live to a ripe old age makes no difference to his steadfastness of purpose. It is through awaiting whatever is to befall him with a perfected character that he stands firm on his proper destiny [*ming*]."

76. Chan, *A Source Book,* pp. 107–108.

77. For a superb discussion of *cheng* as used in the *Mean,* see Tu Wei-ming, *Centrality and Commonality: An Essay on Confucian Religiousness* (Albany: State University of New York Press, 1989), pp. 67–91.

78. Ibid., p. 84.

79. *RSS,* vol. 4, p. 27.

80. Ibid., p. 26.

81. *SOZS,* p. 191. The last sentence is roughly equivalent to saying, "This is built into the cosmic pattern."

82. Ibid., p. 192.

83. Ibid., p. 30.

84. Ibid., p. 193.

85. Ibid., p. 127.

86. Ibid., p. 130.

87. *Analects,* 6:10. Words spoken by Confucius upon seeing Bo Niu sick and dying.

88. *SOZS,* p. 158.

89. *Kyūyō,* no. 27.

90. Ibid., no. 224.

91. Ibid., no. 250.

(HAPTER 4 **Re-Creating Ryukyu**

1. Maehira, "Kōkai to shinkō," p. 10.

2. Tomiyama, "Ōken girei," pp. 191–194.

3. Ibid., pp. 195–196, 199.

4. No. 730.

5. Quoted in Tomiyama, "Ōken girei," p. 197. Although this passage is from six years prior to the formal revision of the rite, its style and content are typical of post-1719 supplications.

6. Ibid., p. 198.

7. Ibid.

8. Ibid., p. 201.

9. Ibid., pp. 199–200.

10. Ibid., pp. 201–202.

11. Ibid., p. 217.

12. Tasato Osamu, "Magiri to kuji," in *Shin Ryūkyūshi, kinsei hen,* vol. 2 (Naha: Ryūkyū shinpōsha, 1990), p. 106.

13. Nakama Yūei and Zhou Yaming, "Sanrin shinpi," *Chiiki to bunka* 37–38 (June 15, 1986):22, 23. The version here is more accurate than that found in *SOZS.*

14. *Kyūyō,* no. 1008. This description is a close paraphrase of a passage in *Sai-uji kafu,* p. 371.

15. *OKS,* vol. 6, p. 203. Sai On included this entire report verbatim in *One Man's Views.* Although the report was published under the seals of the three forestry commissioners, Hamakawa Peekumi, Yamauchi Peekumi, and Asato Ueekata, Amano Tetsuo says that Sai On was in fact the author (*ODJ,* vol. 2, p. 634).

16. *OKS,* vol. 6, pp. 203–204.

17. *Sai-uji kafu,* p. 371. The post of forestry commissioner had existed at various times in the past, but there is no indication that the commissioners prior to those Sai On appointed had any effect on forest use. The full staff of the office consisted of one *sō-yamabugyō,* two *yamabugyō,* three *bugyō zashiki,* three *kari-bugyō,* three *ōyako,* three secretaries, three apprentice secretaries, and thirty-seven other support staff (*ODJ,* vol. 3, p. 757).

18. *Sai-uji kafu,* p. 372.

19. Ibid. There is a similar account in *Kyūyō,* no. 1026.

20. Sai On wrote *Somayama hōshikichō* in 1737, which the Hyōjōsho and the Forestry Commissioners' Office promulgated as official policy. It consists of twenty-eight sections organized around three general topics: (1) how to supervise forest lands; (2) how to nurture forest lands; and (3) how to look after distant forest lands.

His next work was the *Yamabugyōsho kimochō* (alternate title: *Somayama kimochō*), completed in 1738. It, too, was issued as official policy by the Hyōjōsho and the Forestry Commissioners' Office. It contains thirty-one sections covering such topics as basic administrative rules for agencies charged with forest administration, protective supervision of forests, methods for nurturing trees, and the policing of forests, including penalties for those who violate forest use laws. The same year, Sai On also compiled *Somayama sōbakari no tsuite no jōjō*, which he issued under the seals of the forestry commissioners.

In 1747, Sai On and other Council of Three members jointly wrote *Somayama hōshiki shitsugi*, a continuation of the 1737 *Somayama hōshikichō*. The later book covered methods for handling various types of trees used for constructing forests, forest soils, and other topics in eighteen sections.

Finally, in 1751, just prior to his retirement, Sai On supervised the creation of two additional handbooks on forestry at the request of the forestry commissioners. One, *Yamabugyō kimochō shitsugi*, dealt entirely with penalties. Its thirteen sections strengthened the provisions of the earlier *Yamabugyōsho kimochō*. The other work, *Yamabugyōsho kujichō*, dealt with specific duties and job descriptions of forestry officials below the rank of commissioner, as well as other administrative matters.

21. Nakama Yūei, "Somayama to sonraku kyōdōtai," *Shin Ryūkyūshi, kinsei hen*, vol. 2 (Naha: Ryūkyū shinpōsha, 1991), p. 120. See also *Kyūyō*, no. 1009.

22. Nakama, "Somayama," p. 120.

23. *OKS*, vol. 6, p. 180.

24. Conrad Totman, *The Green Archipelago: Forestry in Preindustrial Japan* (Berkeley: University of California Press, 1989), p. 118.

25. *OKS*, vol. 6, p. 118.

26. *SOZS*, pp. 254–255.

27. As Richard J. Smith points out, "A good site should enjoy only mild breezes and gently moving water. . . . Too much wind or too fast a watercourse at a site causes harm and disperses good influences." See *Fortune-tellers and Philosophers: Divination in Traditional Chinese Society* (Boulder: Westview Press, 1991), p. 143.

28. See Nakama Yūei, "Sai On to rinsei," in *Kinsei no shomondai shiriizu 1: Sai On to sono jidai* (Naha: Richūsha, 1984), pp. 73–74, for a discussion of these techniques.

29. *OKS,* vol. 6, p. 125.

30. Kerr, *Okinawa,* p. 207; Inoue Hideo, "Sai On no kenkyū," *Nihon rekishi* 281 (September 1971):60.

31. "Material force of the mountain" *(shanqi)* is a concept connected with geomancy.

32. *OKS,* vol. 6. p. 196.

33. *Okinawa no nōgyō: kinsei kara gendai e no hensen* (Osaka: Kaifūsha, 1993), pp. 55–59.

34. Kerr, *Okinawa,* p. 207.

35. "Sai On no seiji," in *Kinsei no shomondai shiriizu 1: Sai On to sono jidai* (Naha: Richūsha, 1984), p. 69.

36. "Somayama," p. 120.

37. Ibid., p. 120.

38. For a summary of the *yaadui* system, see Smits, "Politics and Thought," pp. 465–467. For a detailed study, see Tasato Yūtetsu, *Okinawa ni okeru kaitaku shūraku no kenkyū,* comprising the whole of *Hōbungaku kiyō,* shigaku-chirigaku hen 23 (March 1980).

39. *ODJ,* vol. 2, p. 42.

40. *Kyūyō,* no. 1037.

41. *Sai-uji kafu,* p. 372.

42. Tasato, "Sai On no seiji," pp. 69–70.

43. Maeda, *Sai On,* p. 154; and *Sai-uji kafu,* p. 372.

44. Tasato, "Sai on no seiji," pp. 69–70; and Maeda, *Sai On,* pp. 153–154.

45. Maeda, *Sai On,* p. 155, based on work by Toguchi Masakiyo.

46. Ibid.

47. Nakama, "Somayama," p. 120.

48. *ODJ,* vol. 2, p. 42.

49. *Magiri kujichō no sekai,* ed. Okinawa-shi shi henshū jimukyoku, (Okinawa-shi: Okinawa-shi kyōiku iinkai, 1987), p. 58.

50. Ibid., p. 57.

51. Ibid., p. 58.

52. Tasato, "Magiri to kuji," pp. 88–92.

53. Ibid., p. 92.

54. Ibid., p. 95.

55. The term *"shinugu"* indicated a wide variety of agricultural festivals, not all of which necessarily had sexual overtones. Our concern here is only with those *shinugu* that involved naked dancing or some other explicit sexual dimension.

56. Araki, *Shin Okinawashi ron,* p. 78; and Shimabukuro Moritoshi, *Ryūka taikan* (Hakueisha, 1962), p. 488.

57. Shimabukuro, *Ryūka taikan,* p. 488.

58. Araki, *Shin Okinawashi ron,* p. 79.

59. Ibid., p. 80.

60. Maehira, "Kōkai to shinkō," pp. 10–11.

61. Araki, *Shin Okinawashi ron,* pp. 78–82.

62. Ibid., pp. 83–85.

63. This Okinawan deity was nearly identical in function with the kitchen or hearth deity of Chinese popular religion and must have come from China originally.

64. Tasato, "Magiri to kuji," pp. 96–97, 102–103.

65. Ibid., pp. 101–102.

66. Shamans were also numerous in urban areas. According to figures provided by William P. Lebra, shamans outnumbered medical doctors 5.7 to one in the Naha area in 1961. *Okinawan Religion: Belief, Ritual, and Social Structure* (Honolulu: University of Hawai'i Press, 1966, 1985), p. 80.

67. *Kyūyō,* no. 815.

68. Quoted in Takara Kurayoshi, "Yuta mondai no kōzu," in *Shin Ryūkyūshi, kinsei hen,* vol. 1 (Naha: Ryūkyū shinpōsha, 1989), p. 171.

69. Takara, *Ōkokushi,* p. 244.

70. In *Essential Discussion of Popular Customs,* for example, Sai On wrote: "Such things as false doctrines and the deception of shamans are all connected with the beast that destroys proper customs and are the poison that destroys the country. Therefore, enlightened rulers and good ministers must strictly prohibit such things" (*SOZS,* p. 159).

71. *Haneji shioki, OKS,* p. 7.

72. In 1667, Yō Shunshi of Kumemura was ordered to undertake calendrical studies in Fujian. He became ill, however, and his brother Yō Shun'ei took over the task.

His work produced a handbook on the calendar, which the royal government printed and had distributed throughout the country. This guide may have been inadequate, however, for in 1687, Sai Chōkō went to Fujian to study the calendar. Upon his return to Okinawa in 1682, he became head calendrical official and distributed handbooks on the calendar throughout the country. See *Kyūyō,* nos. 388, 469, 488; Takara, *Ōkokushi,* p. 218; Xu, pp. 192–193; and Majikina Ankō, *Okinawa kyōiku shiyō* (Naha: Okinawa shoseki hanbaisha, 1965), p. 91.

73. *Kujichō no sekai,* p. 54.

74. Nakamura Akira, "Ryūkyū ōkoku keisei no shisō: seiji shisōshi no ikku to shite," *Okinawa bunka kenkyū* 1 (1974):62.

75. Takara, "Yuta," p. 180.

76. Takara, *Ōkokushi,* p. 232.

77. Ibid., pp. 232–234.

78. Takara, "Yuta," pp. 180–181.

79. For a thorough analysis of Confucian uses of the *Yijing,* see Kidder Smith Jr. et al., *Sung Dynasty Uses of the* I Ching (Princeton: Princeton University Press, 1990).

80. Quoted in Takara, *Ōkokushi,* pp. 249–250. See pp. 250–252 for other examples.

81. Takara, "Yuta," p. 182.

82. *Kyūyō,* no. 785.

83. *OKS,* vol. 6, p. 54.

84. Shimabukuro, *Ryūka taikan,* p. 257. It was customary to write *ryūka* in Japanese "spelling" (for words written in *kana*) but to read them in whichever Ryukyuan language one spoke. The romanization mirrors the "Japanized" spelling of the original. For a similar poem, see p. 488.

85. Here taking the Chinese character read *mae* in Japanese as *"mi,"* (O. *me*) to be consistent with the *kana "mi"* in *Shuri-ganashimi* (O. *Shui-ganashiime*) below.

86. The king.

87. Shimabukuro, *Ryūka taikan,* p. 256.

88. Araki, *Shin Okinawashi ron,* pp. 80, 85.

89. Ibid., p. 85.

90. Tasato, "Magiri to kuji," pp. 105–106.

91. The best modern collection of Heshikiya's novels is Tamae Seiryō, *Junkyō no bungaku: Heshikiya Chōbin no shōsetsu* (Dai-Nippon insatsu, 1984).

92. Ikemiya Masaharu, *Ryūkyū bungaku ron* (Naha: Okinawa taimususha, 1976, 1980), pp. 408–409. For an overview of the major developments in Japanese literature among early-modern Ryukyuans, see Ikemiya Masaharu, "Wabungaku no nagare," in *Shin Ryūkyūshi, kinsei hen,* vol. 2 (Naha: Ryūkyū shinpōsha, 1990), pp. 211–260.

93. Ikemiya, *Ryūkyū bungaku ron,* pp. 401–416.

94. Tamae, *Junkyō no bungaku,* pp. 232–233.

95. Ibid., pp. 105–106.

96. *Mencius,* 6A:11. The passage reads in part: "Mencius said, 'Humanity is man's mind and righteousness is man's path. Pity the man who abandons the path and does not follow it, and who has lost his heart and does not know how to recover it. . . . The way of learning is none other than finding the lost mind.'"

97. *SOZS,* p. 155.

98. Tamae, *Junkyō no bungaku,* p. 68.

99. Ibid., p. 72.

100. Higa Kazuo, *Heshikiya Chōbin,* vol. 2 (Naha: Myaku hakkōjo, 1991), pp. 123–126.

101. *SOZS,* pp. 21–22.

102. Of the forty-one extant *kumiodori,* fourteen feature the theme of loyalty and the rest feature filial piety.

103. Matayoshi Hiroshi, "*Temizu no en* no sakusha wa dareka—Ikemiya Masaharu-shi no ronri," *Aoi umi: Okinawa no sōgō gekkanshi* 138 (December 1984):54–56.

104. Nishime Ikuwa, "Chōbin, *Manzai* e no kyōmi," *Aoi umi: Okinawa no sōgō gekkanshi* 138 (December 1984):38–43.

105. Higa, *Heshikiya Chōbin,* vol. 2, p. 112.

106. Shimabukuro, *Ryūka taikan,* p. 10.

107. In Chinese lore, owls supposedly ate their mothers and are thus a symbol for unfilial, evil, or abominable acts.

108. Quoted in Iha and Majikina, *Go-ijin,* p. 131.

109. Higa, *Heshikiya Chōbin,* vol. 1, pp. 31–32.

110. Quoted in Ikemiya Masaharu, *Kinsei Okinawa no shōzō: bungakusha, geinōsha retsuden,* vol. 1 (Naha: Hirugisha, 1982), p. 163.

111. Ibid., pp. 163–164.

112. Higa, *Heshikiya Chōbin,* vol 1, p. 20.

113. Ibid., pp. 23–24.

114. Ibid., pp. 25–27.

115. Ibid., p. 28.

116. Ibid., pp. 29–32. It is common for modern literary scholars to describe Sai On in the worst of terms.

117. Ikemiya, *Shōzō,* vol. 1, p. 165.

118. Higa, *Heshikiya Chōbin,* vol. 1, pp. 74–75.

119. Ibid., p. 33. Tamae also suggests that Heshikiya was critical of Satsuma in some of his writings. For example, Tamae interprets several of Heshikiya's poems as hopelessness in the face of Ryukyu under Satsuma's control (*Junkyō no bungaku,* pp. 230–231).

120. Higa, *Heshikiya Chōbin,* vol. 1, p. 33.

121. Ibid., vol. 2, p. 160.

122. Ibid., pp. 164–165.

123. See Takara, *Rekishi monogatari,* pp. 119–124, for a discussion of this topic and a modern Japanese translation of parts of the monument inscription. The full text is found in *Sai-uji kafu.*

124. *Sai-uji kafu,* pp. 372–373.

125. Ibid., p. 373.

126. "Fūsui," in *ODJ,* vol. 3, p. 345.

127. *Sai-uji kafu,* p. 373.

128. Ibid.

129. Here, Tenson functions for Sai On much like the equally ancient, mysterious, and legendary sage Fuxi did for Zhu Xi. Fuxi supposedly translated the moral pattern of the universe into diagrammatic form to create the eight trigrams. What appealed to Zhu was that Fuxi "was able to see the unity of the natural and moral pattern without engaging in learning *(hsüeh),*" because he possessed the mind of a sage (Kidder Smith Jr. et al., *Uses of the* I Ching, p. 223). Likewise, Sai On's primeval sage used his "spiritual insight" to select Shuri, an insight far superior to the scholarship and arguments of Sai On's ordinary human opponents.

130. *Sai-uji kafu,* p. 373.

131. Ibid.

132. Takara, *Rekishi monogatari,* p. 123.

133. See, for example, Miyata Toshihiko, "Sai On kafu ni tsuite," *Nantō shigaku* 8 (1976):49.

134. Takara, *Rekishi monogatari,* p. 123.

CHAPTER 5 Contested Visions of Sai On's Ryukyu

1. For a thorough examination of the aggrandizement of the Ryukyuan monarchs as depicted in posthumous portraits, see Tomiyama Kazuyuki, "Changes in Sovereign Power and the Royal Cult as Revealed in Posthumous Portraits of Ryukyuan Kings," paper presented at the 48th annual meeting of the Association for Asian Studies, Honolulu, April 15, 1996. The portraits indicate two points at which the kings were depicted with greater prestige than their predecessors: Shō Tei (r. 1669–1709) and Shō Boku.

2. *Kyūyō,* nos. 1332, 1425; and *ODJ,* vol. 2, p. 434.

3. *ODJ,* vol 2, p. 434.

4. *Kyūyō,* no. 1315.

5. Quoted in Miyagi Eishō, "Ryūkyū karitsu ni tsuite," *Nihon rekishi* 155 (March 1961):12–13.

6. Ibid., pp. 13–16.

7. Although high, *ueekata* status was lower than princely status and the *aji.*

8. For a detailed history of the *kanshō* system in Ryukyu, see Xu, *Kōryūshi,* pp. 179–200.

9. According to Iha Fuyū, Sai Seishō's political ambition drew him close to the elite *yukatchu* of Shuri and away from Kumemura ("Kanshō sōdō ni tsuite," in *Ko-Ryūkyū* [Seijisha, 1942], pp. 120–121).

10. Ibid., pp. 121–122, quoted passage on p. 122.

11. Ibid., pp. 122–123; and *ODJ,* vol. 1, p. 798.

12. Iha, "Kanshō sōdō," pp. 123–124.

13. Ibid., pp. 126–127; and *ODJ,* vol. 1, p. 798.

14. Iha, "Kanshō sōdō," pp. 128–129.

15. Based on the version provided by Iha in *Ko-Ryūkyū,* p. 134.

16. Ibid.

17. Ibid., p. 138.

18. Quoted in Majikina, *Kyōiku,* p. 121.

19. *SOZS,* p. 84.

20. Majikina, *Kyōiku,* p. 81. See also Maeda, *Yogawari no shisō,* p. 185.

21. Maeda, *Yogawari no shisō,* p. 185.

22. Majikina, *Kyōiku,* pp. 164–168.

23. *RSS,* vol. 4, p. 180.

24. Maeda, *Yogawari no shisō,* p. 187.

25. Iha, "Kanshō sōdō," p. 127.

26. *ODJ,* vol. 2, p. 418.

27. Uehara, *Han bōeki,* pp. 126–129.

28. Sakihara, "The Significance of Ryukyu," p. 215.

29. Uehara, *Han bōeki,* pp. 130–134.

Epilogue and Conclusions

1. For an excellent analysis of the complexities and difficulties inherent in the concept of culture, see Judith B. Farquhar and James L. Hevia, "Culture and Postwar American Historiography of China," *Positions: East Asia Cultures Critique* 1.2 (fall 1993):486–525.

2. On the nature and principles of sovereignty in Tokugawa Japan, see Ravina, "State-building," esp. pp. 1007–1013.

3. Nishizato Kikō presents a sophisticated analysis of the international dimension of the *Ryūkyū shobun* that gives due weight to Ryukyuan agency. See "Ryūkyū bunkatsu kōshō to sono shūhen," in *Shin Ryūkyūshi, kindai/gendai hen* (Naha: Ryūkyū shinpōsha, 1992), pp. 23–62.

4. For a particularly severe critique, see Makise Tsuneji, *Nihonshi no genten Okinawashi* (Honpō shoseki, 1984, 1989), esp. pp. 294–312.

5. Makise points out that the *Ryūkyū shobun* was not an attempt to unite the people of Japan (including Ryukyuans, members of the same ethnic group [*minzoku*] as other Japanese in his view) from the bottom up, but a way of expanding Japanese territory (ibid., p. 294). Many other works in Japanese come similarly close to characterizing Ryukyu/Okinawa as Japan's first colony, but never explicitly do so. Christy, however, is not so reticent, pointing out that "the case of Okinawa is now routinely ignored in examinations of Japanese colonialism." See "Imperial Subjects," p. 608.

6. Nishizato, "Ryūkyū bunkatsu," pp. 29–30.

7. Shinzato et al., *Okinawa-ken no rekishi*, pp. 155–157.

8. Nishizato, "Ryūkyū bunkatsu," pp. 33–44.

9. Shinzato et al., *Okinawa-ken no rekishi*, pp. 168–170.

10. The issue of what motivated the *yukatchu* who fled to China is debatable. The standard interpretation is that they were motivated by greed and selfishness, which is why most returned to Okinawa after 1884 under Iwamura. Makise stresses this theme with particular vigor owing to his vision of a united *minzoku* (Japan and Okinawa as one) and its having been thwarted first by the Meiji state and later by U.S. occupation. He argues that the very idea of Ryukyu having ties to both China and Japan is an incorrect "ethnic [racial?] consciousness" *(minzoku ishiki)*. The former *yukatchu* simply sought to hang on to their former "parasitic" mode of life, not to resist the injustices of the Meiji state. See *Nihonshi no genten Okinawashi*, pp. 299–303. By contrast, Nishizato portrays Ryukyuan exiles as selfless patriots and certainly provides compelling evidence that at least some were (Rin Seikō, for example, took his life in 1880 to dramatize his written plea to China to do more to aid Ryukyu). See "Ryūkyū bunkatsu," esp. pp. 52–53. Undoubtedly there were a variety of motives at work among the Ryukyuan exiles.

11. Shinzato et al., *Okinawa-ken no rekishi*, pp. 166–167.

12. Ibid., pp. 174–175.

13. Ibid., pp. 197–200.

14. Christy, "Imperial Subjects," pp. 608–610.

15. Ibid., pp. 611–634.

16. Quoted in Tomiyama Ichirō, "Okinawa sabetsu to puroriteria-ka," in *Shin Ryūkyūshi, kindai/gendai hen* (Naha: Ryūkyū shinpōsha, 1992), p. 171. See also Christy, "Imperial Subjects," pp. 607–608. For the nearly complete text of the several articles about the matter appearing in the *Ryūkyū shinpō*, see *Naha-shi shi, shiryō hen*, ed. Naha-shi shi henshū iinkai, vol. 2, no. 1 *(jō)* (Kumamoto-shi: Shirono insatsujo, 1966), pp. 77–78.

17. Anderson, *Imagined Communities.*

18. Ibid., pp. 6–7; Gellner, *Nations and Nationalism*, p. 1 ("Nationalism is primarily a political principle, which holds that the political and the national unit should be congruent."); Duara, *Rescuing History*, pp. 17–33.

19. Duara, *Rescuing History*, pp. 17–33.

20. For an excellent analysis of national imagining and the fashioning of historical

narratives, see Stefan Tanaka, *Japan's Orient: Rendering Pasts into History* (Berkeley: University of California Press, 1993).

21. Higashionna, "Satsuma no Ryūkyū ni taisuru ni seisaku," p. 234. For the whole address, see pp. 224–235.

22. *Ko-Ryūkyū,* p. 14.

23. Ibid., p. 35.

24. Shinzato et al., *Okinawa-ken no rekishi,* p. 196.

25. Ibid., pp. 192–193. This move prompted a strike by the middle school students.

26. The declining domestic sugar industry combined with high taxes resulted in conditions commonly called the "Sotetsu palm hell" *(sotetsu jigoku),* the almost tasteless fruit of the *sotetsu* being a food of last resort during times of famine. See ibid., pp. 197–202; Christy, "Imperial Subjects," pp. 611–616; and Mukai Kiyoshi, "Sotetsu jigoku," in *Shin Ryūkyūshi, kindai/gendai hen* (Naha: Ryūkyū shinpōsha, 1992), pp. 193–212.

27. Christy, "Imperial Subjects," pp.612–614; and Tomiyama, "Okinawa sabetsu," pp. 179–185.

28. Shinzato et al., *Okinawa-ken no rekishi,* p. 208.

29. Ibid., p. 209.

30. Ibid.

31. *ODJ,* vol. 3, p. 444.

32. Christy, "Imperial Subjects," pp. 612–614. Although my stress here is on mainland images of Okinawans, I do not mean to suggest that Okinawan lack of proficiency in Japanese was not a real problem for those seeking mainland employment.

33. *ODJ,* vol. 3, p. 320.

34. Haruko Taya Cook and Theodore F. Cook, *Japan at War: An Oral History* (New York: The New Press, 1992), p. 475. See also pp. 354–372.

35. An excellent analysis is given by Norma Field, *In the Realm of a Dying Emperor: Japan at Century's End* (New York: Vintage Books, 1993), pp. 33–104.

36. An account of this event and Chibana's subsequent trial and other activities is found in ibid. For Chibana's account, see Chibana Shōichi, *Yakisuterareta hino-maru: kichi no shima Okinawa Yomitan kara* (Shinsensha, 1988).

37. For an analysis of certain aspects of this contestation, see Gerald A. Figal, "Historical Sense and Commemorative Sensibility at Okinawa's Cornerstone of Peace," *Positions: East Asia Cultures Critique* 5.3 (winter 1997):745–778.

38. Sakihara ("The Significance of Ryukyu") and Matsuda ("Government") both tend to situate Ryukyu on the Japan side of the China-Japan divide. These studies, however, tend to be ambivalent, stating that Ryukyu was part of Japan much like the various domains *(han)* in some places but also suggesting a high degree of autonomy in others.

39. Ch'en, "Investiture of Liu-Ch'iu Kings," p. 160. Italics mine.

40. Smits, "Politics and Thought."

41. Ibid., pp. 467–473.

42. For a thorough discussion of this issue, see Watanabe Hiroshi, *Kinsei Nihon shakai to sōgaku* (Tōkyō daigaku shuppankai, 1985), pp. 49–60; Bob Tadashi Wakabayashi, *Anti-Foreignism and Western Learning in Early-Modern Japan: The New Theses of 1825* (Cambridge, MA: Council on East Asian Studies, Harvard University, 1986), pp. 17–57; and Kate Wildman Nakai, *Shogunal Politics: Arai Hakuseki and the Premises of Tokugawa Rule* (Cambridge, MA: Council on East Asian Studies, Harvard University, 1988), pp. 320–339.

43. The older notion of the bakufu's imposing Cheng-Zhu Neo-Confucianism on Japan has been thoroughly refuted by recent scholarship. See Watanabe, *Kinsei Nihon shakai,* esp., pp. 33–188; and Ooms, *Tokugawa Ideology.*

44. Tetsuo Najita, *Visions of Virtue in Tokugawa Japan: The Kaitokudō Merchant Academy of Osaka* (Chicago: University of Chicago Press, 1987), p. 61.

45. Tessa Morris-Suzuki, "Rewriting History: Civilization Theory in Contemporary Japan," *Positions: East Asia Cultures Critique* 1.2 (fall 1993):540.

46. Takara Kurayoshi, *Ryūkyū ōkoku no kōzō* (Yoshikawa kōbunkan, 1987), pp. 236–250.

47. Anderson, *Imagined Communities,* p. 5.

48. For one example, see Mashiko Hidenori, "Kokugo no hatsumei, hōgen no hatsumei, kokushi no hatsumei," *Okinawa bunka kenkyū* 23 (March 1997):173–200.

49. Ravina, "State-building," esp. pp. 1017–1019.

50. Ibid., p.1012.

51. Iha and Majikina, *Go-ijin,* p. 81.

52. Ibid., pp. 111–112.

53. Ibid, pp. 128–129. This tale had been passed down by word of mouth.

54. Recall Christy's analysis of Japanese portrayals of the mainland as "modern" or "advanced" in contrast with a "backward," tradition-bound Okinawa.

Works Cited

The place of publication for Japanese works is Tokyo unless otherwise indicated.

Anderson, Benedict. *Imagined Communities: Reflections on the Origin and Spread of Nationalism.* Rev. ed. London: Verso, 1991.

Araki Moriaki. *Shin Okinawashi ron.* Naha: Okinawa taimususha, 1980.

Bhabha, Homi K., ed. *Nation and Narration.* London: Routledge, 1990.

Bollinger, Edward E. *Saion, Okinawa's Sage Reformer: An Introduction to His Life and Selected Works.* Naha: Ryukyu Shimpō Newspaper, 1975.

Brokaw, Cynthia J. *The Ledgers of Merit and Demerit: Social Change and Moral Order in Late Imperial China.* Princeton: Princeton University Press, 1991.

Chan, Wing-tsit. *Chu Hsi: New Studies.* Honolulu: University of Hawai'i Press, 1989.

———, trans. and comp. *A Source Book in Chinese Philosophy.* Princeton: Princeton University Press, 1963.

———, trans. and ed. *Neo-Confucian Terms Explained (The Pei-hsi tzu-i) by Ch'en Ch'un, 1159–1223.* New York: Columbia University Press, 1986.

Ch'en, Ta-tuan. "Investiture of Liu-Ch'iu Kings in the Ch'ing Period." In *The Chinese World Order: Traditional China's Foreign Relations,* edited by John King Fairbank. Cambridge, MA: Harvard University Press, 1968.

Chibana Shōichi. *Yakisuterareta hinomaru: kichi no shima Okinawa Yomitan kara.* Shinsensha, 1988.

Christy, Alan. "The Making of Imperial Subjects in Okinawa." *Positions: East Asia Cultures Critique* 1.3 (winter 1993):607–639.

Connor, Walker. *Ethnonationalism: The Quest for Understanding.* Princeton: Princeton University Press, 1994.

Cook, Haruko Taya, and Theodore F. Cook. *Japan at War: An Oral History.* New York: The New Press, 1992.

Crawcour, Sidney. "Notes on Shipping and Trade in Japan and the Ryukyus." *The Journal of Asian Studies* 23.3 (May 1964):377–381.

Dana Masayuki. "Kinsei Kumemura no seiritsu to tenkai." In *Shin Ryūkyūshi, kinsei hen,* vol. 1, pp. 205–230. Naha: Ryūkyū shinpōsha, 1989.

———. *Okinawa kinseishi no shosō.* Naha: Hirugisha, 1992.

Duara, Prasenjit. *Rescuing History from the Nation: Questioning Narratives of Modern China.* Chicago: University of Chicago Press, 1995.

Elisonas, Jurgis. "The Inseparable Trinity: Japan's Relations with China and Korea." In *The Cambridge History of Japan.* Vol. 4, *Early Modern Japan,* pp. 235–300. Edited by John Whitney Hall. New York: Cambridge University Press, 1991.

Fairbank, John King, ed. *The Chinese World Order: Traditional China's Foreign Relations.* Cambridge, MA: Harvard University Press, 1968.

Farquhar, Judith B., and James L. Hevia. "Culture and Postwar American Historiography of China." *Positions: East Asia Cultures Critique* 1.2 (fall 1993):486–525.

Field, Norma. *In the Realm of a Dying Emperor: Japan at Century's End.* New York: Vintage Books, 1993.

Figal, Gerald A. "Historical Sense and Commemorative Sensibility at Okinawa's Cornerstone of Peace," *Positions: East Asia Cultures Critique* 5.3 (winter 1997): 745–778.

Gellner, Ernst. *Nations and Nationalism.* Ithaca, NY: Cornell University Press, 1983.

Gotō Yōichi and Tomoeda Ryūtarō, eds. *Kumazawa Banzan.* Nihon shisō taikei 30. Iwanami shoten, 1971.

Hall, David L., and Roger T. Ames. *Thinking Through Confucius.* Albany: State University of New York Press, 1987.

Higa Kazuo. *Heshikiya Chōbin.* 2 vols. Naha: Myaku hakkōjo, 1991.

Higashionna (Higaonna) Kanjun. "Sai On no gakutō." In *Higashionna Kanjun zenshū,* vol. 4, pp. 78–81. Compiled by Ryūkyū shinpōsha. Daiichi shobō, 1978.

———. "Satsuma no Ryūkyū ni taisuru ni seisaku." In *Higashionna Kanjun zenshū,* vol. 5, pp. 224–235. Compiled by Ryūkyū shinpōsha. Daiichi shobō, 1978.

———."Shimazu-shi no Ryūkyū tōji kikan." *Higashionna Kanjun zenshū,* vol. 1, pp. 67–69. Compiled by Ryūkyū shinpōsha. Daiichi shobō, 1978.

Hobsbawm, E. J. *Nations and Nationalism since 1780: Programme, Myth, Reality.* 2d ed. Cambridge: Cambridge University Press, 1994.

Iha Fuyū. "Kanshō sōdō ni tsuite." In *Ko-Ryūkyū,* pp. 117–132. Seijisha, 1942.

———. *Ko-Ryūkyū.* Seijisha, 1942.

——— and Majikina Ankō. *Ryūkyū no go-ijin.* Naha: Okinawa Sankei shinbunsha shuppan jigyōbu, 1965.

Iinuma Jirō. *Okinawa no nōgyō: kinsei kara gendai e no hensen.* Osaka: Kaifūsha, 1993.

Ijichi Sueyasu. *Kangaku kigen.* In *Zoku-zoku gunsho ruijū,* vol. 10, pp. 558–746. Kokusho kankōkai, 1907.

Ikemiya Masaharu. *Kinsei Okinawa no shōzō: bungakusha, geinōsha retsuden.* 2 vols. Naha: Hirugisha, 1982.

———. *Ryūkyū bungaku ron.* Naha: Okinawa taimususha, 1976, 1980.

———. "Wabungaku no nagare." In *Shin Ryūkyūshi, kinsei hen,* vol. 2, pp. 211–260. Naha: Ryūkyū shinpōsha, 1990.

Inoue Hideo. "Sai On no kenkyū." *Nihon rekishi* 281 (September 1971):49–65.

Ishida Ichirō and Kanaya Osamu. *Fujiwara Seika, Hayashi Razan.* Nihon shisō taikei 28. Iwanami shoten, 1975, 1982.

Ishige Tadashi. "Sengoku, Azuchi-Momoyama jidai no shisō." In *Shisōshi,* vol. 2. Edited by Ishida Ichirō. Yamakawa suppansha, 1976, 1984.

———. "*Shingaku gorinsho* no seiritsu jijō to sono tokushitsu: *Kana shōri, Honsaroku* rikai no zentei toshite." In *Fujiwara Seika, Hayashi Razan.* Nihon shisō taikei 28. Edited by Ishida Ichirō and Kanaya Osamu. Iwanami shoten, 1975, 1982.

Itokazu Kaneharu. "Hyōchaku kankei no torishime kitei ni tsuite." In *ROHM,* vol. 1, pp. 15–29.

———. "Sai On to shushigaku: kinsei Ryūkyū ni okeru sono Shisōshijō no ichizuke." Edited by Shimajiri Katsutarō et al. *Kyūyō ronsō,* pp. 263–292. Naha: Hirugisha, 1986.

Kagoshima daihyakka jiten. Edited by Kagoshima daihyakka jiten henshūshitsu. Kagoshima: Minami Nihon shinbunsha, 1983.

Kamiya Nobuyuki. *Bakuhansei kokka no Ryūkyū shihai.* Azekura shobō, 1990.

———. "Edo nobori." In *Shin Ryūkyūshi, kinsei hen,* vol. 2, pp. 11–36. Naha: Ryūkyū shinpōsha, 1990.

———. "Satsuma no Ryūkyū shinnyū." In *Shin Ryūkyūshi, kinsei hen,* vol. 1, pp. 33–72. Naha: Ryūkyū shinpōsha, 1989.

Kerr, George H. *Okinawa: The History of an Island People.* Rutland, VT: Charles E. Tuttle Company, 1958.

Kyūyō. Edited by the Kyūyō kenkyūkai. 2 vols. (one in classical Chinese; one in *yomikudashibun*). Kadokawa shoten, 1974.

Lebra, William P. *Okinawan Religion: Belief, Ritual, and Social Structure.* Honolulu: University of Hawai'i Press, 1966, 1985.

Maeda Giken. *Nago Ueekata Tei Junsoku hyōden.* Haebaru-chō: Okinawa Insatsu Danchi shuppanbu, 1982.

———. *Okinawa, yogawari no shisō: hito to gakumon no keifu.* Naha: Daiichi kyōiku tosho, 1972.

———. *Sai On: denki to shisō.* Naha: Gekkan Okinawasha, 1976.

Maehira Fusaaki. "Kinsei Nihon ni okeru kaigai jōhō to Ryūkyū no ichi." *Shisō* 796 (October 1990):67–89.

———. "Kinsei Ryūkyū ni okeru kōkai to shinkō: 'tabi' no girei o chūshin ni." *Okinawa bunka* 77 (January 1993):1–16.

———. "Ryūkyū ōkoku no sappō girei ni tsuite." Edited by Kubo Noritada sensei Okinawa chōsa nijūnen kinen ronbunshū kankō iinkai. In *Okinawa no shūkyō to minzoku,* pp. 167–200. Daiichi shobō, 1988.

Magiri kujichō no sekai. Edited by Okinawa-shi shi henshū jimukyoku. Okinawa-shi: Okinawa-shi kyōiku iinkai, 1987.

Majikina Ankō. *Okinawa kyōiku shiyō.* Naha: Okinawa shoseki hanbaisha, 1965.

Makise Tsuneji. *Nihonshi no genten Okinawashi.* Honpō shoseki, 1984, 1989.

Mashiko Hidenori. "Kokugo no hatsumei, hōgen no hatsumei, kokushi no hatsumei." *Okinawa bunka kenkyū* 23 (March 1997):173–200.

Matayoshi Hiroshi. "*Temizu no en* no sakusha wa dare ka—Ikemiya Masaharu-shi no ronri." *Aoi umi: Okinawa no sōgō gekkanshi* 138 (December 1984):52–56.

Matsuda, Mitsugu. "The Government of the Kingdom of Ryukyu, 1600–1872." Ph.D. diss., University of Hawai'i, 1967.

Metzger, Thomas. *Escape from Predicament: Neo-Confucianism and China's Evolving Political Culture.* New York: Columbia University Press, 1977.

Miyagi Eishō. "Ryūkyū karitsu ni tsuite." *Nihon rekishi* 155 (March 1961):12–21.

Miyata Toshihiko. *Ryūkyū, Shinkoku no kōekishi: nishū* Rekidai hōan *no kenkyū.* Daiichi shobō, 1984.

———. "Sai On kafu ni tsuite." *Nantōshi* 8 (May 1976):35–52.

Mori Toshihiko. "Satsuma han to Ryūkyū ōkoku." *Nihongaku* 11, Meicho kankōkai (March 1988):86–90.

Morris-Suzuki, Tessa. "Rewriting History: Civilization Theory in Contemporary Japan." *Positions: East Asia Cultures Critique* 1.2 (fall 1993):526–549.

Mukai Kiyoshi. "Sotetsu jigoku." In *Shin Ryūkyūshi, kindai/gendai hen,* pp. 191–213. Naha: Ryūkyū shinpōsha, 1992.

Naha-shi shi, shiryō-hen, daiichi kan jūichi, Ryūkyū shiryō, vol. 2. Edited by Naha-shi kikakubu bunkaka. Naha: Naha-shi yakusho, 1991.

Naha-shi shi, shiryō hen, vol. 2, no. 1 *(jō).* Edited by Naha-shi shi henshū iinkai. Kumamoto-shi: Shirono insatsujo, 1966.

Najita, Tetsuo. *Visions of Virtue in Tokugawa Japan: The Kaitokudō Merchant Academy of Osaka.* Chicago: University of Chicago Press, 1987.

Nakai, Kate Wildman. *Shogunal Politics: Arai Hakuseki and the Premises of Tokugawa Rule.* Cambridge, MA: Council on East Asian Studies, Harvard University, 1988.

Nakama Yūei. "Sai On to rinsei." In *Kinsei no shomondai shiriizu 1: Sai On to sono jidai,* pp. 71–83. Naha: Richūsha, 1984.

———. "Somayama to sonraku kyōdōtai." *Shin Ryūkyūshi, kinsei hen,* vol. 2, pp. 109–128. Naha: Ryūkyū shinpōsha.

——— and Zhou Yaming. "Sanrin shinpi." *Chiiki to bunka* 37–38 (June 15, 1986): 20–25.

Nakamura Akira. "Ryūkyū ōkoku keisei no shisō: seiji shisōshi no ikku to shite." *Okinawa bunka kenkyū* 1 (1974):1–78.

Nishime Ikuwa. "Chōbin, *Manzai* e no kyōmi." *Aoi umi: Okinawa no sōgō gekkanshi* 138 (December 1984):38–43.

Nishizato Kikō. "Ryūkyū bunkatsu kōshō to sono shūhen." In *Shin Ryūkyūshi, kindai/gendai hen,* pp. 23–62. Naha: Ryūkyū shinpōsha, 1992.

Nivison, David S. *The Life and Thought of Chang Hsüeh-ch'eng.* Stanford: Stanford University Press, 1966.

Okinawa daihyakka jiten. 4 vols. Edited by Okinawa daihyakka jiten kankō jimukyoku. Naha: Okinawa taimususha, 1983.

Okinawa-ken shiryō. 19 vols. Compiled by Okinawa kenritsu toshokan shiryō henshūshitsu. Naha: Okinawa-ken kyōiku iinkai, 1978–1991.

Ooms, Herman. *Tokugawa Ideology: Early Constructs, 1570–1680.* Princeton: Princeton University Press, 1985.

Ōshiro Tatsuhiko. *Ryūkyū no eiketsutachi.* Purejidentosha, 1992.

Ravina, Mark. "State-building and Political Economy in Early-Modern Japan." *The Journal of Asian Studies* 54.4 (November 1995):997–1022.

Ricoeur, Paul. *Hermeneutics and the Human Sciences.* Edited and translated by John B. Thompson. New York: Cambridge University Press, 1981.

Ryūkyū ōkoku hyōjōsjo monjo. 18 vols. Edited by Ryūkyū ōkoku hyōjōsho monjo henshū iinkai. Naha: Hirugisha, 1988–.

Ryūkyū shiryō sōsho. 5 vols. Edited by Iha Fuyū, Higashionna Kanjun, and Yokoyama Shigeru. Hōbun shokan, 1940, 1988. (Iha "Fuken" on title page is incorrect.)

Sai On zenshū. Edited by Sakihama Shūmei. Honpō shoseki, 1984.

Sai-uji kafu. Edited by Naha-shi kikakubu bunkaka. In *Naha-shi shi, shiryō hen,* vol. 6, pp. 362–377. Naha: Naha-shi yakusho, 1966.

Sakai, Robert. "The Satsuma-Ryūkyū Trade and the Tokugawa Seclusion Policy." *The Journal of Asian Studies* 23.3 (May 1964):391–403.

Sakihara Mitsugu. "The Significance of Ryukyu in Satsuma Finances During the Tokugawa Period." Ph.D. diss., University of Hawai'i, 1971.

———. "Totōgin to Satsu-Ryū-Chū bōeki." *Nihon rekishi* 323 (April 1975).

Sakima Toshikatsu. *"Omoro" no shisō.* Yonabaru-chō: Ryūkyū bunka rekishi kenkyūjo, 1991.

Shimabukuro Moritoshi. *Ryūka taikan.* Hakueisha, 1964.

Shimajiri Katsutarō. *Kinsei Okinawa no shakai to shūkyō.* San'ichi shobō, 1980.

———, comp. *Ryūkyū kanshi sen.* Translated by Uesato Ken'ichi. Naha: Hirugisha, 1990.

Shinzato Keiji, Taminato Tomoasa, and Kinjō Seitoku. *Okinawa-ken no rekishi.* Yamakawa shuppansha, 1972.

Shisho shūchū. Editing supervised by Yasuoka Masahiro and Morohashi Tetsuji. Shushigaku taikei, vol. 7. Meitoku shuppansha, 1974.

Smith, Kidder, Jr., et al. *Sung Dynasty Uses of the* I Ching. Princeton: Princeton University Press, 1990.

Smith, Richard. *Fortune-tellers and Philosophers: Divination in Traditional Chinese Society.* Boulder: Westview Press, 1991.

Smits, Gregory. "The Intersection of Politics and Thought in Ryukyuan Confucianism: Sai On's Uses of *Quan.*" *Harvard Journal of Asiatic Studies* 56.2 (December 1996):443–477.

———. "Sai On (1682–1761) and Confucianism in the Early-Modern Ryukyu Kingdom." 2 vols. Ph.D. diss., University of Southern California, 1992.

———. "Sai On no gakutō to shisō: toku ni bukkyō/Shaka ron o chūshin to shite." *Okinawa bunka kenkyū* 23 (March 1997):1–38.

———. "Unspeakable Things: Ryukyuan Confucian Sai On's Ambivalent Critique of Language and Buddhism." *Japanese Journal of Religious Studies* 24.1–2 (spring 1997).

Takara Kurayoshi. "Kinsei Ryūkyū e no sasoi." In *Shin Ryūkyūshi, kinsei hen,* vol. 1, pp. 13–31. Naha: Ryūkyū shinpōsha, 1989.

———. Okinawa rekishi monogatari. Naha: Hirugisha, 1984.

———. *Ryūkyū ōkoku no kōzō.* Yoshikawa kōbunkan, 1987.

———. *Ryūkyū ōkokushi no kadai.* Naha: Hirugisha, 1990.

———. "Shō Shōken no ronri." In *Shin Ryūkyūshi, kinsei hen,* vol. 1, pp. 159–182. Naha: Ryūkyū shinpōsha, 1989.

———. "Yuta mondai no kōzu." In *Shin Ryūkyūshi, kinsei hen,* vol. 2, pp. 169–182. Naha: Ryūkyū shinpōsha, 1990.

Tamae Seiryō. "Heshikiya Chōbin no shisō to geijutsu." *Aoi Umi: Okinawa no sōgō gekkanshi* 138 (December 1984):31–37.

———. *Junkyō no bungaku: Heshikiya Chōbin no shōsetsu.* Dai-nippon insatsu, 1984.

Tanaka, Stefan. *Japan's Orient: Rendering Pasts into History.* Berkeley: University of California Press, 1993.

Tasato Osamu. "Magiri to kuji." In *Shin Ryūkyūshi, kinsei hen,* vol. 2, pp. 85–107. Naha: Ryūkyū Shinpōsha, 1990.

———. "Sai On no seiji." In *Kinsei shomondai shiriizu 1, Sai On to sono jidai,* pp. 64–76. Naha: Richūsha, 1984.

———. "Sangyō no imeeji." In *Kinsei shomondai shiriizu 5, kinsei no sangyō,* pp. 5–20. Urasoe: Urasoe-shi Kyōiku iinkai, 1987.

Tasato Yūtetsu. *Okinawa ni okeru kaitaku shūraku no kenkyū.* Comprising the whole of *Hōbungaku kiyō, shigaku chirigaku hen* 23 (March 1980). Ginowan: Ryūkyū daigaku.

Toby, Ronald. *State and Diplomacy in Early Modern Japan: Asia in the Development of the Tokugawa Bakufu.* Princeton: Princeton University Press, 1984.

Toguchi Masakiyo. *Kinsei no Ryūkyū.* Hōsei daigaku shuppankyoku, 1975.

Tomishima Sōei. "Minmatsu ni okeru Kumemura no suitai to shinkōsaku ni tsuite." In *Dayijiai Zhong-Liu lishi guanxi guoji xueshu huiyi lunwenji,* pp. 469–488. Taibei: Lianhebao wenhua jijinhui guoxue wenxiangguan, 1987.

Tomiyama Ichirō. "Okinawa sabetsu to puroriteria-ka." In *Shin Ryūkyūshi, kindai/gendai hen,* pp. 169–190. Naha: Ryūkyū shinpōsha, 1992.

Tomiyama Kazuyuki. "Changes in Sovereign Power and the Royal Cult as Revealed in Posthumous Portraits of Ryukyuan Kings." Paper presented at the 48th annual meeting of the Association for Asian Studies, Honolulu, April 15, 1996.

———. "Hanzai to keibatsu." In *Shin Ryūkyū shi, kinsei hen,* vol. 1, pp. 259–280. Naha: Ryūkyū shinpōsha, 1989.

———. "Kannin seido no issokumen." In *Shin Ryūkyūshi, kinsei hen,* vol. 2, pp. 63–83. Naha: Ryūkyū shinpōsha, 1990.

———. "Ryūkyū no ōken girei—saiten girei to sūbyō saishi o chūshin ni." Edited by Akasaka Norio. In *Ōken no kisō e,* pp. 188–224. Shinyōsha, 1992.

———. "Sappō no yōsō." In *Shin Ryūkyūshi, kinsei hen,* vol. 1, pp. 73–96. Naha: Ryūkyū shinpōsha, 1989.

———. "Tōitsu ōkoku keiseiki no taigai kankei." In *Shin Ryūkyūshi, ko-Ryūkyū hen,* pp. 141–162. Naha: Ryūkyū shinpōsha, 1991.

Totman, Conrad. *The Green Archipelago: Forestry in Preindustrial Japan.* Berkeley: University of California Press, 1989.

Tsuzuki Akiko. "Kinsei Okinawa ni okeru fūsui no juyō to sono tenkai." Edited by Kubo Noritada. *Okinawa no fūsui,* pp. 15–58. Hirakawa shuppansha, 1990.

———. "Sai On no juka shisō ni tsuite: *Yōmu ihen* o megutte." *Ryūkoku daigaku ronshū* 445 (February 1995):285–308.

Tu, Wei-ming. *Centrality and Commonality: An Essay on Confucian Religiousness.* Albany: State University of New York Press, 1989.

Uehara Kenzen. "Bōeki no tenkai." In *Shin Ryūkyūshi, kinsei hen,* vol. 1, pp. 119–157. Naha: Ryūkyū shinpōsha, 1989.

———. *Sakoku to han bōeki: Satsuma-han no Ryūkyū mitsubōeki.* Yaetake shobō, 1981.

Uehara Nario. "Sai On ron." *Shin Okinawa bungaku* 66 (winter 1985):158–167.

Umeki Tetsuto. "Kinsei nōson no seiritsu." In *Shin Ryūkyūshi, kinsei hen,* vol. 1, pp. 181–204. Naha: Ryūkyū shinpōsha, 1989.

Wakabayashi, Bob Tadashi. *Anti-Foreignism and Western Learning in Early-Modern Japan: The New Theses of 1825.* Cambridge, MA: Council on East Asian Studies, Harvard University, 1986.

Watanabe Hiroshi. *Kinsei Nihon shakai to sōgaku.* Tōkyō daigaku shuppankai, 1985.

Xu Gongsheng. *Chūgoku-Ryūkyū kōryūshi.* Translated by Nishizato Kikō and Uezato Ken'ichi. Naha: Hirugisha, 1991.

Zhuzi yulei. 8 vols. Edited by Li Jingde. Beijing: Zhonghua shuju, 1986.

Index

Amanao Tetsuo, 188n. 15
Amplification of the Six Maxims, 63, 64
Anderson, Benedict, 3, 4, 5, 6, 150, 160,
    161
Arai Hakuseki, 21, 47–48, 158
Araki Moriaki, 34, 35, 113, 119
Articles of Instruction, 82, 83, 123, 128,
    162
assimilation (*dōka*): problems of, 149–155

Battle of Okinawa, 154
Beixi ziyi, 90
*Brief Account of the Construction of the
    Confucian Temple and the
    Establishment of Learning,* 66–69
Brokaw, Cynthia, 88
Bunei, 61, 94–95

Chatan-Eso Affair, 24–25, 32, 51, 57,
    58, 128
Ch'en, Ta-tuan, 157, 171n. 12
Chibana Shōichi, 155, 198n. 36
Christy, Alan, 149, 154, 196n. 5, 199n.
    54
Chūzan seikan. See *Mirror of Chūzan*
civil service examinations (O. *kō,* J. *ka*),
    14, 139
Classified Conversations of Master Zhu, 89
Concealment of ties with Japan, 21–23
Conversation of the Three Birds, 136–137
Conversations with a Rustic Old Man, 87,
    96

Council of Fifteen, 135–136
Council of Three, 17, 25, 78, 123, 134,
    135–136, 171n. 10
Crawcour, Sydney, 174n. 74

Dana Masayuki, 40, 59, 140, 180n. 46
Dialect Dispute (*hōgen ronsō*).
    See language policies
Directives of Haneji, 51–52, 55
dispute over moving the capital, 129–132
Domain of Ryukyu (*Ryūkyū han*), 143,
    145
Duara, Prasenjit, 4–6, 7, 150–151, 162

Edo nobori, 27–29
Eiso, 61
Elisonas, Jurgis, 173n. 50
Essential Discussion of Popular Customs,
    75, 121–122, 191n. 70
Essentials of Governance, 86
Essential Views Upon Awakening, 91–94
Expeditious Household Regulation, 96, 97

Farquhar, Judith B., 196n. 1
Field, Norma, 198n. 35
Fifteen Injunctions, 17–18
Fifth Industrial Exhibition, 149–150
Figal, Gerald, 198n. 37

gechiyaku, 134, 148
Gellner, Ernest, 4, 5, 6, 161, 197n. 18
Genealogy of Chūzan, 94–95

General Meaning of the Amplification of the Six Maxims, 63
Geomancy (O. *funshii*), 7, 43, 75–76, 81, 106, 126–132
Gihon, 61, 95
Go-Kyōjō. See *Articles of Instruction*
Great Learning (*Daxue*), 73, 75, 97
Guide to Navigation, 63–64
gyorinkei zōrinpō, 107–108

Haneji shioki. See *Directives of Haneji*
Hangaa jiken. See Valuation Incident
Heshikiya Chōbin, 6, 7, 15, 119–128, 156, 161; and Buddhism 121, 122–123; conflict with Sai On 121–128; Heshikiya-Tomoyose Incident 125–128; literary works 120–124
Heshikiya Chōbin, 125
Hevia, James L., 196n. 1
Higa Kazuo, 123, 125, 126–127, 128
Higaonna Kanjun. *See* Higashionna Kanjun
Higashionna Kanjun, 7, 11, 23, 151, 162, 170n. 10
Hinpun-gajumaru, 128
Hinpunshii. See *Sanfu Longmai-bei*
Hitori monogatari. See *One Man's Views*
Honsaroku, 12

Iha Fuyū, 7, 126–127, 140, 151–152, 162, 171n. 10, 195n. 9
Iinuma Jirō, 107
Ikemiya Masaharu, 57, 120, 123, 127
Information: Ryukyu as conduit of, 30–31
Inoue Hideo, 190n. 30
Iwamura Michitoshi, 147

Jana. *See* Tei Dō
Jana Ueekata. *See* Tei Dō

Jianmiao lixue jilüe. See *Brief Account of the Construction of the Confucian Temple and the Establishment of Learning*
jireisho, 41–42

Kadōkun, 79
Kaibara Ekken, 79
Kamiya Nobuyuki, 20, 44
kanshō, 38, 39, 68, 135–136, 139, 157
Kenbyō ritsugaku kiryaku. See *Brief Account of the Construction of the Confucian Temple and the Establishment of Learning*
Kerr, George, 107
Kobashigawa Niya, 73
Kodama Kihachi, 152
Kōdōkai, 148–149
Kokugaku. See national university
kokushi (state instructor), 76
kujichō, 110–113, 115
Kumazawa Banzan, 20–21, 48
Kumemura, 11, 14, 38–41, 42, 43, 62, 63, 66, 67, 69, 71, 72, 77, 98, 101, 102–103, 112, 115, 119, 132, 135–140, 150; rioting in 136–137, 157
kumiodori, 83, 120, 123, 193n. 102
Kyan nikki, 170–171n. 10
Kyūyō, 44, 53, 55, 72, 75, 76, 77, 98–99, 101, 104, 109, 114, 117, 134, 173n. 46, 175n. 83, 175n. 88

language policies, 148, 152–154
Lebra, William P., 191n. 66
Li Hongzhang, 145
Liuyu Yanyi. See *Amplification of the Six Maxims*
local festivals, 111–113

Maeda Giken, 139

Maehira Fusaaki, 21, 30–31, 41, 44, 54, 100
Majikina Ankō, 7, 64, 126, 138
Makise Tsuneji, 196n. 4–5, 197n. 10
Makishi-Onga Affair, 144, 145, 157
Mashiko Hidenori, 199n. 48
Matayoshi Hiroshi, 123
Matayoshi Yōshi, 127–128
Matsuda, Mitsugu, 176n. 101, 179n. 34, 199n. 38
Matsuda Michiyuki, 145–146, 157
Matsukata Masayoshi, 147, 149
Mean (Zhongyong), 73, 94
Meirindō, 64, 138, 139
Mesaki Shigekazu, 130
Metzger, Thomas, 90–91
military bases, 155
Mirror of Chūzan, 58–62, 95, 98
Miyagi Eishō, 134–135
Miyata Toshihiko, 34, 35
Miyazaki Yasusada (Antei), 106
Morris-Suzuki, Tessa, 159
Mukai Kiyoshi, 198n. 26
Muro Kyūsō, 63

Nago Ueekata zenkō den. See Record of the Good Deeds of Nago Ueekata
Najita, Tetsuo, 158
Nakai, Kate Wildman, 199n. 42
Nakama Yūei, 109, 188n. 13
Nanpo Bunshi, 51, 67, 68
national university, 14, 137–139
Ne-no-hō, 101–102, 111
Nichiryū dōso ron, 56–57. See also *Nichiryū jinshu dōkei ron*
Nichiryū jinshu dōkei ron, 162
Nihon Mingeikai, 153, 154
Nishizato Kikō, 196n. 3, 197n. 10
Nogyō zensho, 106
Nōmuchō, 106
noro (nuru), 115

Ogyū Sorai, 63, 158
okazugaki, 41–42
One Man's Views, 80–86, 97, 138
Onna Nabe (Onna Nabii), 118, 124
Ooms, Herman, 199n. 43
Ōshiro Tatsuhiro, 58

preserving old customs (*kyūkan hozon*), 147–149
pro-Nago faction. *See* dispute over moving the capital
pro-Shuri faction. *See* dispute over moving the capital
prostitution, 50, 57, 117, 120–121

Qing military power: effect on Ryukyuan autonomy 20–22; Japanese anxiety concerning, 20–21, 22, 27, 33

Ravina, Mark, 49, 160, 196n. 2
Record of the Good Deeds of Nago Ueekata, 69–70
Reflections of Things at Hand, 38, 76
Ricoeur, Paul, 185n. 33
Rikuyu Engi. See Amplification of the Six Maxims
Rikuyu engi tai'i. See General Meaning of the Amplification of the Six Maxims
Ryukyuan terminology, 9–11
Ryūkyūjin odori, 28
Ryūkyū karitsu, 134
Ryūkyū shobun, 143–146; negotiations between Japan and China 146; Okinawa as colony 149
Ryūkyū shinpō, 150

Sai En, 72
Saigō Tsugumichi, 144
Sai Seishō, 135–136, 140

Sai On, 6–9, 13–15, 69, 70, 133, 140,
142, 147, 155, 161, 162;
biography 71–80; distinctive
qualities of his Confucianism,
157–159; encounter with recluse,
73–75; forest management,
103–108; Genbun Survey,
108–110; intellectual orientation,
79–80; opposition to, 118–132;
promoter of Ryukyuan
subjectivity, 71, 79, 80, 84,
86–89, 91–99, 159, 160, 161;
suppression of shamanism,
113–117; theory of the Ryukyuan
state, 80–86, 103; understanding
of destiny (*ming*), 86–89, 91–99;
view of profit (*li*), 105
Sai Taku, 72
Sai-uji kafu, 72, 77, 105, 109
Sakai, Robert, 32, 34, 35
Sakihara, Mitsugu, 169n. 2, 199n. 38
Sanfu Longmai-bei, 129, 132
Sanlin zhenbi. See *Secrets of Forestry*
Sanpu Ryūmyaku-hi. See Sanfu
Longmai-bei
Sanrin shinpi. See *Secrets of Forestry*
Sanshikan. See Council of Three
Saō hengen. See *Conversations with a
Rustic Old Man*
Satto, 39, 60, 94
Secrets of Forestry, 103
Setsudō enyūsō. See *Setsudō's Travels to
Beijing*
Setsudō's Travels to Beijing, 63
Shimazu Hisamitsu, 144
Shimazu Iehisa, 16, 19, 20, 59
Shimazu Mitsuhisa, 22
Shimazu Nariakira, 144, 145
Shimazu Yoshitaka, 27
Shinan kōgi. See *Guide to Navigation*
shinugu ashibi, 112, 118–119

Shō Boku, 14, 133–134, 139
Shō Ei, 139
Shō Eki, 76–77
Shō En (king), 60
Shō En (prince), 148
Shō Hashi, 94, 130
Shō Hō, 51
Shō Iku, 141
Shō Kei, 76, 78, 101, 103, 115, 132,
133, 138, 139
Shō Kō, 140, 141
Shō Nei, 15, 16, 18, 19, 58, 59
Shō On, 14, 133, 135, 137–139, 157
Shō Sei, 39, 42
Shō Shin, 115, 136, 139
Shō Shitsu, 24
Shō Tai, 141, 145, 148
Shō Toku, 60
Shō Shōken, 6–8, 13, 15, 32, 51, 69,
71, 98, 115, 117, 152, 156, 161,
162; and attempt to distinguish
public and private realms, 51–52;
biography, 51–52; as historian,
58–62, 67, 95; *ishiki kakumei*,
53–55; opposition to female
officials, 52–53, 54–55, 103; and
Satsuma, 51, 52, 53, 55, 57–62, 66
Shō Tei, 22, 32, 41, 42, 44, 76–77, 82,
103
Smith, Richard J., 189n. 27
state ceremonial, 42–43, 82, 100–103
Suoweng pianyan. See *Conversations with
a Rustic Old Man*
Suxi yaolun. See *Essential Discussion of
Popular Customs*

Taiwan Incident, 144–145
Takara Kurayoshi, 19, 48, 50, 52, 53,
56, 159–160
Takarashima (Tokara), 44–46
Tamae Seiryō, 120–121, 194n. 119

Tanaka, Stefan, 198n. 20
Tasato Osamu, 103, 109, 110
Tasato Yūtetsu, 190n. 38
Tei Dō, 17, 18, 58–59, 61, 67, 98,
    170–171n. 10
Tei Junsoku, 6, 7, 13, 15, 47–48, 51,
    69, 71, 77–78, 98, 132, 156, 157;
    biography, 62–64, 181n. 55;
    China as cultural model, 64–69;
    as historian 66–69; posthumous
    reputation, 62, 69–70
Tei Kōtuku, 136
tentō (*tendō*), 12, 59–61, 95, 156, 161,
    186n. 66
Toby, Ronald, 30, 48, 172n. 40
Toguchi, Masakiyo, 164n. 2
Tōjin odori. See Ryūkyūjin odori
Tōji yōden. See Essentials of Governance
Tokara. *See* Takarashima
toki, 114–116
Toki, yuta togasadame, 114
Tomari Jochiku, 51, 57, 67
Tomiyama Ichirō, 197n. 16
Tomiyama Kazuyuki, 17, 41, 42–43,
    101–102, 177n. 106, 195n. 1
Totman, Conrad, 189n. 24
Tributary relations with China, 35–37,
    48, 77–78; education, 38–39;
    Satsuma's connections with, 23–27,
    29, 32–34, 174n. 74; trade, 19–20,
    21, 34–35; See also *kanshō*
Tu Weiming, 94
*Tuzhi yaochuan. See Essentials of
    Governance*

uchihare asobi. See shinugu ashibi
Uehara Kenzen, 23, 25, 28, 32
Uesugi Shigenori, 146–147

Umeki Tetsuto, 53

Valuation Incident, 77–78, 103, 132

Wakabayashi, Bob Tadashi, 199n. 42
Watanabe Hiroshi, 199n. 42, 199n. 43

Xiaoxue (*Elementary Learning*), 76
Xingli daquan, 76
Xu Gongsheng, 38
*Xuetang yanyoucao. See Setsudō's Travels
    to Beijing*

yaadui, 109, 147
Yanagi Muneyoshi, 153
Yaowu huibian, 76
Yijing, 116, 192n. 79
Yōmu ihen. See Yaowu huibian
yukatchu, 40, 42–44, 48, 53, 73, 80, 81,
    109, 114, 117, 119, 120, 132,
    134, 138–140, 156, 162, 176n.
    95; after annexation, 146–149,
    197n. 10; flight to China, 147,
    197n. 10
yuta, 57, 114–116

Zhinan guangyi. See Guide to Navigation
*Zhongshan shipu. See Genealogy of
    Chūzan*
Zhou Yaming, 188n. 13
Zhu Xi, 38, 75, 194n. 129;
    understanding of destiny (*ming*),
    89–91, 94
*Zhuzi yulei. See Classified Conversations
    of Master Zhu*
*Zokushū yōron. See Essential Discussion of
    Popular Customs*
Zongli Yamen, 144–145

About the Author

Gregory Smits is associate professor of East Asian history at Pennsylvania State University. He received his Ph.D. from the University of Southern California and has published several articles on Ryukyuan and Japanese intellectual history.